perly

How to DJ

The art and science of playing records

properly

Frank Broughton and Bill Brewster

BANTAM PRESS

LONDON · TORONTO · SYDNEY · AUCKLAND · JOHANNESBURG

TRANSWORLD PUBLISHERS
61-63 Uxbridge Road, London W5 5SA
a division of The Random House Group Ltd

RANDOM HOUSE AUSTRALIA (PTY) LTD
20 Alfred Street, Milsons Point, Sydney,
New South Wales 2061, Australia

RANDOM HOUSE NEW ZEALAND LTD
18 Poland Road, Glenfield, Auckland 10, New Zealand

RANDOM HOUSE SOUTH AFRICA (PTY) LTD
Endulini, 5a Jubilee Road, Parktown 2193, South Africa

Published 2002 by Bantam Press
a division of Transworld Publishers
Reissued 2006

A catalogue record for this book is available from the British Library.
ISBN 9780593049662

Design by Julia Lloyd
Photography by John Bland
Illustrations by Trudi Cross

Printed in Great Britain by Butler Tanner and Dennis, Frome

MIX
Paper from
responsible sources
FSC® C023561
FSC
www.fsc.org

5 7 9 10 8 6

For **Francis Grasso** (1948-2001)
and **Steve D'Acquisto** (1953-2001)

They did it for love and made less than the bartender.

and **Adam Goldstone** (1969-2006)

He always did it properly.

S INCE THIS BOOK FIRST CAME OUT we've had a flood of heart-warming emails from readers who've gone from being nervous novices to throwing their own successful parties and club nights. It's great to know we've helped so many people have fun.

This book goes into great detail about the nuts and bolts of performing with recorded music, but it also tries to encourage a deeper understanding of what DJing is and why it can be so powerful. The most important thing about DJing is loving the music you play; everything else you can pick up with practice.

It used to be that the only reason to be a DJ was an impractical and overwhelming passion for music. Now that playing records is a glamorous career option, many kids' reasons for taking it up are far less noble. We're happy to teach them the skills they need to chase their dreams of money and celebrity, but to get to them they'll also have to read our propaganda about how the craft should really be practised.

DJing is a thoroughly mystical activity, ruled by improvisation and emotions and a profound understanding of what makes people tick. What you need to DJ (properly) is experience, sensitivity and a lover's drive to share musical pleasure. Without these you could perhaps be a successful DJ, but we don't think you'd ever be a great one.

If you're going to play records in public the most important thing is to do it your way and no-one else's. This is a collection of possibilities, not a rulebook. Have fun with it and don't believe everything we say.

Frank and Bill, 2006

The masterclass

The industry

The extras

The craft

How to DJ properly

It's only playing other people's records

DJs track down greatness in music and squeeze it together. Like a master chef who picks just one perfect cherry from each tree to make his pie, a DJ condenses the work and talent of hundreds of musicians into a single concentrated performance. DJs bring all the right things together – that's why we love them so much.

And they make it to measure. None of this off-the-peg, one-size-fits-all rubbish; when you hear a DJ play you're getting a unique performance, exactly suited to the moment. Proper DJs don't just trot out a load of nice tunes, they think carefully about the time, the place and the people in front of them, and choose something that's perfect.

This is the real skill of DJing and it doesn't come easily. Knowing music, finding music, understanding music, is something that takes years. And once you've started there's no end. The real work of a DJ happens behind the scenes – searching dark record stores, devouring endless lists and daunting stacks of vinyl, and sniffing out the wonders they contain. Playing records is rarely hard work, but doing the research and amassing the knowledge to do it well is a full-time job.

The other great task ahead of you is to learn about people. You know your own musical tastes; now you have to understand everyone else's. Not only that, but you must learn about their feelings – what makes them laugh and smile and dance and go crazy. Again, this takes time and experience. Your brain must record and tabulate the wildly different emotions music can generate. A great librarian knows which shelves the raunchiest, most revolutionary books are on; a great guitarist knows where all the good notes live. A great DJ knows which records make people lose themselves.

A musician, however legendary, is trapped by the limitations of their instrument. But as a DJ you have the entire history of recorded sound to play with. Unlike a band, forced to plough through your back catalogue (again) through bad amplifiers, you can choose from every artist, every track, every remix ever made, and you can deliver them with clear, crisp studio perfection. You might pick the funkiest two bars of a musician's entire life and loop them as a little intro. You might take two records made 30 years apart and place them neatly side by side. You might pick the one track Supertramp made that can send a deep house crowd bonkers (we're not telling) and happily dismiss everything else in their entire career as pointless. We won't deny that the average musician is probably far more skilled than the average DJ, but doubtless the DJ controls more musical power than the musician ever did.

A respectable job?

As a DJ you become the focus for the greatness in the music you play. All the emotional force, the lyrical, spiritual impact of your records gets reflected back to you – even if you're tired and slightly shit-faced and keen to see the end of the night. Track down some good tunes, patchwork them together, and people act as if you've made all this music from scratch. It becomes truly *your* performance. 'Curses,' say the world's rock stars. 'Here's my room number,' says the DJ.

Added to this is the job's enviable cultural clout. The DJ is the tastemaker, the discoverer, the champion of a new sound or scene. No musical movement can spread its wings too far without the DJ's approval. People still write endless books about how Muddy Waters, The Beatles and Bob Dylan changed music. The truth is they wouldn't have affected much beyond their own backyards without DJs playing their records. And a good DJ is by definition a permanent revolutionary. While musicians live in a time capsule built around their one greatest year, a DJ is always searching for the next song – 'the *new* Fatboy Slim single', not the old one; 'the *next* U2', not the last lot – never playing the same set twice for fear of losing their reputation as music's evangelist. The DJ is the only figure with any power in the music industry who isn't an indentured slave to the record labels and their conservatism – the greatest freelance music-maker to date.

Thanks to this gunslingin' freedom, the DJ has for nearly 50 years been music's prime mover. The DJ realised his power when he cultivated first rhythm and blues then rock 'n' roll, and despite murderous opposition (ask Alan Freed) spread them across the airwaves. Since then the DJ has snatched the keys to music's patent office and conspired with post-modernism to lock the musician out. Live music sustained itself by dreaming of the next big thing and reheating rock every ten years. Meanwhile the truly novel forms were being created by the collision of vinyl on DJs' turntables. Reggae, disco, hip hop, house, techno, drum & bass, garage – all forms born and bred not by musicians but by the DJ. These genres didn't emerge from some jam-session epiphany: they came from the DJ trying every trick in the book to keep hold of the dancefloor – his high-maintenance lover.

The DJ came of age when he replaced the rock gods as a marketable star. We buy compilations now, not albums, and the name on them is the DJ's. This was the final step in his journey out of the shadows – from someone who helped collect dirty glasses to someone worth more than the club owner. Brand-name status quickly reconnected with the emotional power a DJ has always held over his dancers, and DJing became the sexiest job imagin-able. Clubbers have long known that a great DJ can toy with them like a great lover; now the magazines and the clubs and the labels have caught up with the idea and DJs have been belatedly promoted to the celebrity madhouse. These days the rewards of DJing can be phenomenal. It's no wonder little Johnny and Juliette want to play records when they grow up.

What's your motivation?

You too? You want to get paid for putting on tunes? Well, here's the entrance exam. Do you love music or do you just dream of being Sasha? We won't hammer it home too hard, but if you real-ly want to DJ *properly*, if you want to be great at it, you have to be doing it for the right reasons: not for private jets and power over a dancefloor, but because of a simple and unavoidable need to share music with people. Without the gene for musical evangelism you'll just be a jukebox.

Now that DJing is a respectable career this often gets forgotten – a scary number of kids think it's just about technical skills and access to the most upfront tunes. The saddest things we found while researching were kids' questions on bulletin boards saying, 'I want to be a DJ. What kind of music should I play?' If that's you and you really don't know, then put this book back immediately. Give it to someone who actually cares about music, who lives and dies for their record collection, who knows without question what music they should play – the music they *love*, stupid.

The other great misunderstanding is the obsession with mixing. Today's styles place an unhealthy emphasis on the mechanical side of things, and most of the best DJs do have impressive tech-nical abilities. But don't let this overshadow their more fundamen-tal talents – for discovering music and for playing exactly the right record at exactly the right moment. Sure, you need some technical skills to play records, but not that many, and these skills are far less important than the records themselves and the order you put them in. Some of the world's greatest ever DJs have been pretty ropey mixers. They might have stumbled their way from one track to the next, but the next track was so amazing and perfect for the moment that you didn't care. And the next, and the next...

If your music is boring or badly chosen, the best beatmatching in the world won't save you. Yet there are endless young DJs who develop incredible technical skills without ever once worrying about what they're for (keep battling, turntablists, it *looks* incredi-ble). It's like a photographer spending so much time thinking about f-stops and exposure times that he never bothers to see what's through the lens.

Hopefully we can defuse the obsession with technique, simply by making it available to all. In collating the wisdom garnered over nearly a century of DJing we're hoping you'll quickly get all the boring stuff under your belt and get on with being creative and musical and individual. Learning to mix is only your apprenticeship. It's maybe five per cent of the craft, at most. You don't really start DJing until you're playing for a real dancefloor and using your music to interact with real people. Only then can you begin your life-long accumulation of experience and artistry.

Anyone – your mum, your dad, your dog – could learn to beat-match from this book. And that's our first great secret: PLAYING RECORDS ISN'T ROCKET SCIENCE. The point is that there's a universe of difference between doing it and doing it well. DJing is like running: most people can run to catch a bus, some might manage a jog round the park, but only a tiny few can ever be Olympic champions.

What makes greatness?

We don't know what makes great DJs. We suspect they have all the talents that would have made them great musicians – a heightened aesthetic sense, a great feel for rhythm, perfect pitch, a phenomenal musical memory... If only they'd stuck at those trombone lessons they might be wearing a bow-tie to work instead of a baseball cap.

What probably unites the best DJs is an insane love of music. Not just a minor eccentricity; we're talking about an obsession that crushes normal life in its path. Forget food, there are records that need buying. Didn't talk to anyone today? Turn off the phone and don't worry – you have your music for company. We know some DJs who think of record shopping as an activity that rivals sex for excitement. Given the choice between a weekend of motel passion and a trip to a new collector's shop, rather than packing the baby oil, they'll be updating their wants list.

For a DJ, the need to discover music and then to show it off to the world is like the voice in a serial killer's head. However vast their collection, however encyclopaedic their knowledge, there are always more tunes to hear, always new records to fall in love with. One morning one of us was talking to Danny Tenaglia. It was early; the phone call had woken him up. 'What did you dream about, Mr T?' was our greeting. He collected his thoughts, rubbed sleep from his eyes and said excitedly, 'Records, records and more records.'

15

This book can't give you that kind of passion, but you need to know that it exists. You need to know that DJing isn't really about celebrity, or money, or pulling power, it's about *music*. Music is what motivates the finest DJs: they love it, they live for it. Take away the stardom, the fat paychecks, the pretty girls, the cute boys, and sure, plenty of DJs would have a speedy career change. But the very best of them would still be there, playing as often as they could, just for the love of it, just for the music, just for the sheer orgasm of seeing people go nuts to a record they've discovered.

The bedroom

1. **How to** buy music

Your job starts in the record store, not on the decks. Your worth as a DJ begins and ends with what's on your shelves and in your bag. For every overpaid hour in a club, a good DJ spends days, months and years picking out tunes and learning about music.

The basics

Victorian critic John Ruskin said, 'Have nothing in your home unless you know it to be useful or believe it to be beautiful.' He meant records.

- Is it great music?
- Will it work on a dancefloor?
- Does it fit my style?

Some rules

Buy little and often
Regular shopping is the key to keeping track of things – and catching those elusive gems that are only around for a week or two. It also prevents you going on mad bulk-buying sprees that haul in quantity over quality. Visit your main store weekly.

Only buy records you can't live without
You've picked out a pile of ten. Now force yourself to buy just five. This is the easiest way to buy better records. Remember: killer, not filler.

Don't buy something you've never heard
. . . Unless you can get a refund. Even your favourite producer has the occasional off moment.

Records always sound better in the shop
Don't be fooled by their booming system. And don't buy records under the influence of drugs (or the day after) for similar reasons.

Check the condition
Look for warps, bumps and scratches. If it's a new record, buy a shrink-wrapped copy, not the one that 100 customers have dragged a needle over.

Save your receipts
If your tax return includes income as a DJ (or music journalist) then you can claim the cost of records back against tax – they're a business expense.

Save our stores

We love buying music online, we really do. But the omnipotent rise of the internet means bricks and mortar record stores are closing faster than coal mines under Margaret Thatcher. It's great to grab an eBay bargain, but for real discoveries nothing can replace some serious digging at disco's coalface. To keep your local store alive you need to keep getting your fingers properly dusty. Those shops need you!

20

In a big city with lots of dance stores, find the one that best fits your style and make it your headquarters. But check out other places regularly as well – you'll expand your tastes and find secrets that others on your scene don't know about. In smaller towns you're probably stuck with a mainstream chainstore or a lone dance shop selling commercial tunes and a few underground biggies. Here you'll have to work much harder to be individual.

Secondhand
Secondhand sources range from collectors' shops run by experts where everything's carefully organised, to car-boot stalls that also sell ten-pound sacks of custard creams. Prices usually relate to the amount of digging required. There's more on buying secondhand on p152 *How to build a collection*.

Online/mail order
Certain dance stores have teamed up with the postman to serve people living beyond civilisation. You'll find their ads (with long lists of records) in the dance mags. Many websites let you hear snippets of tunes before you buy.

Buying online

3 Beat www.threebeatrecords.co.uk

45 rpm www.45rpm.co.uk

Bang Bang www.bangbangrecords.com

Catapult www.catapult.co.uk

City Sounds www.city-sounds.co.uk

City 16 www.city16.com

Dusty Groove www.dustygroove.com

Global Groove www.globalgroove.co.uk

Hard To Find www.htfr.com

HMV www.hmv.co.uk

Juno www.juno.co.uk

Phonica www.phonicarecords.co.uk

Piccadilly Records www.piccadillyrecords.com

Selectadisc www.selectadisc.co.uk

Tunes www.tunes.co.uk

Turntable Lab www.turntablelab.com

Ultimate Dance Music www.ultimatedancemusic.co.uk

Uptown www.uptownrecords.com

Where to buy music

'McDonalds had just come out and my friends would buy double cheeseburgers, but I'd go off and buy records. They'd come back having eaten it and gone "wicked". And I'd come back and say, "This record by Brass Construction is unbelievable".'

Carl Cox, !Jamming.net

For DJ download sites see p96 *How to DJ digitally*.

For a huge list of the world's online record stores: www.moremusic.co.uk/links/world_sh.htm

How to find out about music

They keep it quiet to maintain their pulling chances, but DJs are all obsessive anal retentives. You must join their ranks and become a true trainspotter – a dance music librarian who gets very excited by lists of records. Musical knowledge is musical power. Get it wherever you can.

DJ charts
If you like a certain DJ, you'll like the records they put in their playlist. You'll find these in magazines, fanzines and websites.

Buzz charts
These are useful indicators of what's going to be big. They're usually made by combining and comparing charts from lots of different DJs.

Sales charts
These are less useful because they only show what's already popular. But they're still a good round-up of what's out there that you might want to hear.

Store charts
These usually list the records the staff think they'll sell the most of. If it's your main store, you should at least give them a listen.

Reviews
Invaluable as a guide to what's coming out, who made it and where it came from, plus a vague idea of what it sounds like. Get to know which reviewers you can trust. If online, you might also be able to hear a sample.

Radio
From Gilles Peterson and Rob Da Bank to Tim Westwood and Mr Tong himself, you'll find radio shows filled with what's new and wonderful. You can find track-listings (in magazines and websites) for certain mix shows. Specialist shows are great for learning about other genres.

Recommendations
Listen and learn – from DJ mates, record store staff, even acquaintances you meet on the scene. Most will spill the beans – if they know something you don't, they'll be happy to rub it in.

Your ever-growing wants list
Keep one. You never know when you might find that obscure Mood II Swing track. Was it the 4am dub or the mental mahogany mix you were after?

Follow producers
If you like a record, find out who made it and watch for their name. The same goes for particular labels.

Online forums
The web is full of DJs swapping notes on their favourite music. Try googling your favourite genre or go to some of the DJ-related sites mentioned on p210 *How to join the DJ community*. For a busy forum of the world's spottiest spotters you can't beat our site www.djhistory.com

Be curious
Explore, investigate, accumulate knowledge. Ask what that killer track was. Sniff out classics. Learn about your music's roots. Listen to obscure radio stations. Surf strange websites. Borrow music. Swap tapes. Ask the cab-driver about that funky bhangra track. Stay after the movie and read the song credits. It's endless.

'I used to only date women whose mother, or brother, had records in their house. I'd enquire, "'Scuse me, do you have any records you don't want?" They'd open the closet and it'd be a gold-mine in there, and I'd be: "OK, this person has to be my girlfriend for a minute".'

Grandmaster Flash

23

How to win in a dance store

There's a certain attitude and etiquette in most dance stores that can be intimidating, especially to the newcomer. But don't be put off. The people behind the counter are bound to know more about the records they're selling than you do – that's their job. You're not there to impress anyone, you just need to listen to records and decide which ones sound amazing.

In any case, record retailers are having a tough time of it, and that's good news for you because they're putting more effort into being nice to customers. That means more cheery advice and more listening decks.

- Find a place with music you like.
- Visit at quiet times of day and take your time.
- Visit your favourite shop at least once a week.

Stand firm at all times

It's all about you. You're there to buy music that you think is great – don't be pressured into buying records because someone else is raving about them. Give them a listen, but make sure they pass the test before you add them to your bill.

Get friendly with the staff

Once you're a regular they'll know your style and stack you up with tunes as soon as you walk through the door, put hot imports aside for you and offer you promos that don't get racked. That's usually what's in those bags of records behind the counter. And to get the very best from a record store? Get a job in it.

It's a wrap

Open a shrink-wrapped record in style by slicing its edge back and forth against your jeans. Practise at home.

24

How to choose your tunes

>> **Ask the staff to pass you particular records**
Listen to them on headphones. Choose some you like. Ask for more suggestions along the same lines.

>> **Hang out and listen to what they play in the store**
This way you'll hear records played on a decent system. When you hear something you like, ask for a copy.

>> **Describe your style and have them pick out a stack**
The fun comes in your description – something like 'Leftfield breaks with strong basslines' or 'Soulful house but not too jazzy'. Or name labels or producers or recent tracks. Sort through the stack on headphones, then rave about the ones you liked. They'll find you more up that street.

>> **Pass them a wants list**
This only works if they're recent tracks and the shop's not busy. Even if they don't have the records, it'll help them figure out your tastes.

>> **Hum a tuneless version of a track you heard last night**
The best way to look daft. But really knowledgeable staff may surprise you.

What they say	What they mean
Tongy's been caning that	It's in the charts, you moron
That's huge in Ayia Napa	**There's a vaguely garage remix**
Very deep	It'll clear the floor in seconds
Nicely minimal, that one	**Unbelievably boring**
It's a secret Robbie Rivera project	My mate made it last week
That's been flying off the shelves	**Now I've got rid of both copies**
That was the tune in Miami	It's on my friend's label
It's a grower	**You'll hate it**

25

2. **How to** buy equipment

It's pricey, but go for the best stuff you can afford. Decent decks are essential; spend as much as you can on turntables and then sort out the rest of your gear with the money left over.

What you'll need

Vinyl	CD
Two turntables	Two CD decks
Two cartridges (with needles)	(or one double CD deck)
Two slipmats	
One mixer	
Headphones	
An amplifier and speakers (or a hi-fi system you can plug your mixer into)	

Check out the equipment reviews and ads in the back of dance mags. Test drive other people's equipment, and talk to anyone you can about what's good and what isn't. Equipment stores should be pretty helpful: ask to play with their goodies and don't believe everything they say.

Where to shop

Online stores

DJ Empire www.djempire.co.uk

DJ Store www.djstore.com

DJ Superstore www.djsuperstore.co.uk

Guildford Sound & Light www.guildfordsoundandlight.com

JB's Music www.jbsmusic.com

Richer Sounds www.richersounds.com

Sapphires www.decks.co.uk

The DJ Shop www.thedjshop.co.uk

Manufacturers websites

Allen & Heath www.allen-heath.co.uk
Citronic www.citronic.com
Denon www.denon.dj
Gemini www.geminidj.com
Kam www.kam.co.uk
Numark www.numark.com
Ortofon www.ortofon.com
Pioneer www.pioneer.co.uk

Sennheiser www.sennheiser.com
Shure www.shure.com
Sony www.sony.co.uk
Stanton www.stantonmagnetics.com
Tascam www.tascam.co.uk
Technics www.technics1210.com
Vestax www.vestax.co.uk

Which turntables?

The essentials

>> **Direct drive**
Direct drive turntables are the only kind to use for DJing. Don't buy belt-drive decks: they use rubber bands and are disastrous for mixing.

>> **Decent torque**
Torque is twist power. Put a record and a slipmat on the turntables you're thinking of buying. Can you hold the record still while the platter turns underneath? If the platter slows down a lot the motor is too weak.

>> **Pitch control**
Unwavering speed and reliable pitch control are essential for mixing records. How smooth is the adjustment? How long does the platter take to speed up?

>> **Sturdy construction**
You want a heavy, unshakeable platter. A wobbly platter or tone-arm will make your records jump.

Why Technics?

A concert pianist expects a Steinway; a DJ expects Technics. Despite valiant competition, Technics SL1200 turntables remain the undisputed industry standard (the 1210 is the same model in black). Introduced in 1972, they are simple, elegant machines that just get on with the job. They start instantly, they've got torque like a tractor and they're strong enough for mad scratch DJs to do handstands on. Their only fault was that the pitch control could waver when close to zero, but the MkIII version (new in 2001) completely cured this.

Almost every decent club worldwide uses Technics, so if you learn on them you'll have few surprises. Sure they're expensive – a pair of MkIIs costs around £670, with MkVs around £770 – but they have a strong resale value if you change your mind about DJing. A secondhand pair (£250-£450) is a good bet because they're pretty indestructible.

27

The challengers

The top-of-the-range models from Gemini and Numark are fine decks, but for £50 more you can have Technics. You might, however, be swayed by Vestax and their futuristic PDX range. You can change the pitch control to make it much more sensitive; they have digital read-outs, straight tone-arms for better scratching, pitch change up to a massive +/-50%, and a pitch-bend stick; you can even put them in reverse. If gadgets turn you on, they're £650-£700 a pair.

On a budget

OK, they're only for your bedroom, but those really cheap decks simply won't do what you need them to. Even if you're really strapped, you should try and spend at least £400. For that you'll get a serviceable pair of turntables. (Mind you, learning on cheap decks is like playing football barefoot. When you finally get some decent boots, it's suddenly much easier.)

Value packages

Most DJ equipment stores advertise combinations of mixer, cartridges and headphones. If you're happy with the decks and mixer these are usually good value, but never go below £450, and expect the headphones and cartridges to be basic. Avoid the everything-in-one-box 'instant DJ' packages, though: these are toys for babies.

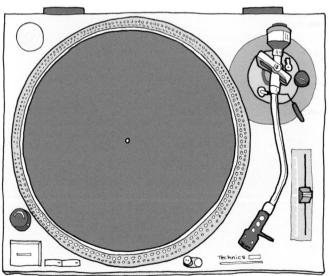

28

Adapter	Fits over the spindle for 7-inch singles with big holes.
Power switch	Turns the whole thing on or off.
Start/stop button	Hit it once and the platter turns. Hit it again and it stops. The better turntables have electromagnetic brakes.
Speed buttons	Set the speed at either 33 or 45rpm (revolutions per minute).
Strobe light	Flashes 50 times a second so you can see how precisely your deck's spinning from the dots on the platter. They stand still when you're at exactly 33 or 45rpm. You don't really use this for DJing but it's a good way of testing whether secondhand decks have any motor or pitch control problems.
Light	A headlight for your needle so you can see if you've got time for a pee.
Platter	The bit that spins.
Spindle	The knob in the middle of the platter.
Stylus	The needle that finds the groove.
Cartridge	Turns the needle's vibrations into electronic signals.
Tone-arm	Can be straight or S-shaped.
Height adjust	Raises or lowers the whole tone-arm. It locks with a little lever.
Anti-skate control	Keeps the needle in the centre of the groove.
Cueing lever	Lifts the tone-arm up off the record or lets it down slowly.
Counterweight	Balances the weight of the cartridge so the needle doesn't dig in too hard.
Pitch control	Speeds up or slows down the rotation so you can match records with different tempos. The standard range is +/-8%, though some decks offer more. The longer the slide the more delicate the changes you can make.
Green light	Comes on when the pitch control is set to zero, ie when the platter's going at exactly 33 or 45rpm.
Phono leads	Plug into your mixer.
Earth lead	Fixes into the screw on the back of your mixer to prevent nasty noises.

Which mixer?

A mixer does exactly what it says on the tin: it takes music from two or more sources and mixes it together. Plus it lets you listen to one record while everyone else hears another.

Provided it has all the basic controls (and the inputs and outputs you need for your set-up), you can learn to mix on the cheapest mixer. Expensive ones just give you better sound quality and more precise control. Secondhand mixers are easy to come by as there's always someone upgrading.

Turntablists

If you're a bit hip hop you might want a mixer with crossfaders designed for scratching, and other turntablist-friendly features, like a hamster switch and adjustable crossfader curves.

Channel one upfader (Channel fader)	Turns up the volume on one deck.
Channel two upfader (Channel fader)	Turns up the volume on the other deck.
Crossfader (X-fader)	Fully over to the left you hear channel one. Fully over to the right you hear channel two. In the middle you hear them both equally. Move this across and it fades one channel out and the other one in.
Cueing	Decides which channel you hear in your headphones. This is completely separate from what's going on with the other controls.
Headphone volume	How loud it is in your ears.
Master volume	How loud the signal going to your amplifier is.
Level indicators	Some records are louder than others. Most mixers have a level meter showing the volume of the record you're cueing so you can match it to what's playing.
Gain	If you've got a quiet record, the gain controls boost its volume.
Line/phono switch	Switches between different things plugged into the same channel, eg your turntable (plugged into 'phono') and your tape or CD player (plugged into 'line').

The extras

Multichannel	More channels let you mix more sound sources – a CD player, keyboards, a sampler, a computer, maybe three turntables... Most mixers have at least four inputs even if they only have two channels.
Mic input	You can plug a microphone into most mixers. Some have a separate volume control; others automatically input it to one of their channels.
Kills	Kill switches turn off the bass, midrange or treble completely. Rotary kills let you turn them each up or down gradually. Many mixers have both.
Split-cue	Lets you hear two channels in your headphones, one in each ear. It's very useful for mixing in a noisy booth or if you don't have a monitor.
Premium crossfaders	A scratch DJ's crossfader gets about a million times more abuse than normal, so it needs to be extra high quality.
Booth output	This adjusts the volume of the monitor speaker in your booth.
Crossfader assign (hamster switch)	This allows you to choose which two channels the crossfader fades between. Scratch DJs use it to give them more flexibility.
Transform (Punch) buttons	Transforming is a scratch where you cut up a long noise with the fader. This button does the hard work for you by punching in the opposite channel.
Crossfader curve adjusts	Some mixers have different settings for how quickly one channel comes up to full volume when you move the crossfader. These can be pictured as curves.
Effects (FX) send and returns	Let you use external effects units (reverb, echo, delay, a sampler...). You 'send' a channel out to it and let the unit 'return' its warped and mutated signal.
Pan	Lets you flit a song from one side of the room to the other. It keeps the bass constant in both speakers but moves the midrange and treble.
BPM counters	These give you a digital read-out of a record's tempo in bpm (beats per minute). Avoid them. Learning to beatmatch is about training your ears to do this. Use a silicon chip to do your dirty work and you'll never figure it out.
Built-in effects	Effects take the signal and mess with it creatively, adding echo, reverb or other crazy things.
Built-in samplers	These let you sample a snatch of a record and loop it up for a bit of live re-editing.

31

Which CD decks?

More and more people are starting their DJing careers with CDs, not least because collecting music this way can be so much cheaper than vinyl. For more about CD decks, see p90 *How to mix CDs*.

Built-in mixers aren't a good idea – to upgrade you'll have to replace everything. Good twin decks start at around £400, but single decks give you the most flexibility for the future (ie if you want to move into vinyl but carry on playing CDs). Decent single decks are about £250 upwards, but you'll find some as low as £150.

What to look for

The major differences are in the controls for cueing and pitch adjustment, extra functions (eg looping and effects), and of course sound quality. Another key thing to test is how fast the 'instant start' is. Get your head around the basic controls before you buy your decks, and never buy the kind without a jog wheel – they're much harder to cue with.

Pioneer

Pioneer CD decks, notably the CDJ800 (about £530 each) and CDJ1000 (about £800 each), are quickly carving out a reputation as the industry standard – the CD equivalent of Technics turntables.

Denon

The other widely established brand is Denon, who pioneered double CD decks for DJs, and you'll find their excellent decks in many clubs.

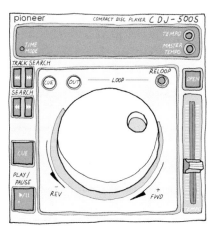

Track search/skip	Takes you to a particular track.
Search	Fast-forwards you to your chosen place in a song.
Jog wheel	Usually has several functions, depending on what you're doing. When you're cueing up a track it lets you move frame-by-frame (ie very slowly) through the music to find your exact starting point. Push it a little further and you go slightly faster. Once you've started the track playing it usually acts as a pitch bend, so you can synchronise the beats with what's playing.
Cue	When the track's paused this sets a cue point. When the track's playing this takes you straight back to it.
Play/pause	The equivalent of a start/stop button.
Tempo control (Pitch control)	Speeds up or slows down the track so you can match songs with different tempos.
Tempo control adjust	Changes the range of the tempo control (eg from +/-10% to +/-16%).
Read-out	Usually shows the track number and the track counter (as time remaining).
BPM counters	Give you a digital read-out of a tune's tempo in bpm (beats per minute).
Anti-shock system	CDs are sensitive to knocks; some players have better protection against this than others.
Vinyl emulation	The best players give you a fake turntable platter so you can control the CD as though it was a record.
Wave display	This feature shows you where the loud and quiet parts of the track are.
Loop controls	Many CD players let you loop up a section of music.
Extra cue points	Fancy models let you mark multiple cue points on a track.
Hot cue	Lets you mark a cue point when the track is playing. You can then go back to that point at the flick of a switch.
Data memory	Lets you save your cue points ready for when you next play the same track. Often saved on to an optional memory card.
Master tempo	Lets you adjust a track's tempo (its bpm) without changing its pitch (its notes).
Reverse	Lets you play backwards.
BPM synch	Some twin decks will beatmatch for you (up to a point).

Cartridges & needles

Spherical stylus

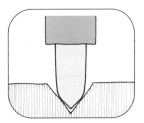

Elliptical stylus

Headshell and cartridge

All-in-one cartridge

The needle, or 'stylus', is a sharp diamond that rides along the groove of a record and vibrates on its tiny bumps. The cartridge ('cart') turns these vibrations into electrical signals, which end up as music.

You could spend thousands on a cartridge. The top-end 'audio-phile' models are marvels of sensitivity and costliness. However, for DJing you need a knock-about one that will stay in the groove. Even the best DJ cartridges are a compromise between rugged-ness and sound quality.

Decks don't usually include cartridges

The store might throw in some basic ones for free (remember to ask), but they might try to get you to spend more for some slightly better ones. Basic carts come in around £50 a pair. Good ones start around £100 a pair and the best DJing ones at £150 each. You need two, obviously. Is the price for a pair or for each one?

Cartridges come complete with a needle

When the needle starts to wear out, you replace it separately. New needles cost about half the price of the total cartridge.

Beginners

If you're starting out, go for basic carts like the Stanton 500AL. These are pretty rugged, and while you're a clumsy beginner there's no point in spending more.

Man-handlers

If you manipulate the vinyl a lot, doing spins and scratching etc, get a headshell-mounted cartridge with a spherical needle. Spherical needles give you better tracking (they don't jump out so easily), however they will wear your records quicker and the sound quality is slightly worse. With a headshell you have more ways to adjust the position of the cartridge and usually more weight holding the needle down.

Smoothies

If your style doesn't depend on whipping the needle all over the place, you're better off with an elliptical needle. This won't track as securely, but the sound quality will be better and your vinyl will survive longer. You can also take advantage of the all-in-one cartridge designs (the long, elegant ones) which are better for see-ing where the needle is in the record.

Headphones

A DJ packs his own headphones, and in the wild they're a matter of life and death. Up in your room you can live with second-raters, but when you're cueing up a record in a noisy booth you have to be able to hear more than a few distorted bass kicks. Top of the range will cost you £100 plus; decent ones are around £50. Anything much cheaper will be a bedroom-only compromise.

Comfortable and rugged
They'll be on your head for hours so go for lightweight and well padded headphones with a long, thick cord. If an adapter is needed to change the plug from Walkman size (3.5mm) to mixer size (6.3mm), a screw-fitting one is best.

Closed back
This means they cover your ears. You want them to cut out as much background noise as possible.

Good sound
Loud and clear, please. They need to have a 'wide frequency response' (from 20-20,000Hz) – the full set of highs and lows – and a 'high sound pressure level' – they go loud without distorting. If you turn up the bass and they go *klumph* or *plopp*, look for another pair.

Low impedance
Impedance is a measure of how hard it is to push electricity through something. Your headphones should match (roughly) your mixer output.

Slipmats

Ditch the rubber mats that came with your turntables and replace them with slipmats – circular felt mats that sit under the record and let it slip. They're your cheapest bit of kit, but crucial. Now you can hold the record still while the platter runs underneath. Let go and it starts instantly.

Slipmats are like t-shirts for decks, so there's a huge choice of design. The most practical are plain ones, however, because too much printing might cause a lack of slip, or even scuff your records. Scratch DJs need the slippiest slipmats so they can whip the record back and forth – they'll often use an extra bit of shiny paper for greater slip; in an emergency you can use a record's inner sleeve.

35

3. **How to** set up

Now you've got your expensive equipment, it's time to hook it up and get cracking.

How to fit it together

Connect everything with the power off and all volume controls (faders, gains and master volume on the mixer; the volume on your amplifier or hi-fi) at zero. Then switch on, play a tune and gradually adjust things. This way you won't blow anything if it's connected wrong. And read the instruction books, dummy.

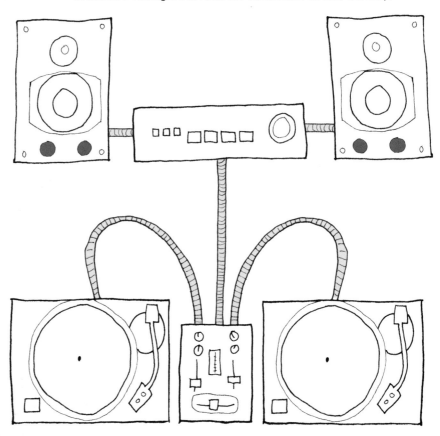

Ground wires

Turntables have little, thin ground wires to protect against static hum. It's important to connect these to the screw on the back of your mixer (or amplifier) marked 'Ground' or 'Gnd' or 'Earth'.

Phono plugs

Most equipment connects using a double cable with two phono plugs on each end ('RCA plugs' in American). (R)ed always carries the (R)ight stereo signal; white or black carries the left.

Mixer inputs

- The input sockets on your mixer will be marked Ch 1, Ch 2, Ch 3, according to which channel they feed into. Each channel should have a choice of 'line' inputs and 'phono' inputs.
- Plug your turntable leads into the 'phono' inputs. If you plug them into the 'line' inputs they'll be too quiet.
- Plug your CD (or tape) player leads into the 'line' inputs. If you plug them into the 'phono' inputs they will distort and could blow something.
- Set the 'phono/line' switch according to the inputs you have used.

Mixer outputs

- The 'master' output should connect to either your amplifier or your hi-fi system. If you're plugging into a hi-fi, plug the mixer into a 'CD', 'aux' or 'tape' input, rather than a 'phono' one.
- Other outputs might include 'rec', which can go to a tape recorder, 'booth', which is for an extra monitor speaker, and 'send', which is for external effects boxes.

37

How to adjust your turntables

It's important that your decks are on a sturdy, level surface. Also, if your speakers are too near them, or resting on the same table, you might get some horrible feedback noises (the needle picking up vibrations from the speakers).

Adjust the counterweight

Think of your tone-arm as a see-saw. The counterweight is the fat kid on one end who balances the needle on the other and stops it digging into your records. Move the fat kid further away from the pivot and the needle gets lighter.

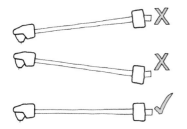

1. Take the tone-arm off its rest but be careful not to bang the needle against anything.

2. Turn the counterweight until it exactly balances the cartridge. The tone-arm should float freely with neither needle nor counterweight pulling down.

3. It's as if the needle weighs nothing, so turn the numbered plastic ring near the counterweight to zero.

4. Now when you turn the counterweight anti-clockwise it moves inwards and makes the needle end heavier. The plastic ring will move with it and the numbers on this tell you how much 'weight' you're adding to the needle.

How much weight should you add? You have three choices.

- Stick to the 'tracking force' or 'stylus pressure' recommended by the cartridge manufacturer. Check on their website. For DJ carts it's usually between two and five grams.
- Add the bare minimum to stop your records jumping during normal DJing.
- Add as much as possible because you're a turntablist and you want better tracking (less jumping). However, this will worsen the sound quality and wear your records and needles out quicker.

Some decks come with an extra screw-in counterweight. You only need this if you have a really heavy cartridge.

38

Adjust the anti-skating

In normal use this should be set to the same level as your stylus pressure. A forward-spinning record pulls the needle to the middle of the platter (that's centripetal force, physics fans). Anti-skating works to correct this and keep the needle in the middle of the groove. However, the moment you spin a record backwards, anti-skating is adding to the problem rather than lessening it. So scratch DJs usually turn it off (ie to zero).

Adjust the tone-arm height

On decks that let you adjust this there's a large ring at the base of the tone-arm assembly (plus a locking lever to hold it in place). Turning this ring raises or lowers everything to allow for cartridges of different heights. When the needle's resting on a record, your tone-arm should be parallel with the surface of the record (ie not sloping). This is how your cartridges and needles were designed to operate. However, most scratch DJs like to have this as high as possible, so the tone-arm slopes down and holds the needle in the groove better. Again, this is pretty harsh on everything.

Fun with Technics

Want to change your 1200's pitch control to +/-12% (or +/-3.3%), tighten up your brake or just change your lightbulb? These amazing websites have the know-how.

http://music.hyperreal.org/dj/sl1200.html
www.backspin.org
www.technics1210.com
www.htfr.com

'Last time I played I switched the power off by accident. I had to look round and go, "Oi, sort it out!"'
Fabio, *Mixmag*

39

4. **How to** get started

All plugged in and nowhere to go? You're probably itching to find the beatmatching chapter. Well don't. Sit still for a minute and learn something.

How to listen to a record

Your first exercise is to listen really closely to a record. You might think this is pointless but actually it's incredibly helpful (and quite Zen).

- Listen to some of your favourite tunes through headphones.
- Try to separate out the different musical elements of each record: the drums, the bassline, the melody. Imagine these are actual instruments played by different people.
- Pick out each element in turn and follow it through the record. Listen to where it starts and stops and where it does something different. Try to ignore all the other sounds on the record.
- Play with your EQ controls (bass, midrange, treble) to help pick out different instruments.

Records to learn with

Choose records that have a clear and simple drum pattern, and where the kick drum is the very first sound on the record. Intros that fade in, weird rhythms, or songs that start with a bassline or melody instead of drums are going to be confusing. 'Bonus beat' mixes and simple dubs of a tune are great to learn with. If you're starting from scratch, it might be a good idea to buy some records that you don't mind wearing out.

Helpful records

These actually introduce the instruments you're listening out for. The last one has Adolf Hitler playing vibes.

Danny Tenaglia	'Elements' (1997)
Technique's	'This Old House' (1995)
King Curtis	'Memphis Soul Stew' (1967)
Bonzo Dog Doo Dah Band	'The Intro And The Outro' (1973)

40

The basic elements

Kick drum

(Or 'bass drum', or 'kick'.) The one that goes *boom*, *boom*, *boom*. In a real drum kit it's the big one with the band's name on it, controlled by a foot pedal (hence the name). In most house records it hits on every beat (ie 1, 2, 3, 4); in most funk and hip hop records it hits 'on the one' (ie 1, -, -, -).

Snare drum

(Or just 'snare'.) The tight, snappy *chip*, *chip* drum-beat which makes the rhythm more complex, often by marking the off-beat in between the kick drum (*boom*, *chip*, *boom*). In a real kit it's the metal-framed drum at the drummer's side. It has steel springs against its lower skin for that distinctive 'biscuit-tin' sound.

Hi-hat

The cymbal that goes *tsst*, *tsst*, *tsst*. It's actually two cymbals which crash against each other, also controlled by a foot pedal. In most house records the hi-hat marks the off-beat.

Other percussion

Tom-toms are quite deep, rolling drums; congas and bongos are played with the hands and have that *slappety slap* sound (congas are bigger and bassier than bongos). You'll just have to figure out the other wonderful percussion noises for yourself: rimshots, timbales, cowbells, claps, kettle drums . . .

Bassline

On a club system you'll *feel* the bassline as well as hear it – that's why it's so important (along with drums) for dance music. Usually the drum and the bass lay down the groove – a repetitive rhythm – while the melody and vocals ride over the top doing something more doodly.

Melody

The bit you can whistle along to. Could be a saxophone, a guitar, an organ, a violin (strings), bells, some horns (brass), or it could be a sample, or a synthesiser programmed to sound like a combination of instruments (or like nothing on earth).

Vocals

Musically, you can think of vocals as a special kind of melody. However, because there's a person singing (or rapping) words that mean something, vocals have an extra emotional and storytelling power. They come in verses and choruses.

'I was DJing when it was still a dirty word. You were just somebody in the corner putting on records. Before I collected my wages I used to have to sweep the dancefloor and collect the empty glasses up.'

Tony De Vit, *Mixmag*

41

5. How to cue

'Cueing' means two things: 1) listening to the next record in your headphones while the dance-floor hears something else; 2) getting the needle in the right place and starting the record.

How to hear two things at once

The first part of cueing is about listening. DJs can listen to two records at once – one in the room and one in the headphones. At first this seems impossible, but after endless practice it becomes easy to separate the information coming from each ear.

1 Put two records on, with the crossfader set so you can hear one through the speakers.

2 Use the cue controls on your mixer to listen in your headphones to the same record that's playing out loud.

3 Change the cue controls so you hear the other record in your headphones. There should be one record in the room and a different one in your headphones.

4 Now hold your headphones so they only cover one ear. You'll be hearing a different record in each ear.

5 Adjust the volume levels (and the position of your head relative to the speakers) so the records sound equally loud.

6 Listen. Try to separate the two records in your head. You'll be doing a lot of this.

7 Change ears. Listen some more. Does one way feel more natural? Practise DJ poses with the headphones. Get someone to take pictures.

Split-cueing
Some mixers have a split-cue button which puts one record in each ear of your headphones, so in theory you can beatmatch without having to hear the speakers. This can be handy for cueing if you don't have a monitor.

Imagine – you finally make it to the top, earning thousands a night, and then you have to retire because your hearing's gone west. As soon as you're born, the nerve cells in your ears start to die. Loud music kills them off much faster, leading to deafness or tinnitus (permanent ringing in the ears). Neither of these is good for business, so start taking care of your hearing now. A DJ taking risks with his ears is like a carpenter leaving his tools in the rain.

How to keep your hearing

Sietech St Mary's Hearing Centre
020 7706 3051
Advanced Communication Solutions
01582 767007
www.hearnet.com/index.shtml
www.hearingcare.co.uk
www.sistersf.com/articles/earplugs.php
Geraldine Daly
55 Harley Street, London W1G 8QY
020 7323 2076.

Avoid unnecessary noise
Headphones create more sound pressure than external sources, so having your Walkman too loud is a common cause of hearing loss. Motorbikes and loud machinery are others. High frequencies are more damaging than low ones.

Give your ears a rest
Strangely, ears get tired, just like the rest of you. Listening for long periods without a break can be damaging on its own, whatever the volume level.

Get some earplugs
You can buy custom-made earplugs that reduce all frequencies by the same amount (up to 25dB), giving you lower volume without any loss in sound quality (so you can DJ with them in). These are pricey (£150) and involve having a mould made of your ear cavity, but vital if you're serious about not becoming a deaf DJ. Basic foam earplugs from the chemist (two pairs for a quid) will muddy the sound as well as reduce it. You should certainly use these when you're out clubbing, and some people find they can even DJ with them.

'DJs are powerful. Whether they want it or not, DJs have the power to change people. It's speaking without speaking.'
Armand Van Helden, *DJ Times*

43

How to man-handle a record

You need to be a superlover – rough enough to have complete control, but sensitive enough to not damage the grooves. Get to know your record's erogenous zones – the shiny parts round the edge and in the middle, plus the label – and then lay on your hands. Don't knock the tone-arm with those sleeves.

1 Use just one deck, playing through the speakers.

2 Use a record that starts with a solid kick-drum beat.

3 Put the needle on the record with the deck switched off and play around, moving it round by hand.

4 Switch on the deck. Play around, starting and stopping the record using the start/stop button. Listen to what it sounds like.

5 Practise holding the record still on the slipmat while the platter spins underneath.

6 Practise starting and stopping the record by hand, letting the platter spin underneath.

7 Practise winding the record backwards and then forwards using your fingers.

8 Practise finding the first beat and moving the record back and forth over it.

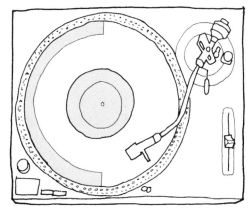

Touch/hold a record here.

Get used to lifting the needle carefully on and off the record by hand (DJs don't use the cueing lever).

44

Slip-cueing is the basis of it all: starting a record right on the beat.

How to slip-cue

1 Use just one deck, playing out loud.

2 Use a record that starts with a solid kick-drum beat.

3 Find the first beat and hold the record still, just behind the beat, with the platter moving underneath.

4 Move the record back and forth over the beat a few times – back, forwards, back, then let go.

5 To make the record start right away, at full speed, you'll have to give it a tiny push – a flick of the finger. The amount of flick you need depends on how good your decks are.

Exercises

• Concentrate on getting an instant start so the song plays at the correct speed right from the beginning.

• Practise hitting that first beat exactly when you want it. Eventually you'll almost feel it.

CD DJs
can slip-cue at the touch of a button.
See p90 *How to mix CDs*.

'There was a time before mixing came in when there was no cueing. You'd cue by looking at the record. You'd try to listen to the needle on top of the record. The guy who could leave the least amount of space in between each record was the top guy.'

Juan Atkins, *Looking For The Perfect Beat*

45

6. How to fade

Let's get to grips with your mixer. Think of it as a multiple volume control: you can turn up deck one, or deck two, or both together. And with the crossfader you can turn one up and the other down at the same time. This, young decksmaster, is the key to joining records together.

How to use your faders

There are two ways to fade between records.

With the crossfader in the centre you can use the upfaders (or 'channel faders') to bring one record down and the other up.

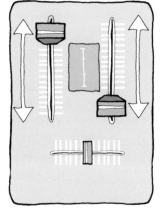

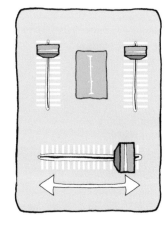

With the upfaders up you can slide the crossfader over from one record to another.

Explore the mixer controls
Put on two similar records and play around with the upfaders and crossfader. Fade from one record to the other.

- See where the two tunes are at equal volume.
- See where one takes over from the other.

Sliders vs knobs

We can thank Schindler's list for giving us the first stereo mixer. Alex Rosner was one of the children included on that life-saving set of names. Saved from the holocaust, Rosner settled in New York and fell in love with the world of recorded sound. After building the very first stereo club system for the 1964 World's Fair, he invented the Rosie, the first mixer designed especially for DJing. Pioneer DJ Francis Grasso used Rosie (it was painted red) in a club called the Haven where he made beatmixing a required skill as early as 1969. Rosner then helped Louis Bozak to develop the first commercially available DJ mixer, the Bozak, which is prized by collectors to this day. Top of the list of vintage mixers, however, is the Urei, a knobs-only (no faders or cross-fader) monster which big clubs have to wire up whenever they book American DJs of a certain age. Weirdly enough, retired boxer Nigel Benn's got a Urei, too.

Crossfaders differ in how quickly one channel comes up to full volume when you move the slider over. This can be pictured as a curve. Some mixers let you adjust the curve settings.

Crossfader curves

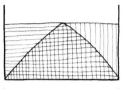

Beatmix curve
This is great for smooth mixing styles because you can move gradually from one channel to the other. There'll be no drop in sound level as you fade across.

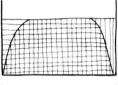

Scratch curve
Designed for scratching. You only need a small movement to bring in the other channel at full volume, so you can use the crossfader more like an on-off switch. Where it goes from on to off is called the 'cut-in point'.

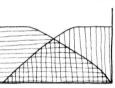

Dipped curve
This is an old-fashioned type and not much use for today's styles. It dips in the middle to compensate for the rise in level that comes when two tracks are mixed.

Your first set

As soon as you can fade you can play records one after the other without a gap. So forget about beatmatching for a moment – you're ready to play your first set.

1. Choose your first record and let it play.
2. Find a record that would be great next. Listen on headphones to make sure. Cue it up at a good starting point.
3. At a suitable point in the first record (you decide), start the next record and fade over to it.
4. Play your favourite records until you need to eat/sleep/pee.
5. Eat/sleep/pee and then go back and make a tape.

Some fades will sound pretty ragged, but some flukey ones might sound quite good. Do quick fades where the beats get tangled up and slow ones where you can (try fading over breakdowns or quiet bits). Some records work best with a gap and a clean beginning.

47

7. **How to** beatmatch

How many of you came straight to this page? Beatmatching – getting two records to play at the same tempo – is a skill you need for most kinds of mixing. It's about hearing which track is faster than the other and adjusting them until they match. Beatmatching is hard and the only way to learn it is to practise.

What you're trying to do

You're aiming to synchronise two tracks so the rhythms sit beautifully on top of each other. These diagrams show different pairs of records. Imagine the dots are the kick-drum beats.

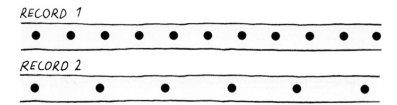

These records are out of synch because one is faster than the other.

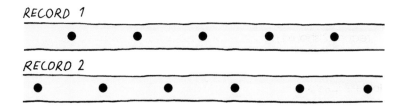

These records are the same speed but still out of synch.

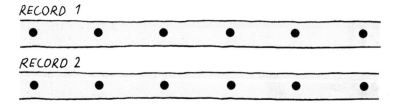

Now they're perfectly lined up.

How to cue up one record in time with another

When you first listen to two records together it just sounds all jumbled up – it's impossible to tell which one is faster. To make it much easier...

Start the second record in time with the beat of the song playing live
This should start them off in synch. If they're adjusted right they'll stay in time; if not, they'll drift apart. And the faster they drift, the more they need adjusting.

1 Use two records with clear, solid drum-beats – the simpler the better (beats-only tracks are great to practise with).

2 Set the mixer so record 1 is playing out loud and record 2 is in your headphones. You should have one record in each ear.

3 Find the first beat on record 2. Move it back and forth in time with the record that's playing – like you're tapping out the rhythm.

4 When you're ready, let go on the beat. The first beat of record 2 should play in time to record 1.

When you can do this accurately, beatmatching will start to seem a lot less impossible.

> **CD DJs**
> can do this at the touch of a button.
> **See p90** *How to mix CDs*.

'There's nothing like it, is there? Making those records work together. That connection with the crowd and that energy that you're putting through the mix. And on the right night when that energy combines – the two forces – there's nothing that comes near that high. For the audience and the DJ as well.'

Danny Rampling

49

How to hear which record is faster

Trust us, you'll only get this with loads of practice. There's no short cut. You're actually rewiring your brain, and that takes sheer, endless repetition. All we can really tell you to do is:

- start your second record in time with the one that's playing
- listen to the drum-beats and decide which is faster.

Just try to do it, over and over, and one day you'll realise you can.

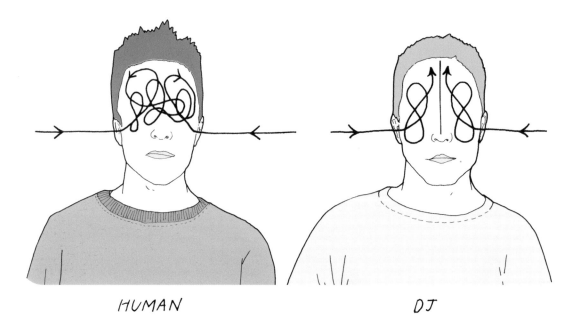

HUMAN   DJ

The following things might help

Make it a race
Listen for which record finishes four bars (or eight bars) first.

Simplify the rhythm
Concentrate on the kick drum and ignore everything else.

Dance to one
Move a little to the record that's playing – tap your foot or nod your head.

Count the other
If you're marking one beat with your body, it leaves your head free to count the other beat.

How do you hear beats on two records at once?
At first you'll have to count, and that's confusing. But with practice you'll just *hear* four beats without counting them (like you just see four dots on a dice).

How do you know if it's faster or slower?
Eventually you'll just be able to hear it. Until then, use trial and error. Take an educated guess, then adjust things. If you guessed right you'll have corrected the problem a bit; if you guessed wrong you'll have made it worse.

How can you tell the two records apart?
One clue is the noise that two records make when they're out of synch. Instead of a clean kick-drum *boom*, you'll hear *b-boom*. Listen carefully to this noise and you can hear whether the extra *b-* is in the headphones or the speakers. This will tell you which record is hitting the beat first.

How can you hear really small differences?
Practise. At first you'll only be able to hear big differences in speeds. But gradually your skill will increase until you can spot tiny ones without consciously trying. The more you practise, the more obvious they'll become.

Do you always count kick drums?
Not necessarily. As you get better you'll be able to hear the beat in all sorts of rhythms, even ones without a kick. Some people beat-match by lining up hi-hats.

Imagine drum-beats stuck together
This is how you perceive beats when you get good at it – like a series of dots stuck with glue. If they go out of time, the glue stretches and you need to pull them back in line.

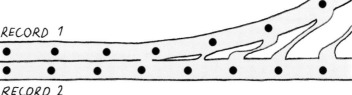

RECORD 1

RECORD 2

Headphone mix

Some mixers let you mix the two tunes in your headphones, so you can do a dry run of the real thing. As you're cueing up a record you can add a bit of the record that's playing and do a final check that everything's lined up and ready. On mixers with this feature you'll find a knob (sometimes a slider) marked 'cue' which goes from 'CUE' (or 'PFL') to 'PGM'.

- On CUE/PFL ('Pre Fader Level') you hear the record you're cueing.
- On PGM ('Programme Monitor') you hear what's in the speakers.
- In between you hear a mix of the two.

This can be handy in a noisy booth or when your monitor is rubbish, and it's a great way to check that your record is cued right. But don't learn to rely on it because not all mixers have it.

How to adjust a record's speed

The pitch control sets the speed of a record and keeps it constant (until you change it). But you have to find the right setting. Most DJs use their hands to give the record a burst of the accelerator or a touch of the brakes, and then move the pitch slider to hold it at its new speed.

>> **Adjust the speed** (by hand).

>> **Set the speed** (with the pitch control).

>> **Test the speed** (by getting the beats back in synch or by cueing up the record again).

You can adjust the speed with your hands in the following ways. The quality of your decks will make a big difference to what happens.

To slow it briefly

Brush the platter very gently.

Nip the spindle between finger and thumb.

Stroke the label gently.

To speed it briefly

Twirl the spindle between finger and thumb.

Push on the edge of the label and walk it round.

CD DJs
can do all this with the 'pitch bend' controls.
See p90 *How to mix CDs*.

53

When you're learning

At first you'll have to keep going back and restarting the second record.

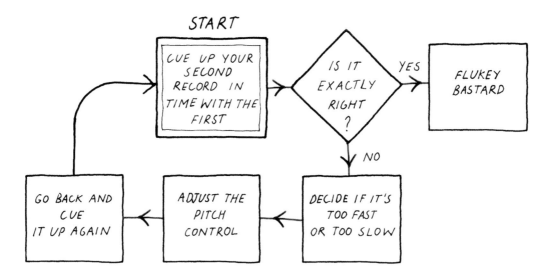

When you're getting good

Soon you'll be able to correct the speed by hand quickly enough to keep the second record from ever going out of synch.

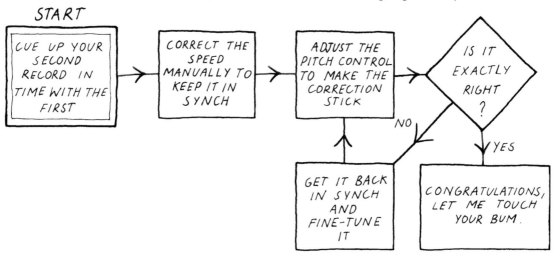

Fine-tuning

The correct speed is there somewhere. You have to find it by making finer and finer adjustments.

- You start with the record at zero. It's too slow.
- You pitch it up to +1, test it, it's still too slow.
- Then you pitch it up to +3, test it, it's too fast.
- Now you know the correct speed is somewhere between +1 and +3.
- You pitch it to +2, test it, it's a tiny bit too fast.
- Now you know the correct speed is somewhere between +1 and +2.

Every time you test it, you narrow down the possibilities until you know exactly where the correct speed is hiding. Eventually you'll be moving the pitch control in hair-breadths.

Is the speed wrong or are the beats just not lined up?

The key is to decide whether the beats are drifting further and further apart, or whether the misalignment is staying pretty constant (a regular *b-boom*). Only if there's drifting do you still need to adjust the pitch. If there's no drifting you just need to tweak the record a little (a quick spindle twirl or a gentle platter rub).

It was too slow, now it's too fast. How do I get it exactly right?

Assuming it's not just a crappy turntable, this happens when you're not making small enough changes to the pitch control. You've tried two settings – the correct speed is somewhere in between.

How can I be sure I've got it right?

Test it. Cue up your second record, start it in time with the first one and listen to it in your headphones for as long as you like. If the beats start to drift away, make a tiny adjustment and try again.

I thought I had them exactly matched, but then they drifted apart

Decide which record is slightly faster and make a really small adjustment to the pitch control. Then get the records back in synch and test them again. This kind of thing will happen for ages; it's just a sign that your ears need more practice. Eventually you'll be able to hear that the two tunes aren't perfectly matched long before they go off into a gallop.

'For a lot of DJs now, blending is the most important thing. When I was coming up we were playing on turntables without pitch control, but you could still set the tone and mood and take people where you wanted to go.'

Ron Trent, *Muzik*

Beatmatching problems

Decks with poor pitch control

This is why bargain turntables aren't such a bargain. Bad decks may waver slightly, speeding up or slowing down when you didn't ask them to.

Decks with weak motors

You gently brush the platter to slow it a little and it stops completely. Or you give the spindle a little tweak and it doubles in speed. Don't say we didn't warn you.

Records that change tempo

Bad edits can throw a record out of synch. And anything with live drums will have fluctuations. Once upon a time all records wavered in tempo because they were powered by real humans. DJs managed to cope and so will you. Don't forget – 'French Kiss' slows down in the middle.

The Godfather of beatmixing

More than anyone else it was Francis Grasso who made beatmixing a required skill for DJs. This Brooklyn-born Italian-American was the first DJ to mix records in a way that DJs do today and the first to make his sets a real performance rather than just a series of tunes. His triumph was to make his nights as much about his personality and tastes as it was about the records he played. And he was doing this not in the eighties, but in 1969. Grasso started in New York clubs The Haven and The Sanctuary, and in his day was a pop star in his home city every bit as big as someone like Carl Cox is today. He dated Liza Minnelli, hung out with Jimi Hendrix and claims to have spent more than his rent on drugs. Together with his close friends Steve D'Acquisto and Michael Cappello, not to mention other pioneers like David Mancuso and Grandmaster Flowers, Grasso rewrote the rules on the way we hear music in clubs. Sadly, on March 18th 2001, he was found dead in his apartment, just one week before his 53rd birthday. If you're a DJ, he was your godfather. DJ Francis, we salute you.

Other beatmatching exercises

We think beatmatching is best learnt by jumping in at the deep end and splashing away until you can swim. But you might want to try these 'arm-band' methods.

Use two copies of the same record

Since they're exactly the same tempo, it makes some of the exercises simpler.

- Set them both at zero so they're the same tempo and practise cueing up one over the other (maybe without headphones: see below).
- Or set the pitch controls so you know one's faster to begin with, and then try correcting it.

Watch it, though – it's harder to separate the two records in your head when they're the same song. Also, be aware that two identical records will behave strangely when they are slightly out of whack – their waveforms will cancel each other out and instead of a double-thump you might hear a whooshing noise. Do this on purpose and it's a clever trick called phasing (see p182 *How to do deck effects*).

Practise without headphones

This keeps it simple when you're learning how to cue up a record in time with another. Put the crossfader in the middle so both records play through the speakers. You can hear your mistakes quicker and you can concentrate on your dexterity without having to worry about rewiring your ears. However, split-hearing is the most crucial skill to develop for beatmatching and this won't help it at all.

Counting bpms

To take the pulse of a record, count how many beats it has in 15 seconds (don't count the beat on which you start your timer), then multiply by four. (Or count for 30 seconds and double it.) This gives you its bpm (beats per minute) count. Some DJs write the bpm on their records, and this can be handy as a guide for programming or as a rough starting point for beatmatching. However, for a precise adjustment you're going to have to use your ears, so don't rely on this. We forbid you to learn with a digital bpm counter for the simple reason that most clubs don't have them.

8. How to blend

A blend is a smooth and gradual transition from one record to another with the beats synchronised. Blends are great for most varieties of house and techno, but genres based on breakbeats (hip hop, breaks, drum & bass, UK garage...) use cuts more than blends. King genre for long, seamless blends is progressive house, where DJs will overlap records for days.

Once you can beatmatch, blends are as easy as one, two, three. In real life you'll learn beatmatching and blends at the same time.

1 Beatmatch.
2 Fade the second record in.
3 Fade the first record out.

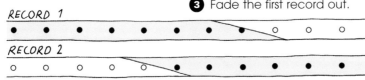

How to blend with the crossfader

1 Start with both upfaders up and the crossfader over to one side, so record 1 is in the speakers.
2 Beatmatch record 2 to the same tempo as record 1. Start it in your headphones in time with record 1.
3 Move the crossfader slowly over to the middle until you have both playing at once.
4 Now move the crossfader slowly the rest of the way until record 2 is playing on its own.

How to blend with the upfaders

This does the same thing but gives you a little more control over the mix.

1 Start with the crossfader in the centre and upfader 1 up, so record 1 is in the speakers.
2 Beatmatch record 2 to the same tempo as record 1. Start it in your headphones in time with record 1.
3 Move upfader 2 slowly up until you have both records playing at once.
4 Now move upfader 1 slowly down until record 2 is playing on its own.
5 Casually strut around the room.

58

How to fine-tune your beatmatching

The aim is to get the next record perfectly beatmatched in your headphones before you start the mix. But even the best DJ has to make small adjustments during the mix, when the dancefloor can hear both records. Here are some rules about these 'nudges':

- Few people will notice you nudging a record if it only has drum-beats playing.
- But don't mess with a record that's playing a melody (especially strings); they'll hear the notes bend.
- All things being equal, it's better to nudge whichever record is quieter in the mix at that moment.
- The needle will pick up the noise of your fingers on the record, so keep manual adjustments to a minimum and if you brush the platter, do it away from the needle.
- Twirling the spindle is preferable to pushing the label round because it's smoother and subtler and because pushing the label risks making the record slip.

How the experts do it

In a perfect world you'd never touch the platter during a mix – you would do your nudges using only the pitch control, giving the slider a little boost up or down then returning it to precisely the same position. But this is easier said than done and few DJs can really do it (you need to be experienced enough to *anticipate* the tracks going out of synch). Top-of-the-range Vestax decks have a special pitch bend lever which does it for you.

CD DJs
often have a master tempo feature which lets them adjust tempo without changing pitch. This is great for hiding nudges.
See p90 *How to mix CDs*.

'The DJ's power is like a parent. It's like a president. The DJ has a responsibility, like any person in power. When you have an audience you better do the right thing and make sure you educate. Let them know what you're about, and make sure you're saying something they want to hear.'

DJ Pierre

How to listen during a mix

When you were cueing you had one record in each ear. But now the speakers are playing a mixture of both records. How on earth do you separate them? Here's where your new split-hearing skills get clever.

To hear record 1
Ignore anything in the mix that's also in the head-phones. Concentrate on what isn't in the head-phones.

To hear record 2
Concentrate on what's in the headphones. Ignore everything else.

Listen to the live mix
It's important to check out what your mix sounds like through the speakers, so you know how the dancefloor's actually hearing it. At first you'll be too busy worrying about your beatmatching, but as you get better you'll have time to come out from your headphones.

Swap the cue
When you're bringing in record 2, have record 2 in your head-phones. But when you start to fade out record 1, it's often helpful to swap the cueing over and have record 1 in your headphones.

Be careful – if you swap which record's in your headphones, make sure you also swap which record you're looking at (and/or touching). Forgetting to do this is how DJs take off the wrong tune.

Get the levels right
Some records are quieter than others, so as you bring in a tune you may need to adjust it to match the one playing. In theory, when you're halfway through the blend, both records should be of equal volume. If this isn't the case, simply adjust the upfader to compensate.

Most mixers have level meters to help you compare volumes *before* you do a mix. For more on using these, see p70 *How to cut*.

How to mix with the bass out

Two records playing together at full volume can sound pretty muddy. EQ controls (separate bass, midrange and treble for each channel) let you clean up your mixes.

1 Turn down the bass on record 2 before you fade it in.
2 Fade in record 2.
3 Turn down the bass on record 1 as you turn up the bass on record 2. (On some mixes you'll do this slowly; on others abruptly, swapping from one bassline to the other.)
4 Fade out record 1.

Experiment with this idea
There's lots more you can do with the EQ during a blend, whether to tidy up a mix or add drama. You might cut the treble to mix just the bass of record 2 into a quiet passage of record 1, or to cut back hi-hats or vocals which are much louder in one record than another. Be creative.

Varying your blends

How you mix two records depends on their sound, their structure and the effect you want to achieve. See p74 *How to place a mix*.

Quick blend
The no-fuss method. For when you don't want to do an abrupt cut, but you also don't want to blur the two songs completely into each other. This works well for hip hop and for tracks with live drummers.

Slow fade in and slow fade out
This works for very repetitive songs which build slowly. Here you're imperceptibly changing from one song to another.

Slow fade in then crash out
If the incoming song starts off by building to a crescendo, you can take advantage of this. Blend it in slowly until the high point arrives, then crash the crossfader over.

Overlays
Two records making love. Sometimes two tracks fit so perfectly you can blend them for a really long time. It takes concentration to keep them in synch, but pull it off and you've made a new track.

61

9. **How to** match phrases

To be a good DJ your mixes have to obey the same musical rules as your records. So when you mix two tracks you have to line up more than just their beats or you'll have a mess on your hands. Get ready for a lot of counting.

On nearly all dance records the action happens in fours and eights. There are four beats to each bar (this is '4/4 time'), and the music is usually arranged in four-bar 'phrases'. These phrases are arranged together to create the structure of a song (eg a 16-bar intro, a 32-bar breakdown, an eight-bar solo...). Even Mozart wrote his music in four and eight-bar chunks.

When you mix you should line up records' phrases as well as their beats.

How to count beats, bars and phrases

Train yourself to divide music into beats, bars and four-bar phrases. Practise counting whenever you hear music – especially if you're out on a dancefloor.

Count beats

- Listen to a dance tune and count out 1, 2, 3, 4, 1, 2, 3, 4... in time with the music. You're counting beats.

Count bars

Each group of four beats is a bar (a 'measure' in American).

- Change it so you're counting **1**, 2, 3, 4, **2**, 2, 3, 4, **3**, 2, 3, 4, **4**, 2, 3, 4... Now you're counting bars.

You might want to count the beats in your head and the bars on your fingers.

> ### Tricky time signatures
>
> Not all dance music is in 4/4 time (four beats in a bar). Some jazz, Latin and African records use different time signatures. **See p85** *How to match rhythms*.

How a musician sees bars

How we see bars

Count four-bar phrases

Start to hear music divided into four-bar phrases. These usually travel in pairs (ie they're repeated to make an eight-bar section). This is very important for understanding song structure and putting your mixes in the right place.

1 Listen to a dance tune.

2 Count its bars.

3 Notice how every four bars there's a little marker in the music (eg an extra twiddle in the drum pattern).

4 And every eight bars there's a bigger marker (eg a cymbal crash).

5 Notice how, if the music changes or a new instrument is introduced, it happens after one of these markers.

As a rough guide, every four bars something little happens, and every eight bars something bigger happens.

How to spot phrases

Musicians and producers are helpful – they put full stops in the music to mark the end of one phrase and the start of another. Listen for these clues in your records:

- a cymbal crash
- a reversed cymbal crash (`ssshuuup`)
- another noise that builds up to a sudden climax, eg a synth woosh, an explosion
- extra drum-beats or percussion in the last bar of a phrase
- missing drum-beats or percussion in the last bar of a phrase
- an instrument finishing a solo or a vocalist finishing a verse or chorus
- James Brown shouting `Hit it!'

> ### Correct terminology
>
> Classical and jazz musicians give the word 'phrase' a slightly different meaning. To them it's any snatch of melody, rhythm or harmonic progression, the same as a 'riff' in rock music or a 'phrase' in speech.

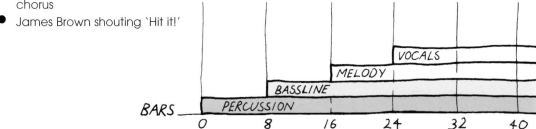

Dance music is built on an eight-bar grid.
Your records are built from pairs of four-bar phrases.

63

How to match phrases

You should mix so you don't break up a record's phrases. If you cut one off halfway or start halfway through a phrase, it will throw your dancers off. Just make sure you synchronise both tunes' phrases when you start your mix.

- Cue up your incoming record so its first beat is the start of a phrase.
- Start the mix at the start of a phrase in the outgoing record.

If you get it right, the two records will groove along within the same structure and their musical 'events' will be synchronised. Get it wrong and you'll create a very confusing mix.

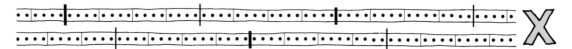

These records are beatmatched but their bars and phrases are out of line.

These records are beatmatched with their bars lined up, but their phrases are still out of line.

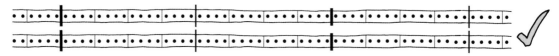

These records are beatmatched with their bars and phrases in line.

64

Once you're aware of these divisions in music, they're hard to ignore. There's more on song structure on p79 *How to place a mix*.

Phrases are instinctive
Dance music's four and eight-bar framework is something you'll have felt whenever you've been on a dancefloor. It's all about expectation and resolution.

- You hear a cymbal crash and expect another one in eight bars' time.
- You listen to the vocals and know when the next verse will start.
- You hear a drum roll and you'd be confused if it climaxed after five bars rather than eight or 16 (or 128 bars if it's trance).

Let phrases be your conductor
Every four or eight bars he gives you a nod (or hits a cymbal, etc), and that's when you can do something to your mix.

- Start off a record you're cueing.
- Move the fader a step in a blend.
- Bring an incoming record to full volume.
- Swap the bass in a blend.
- Finish fading out an old record.
- Cut to a new record.

Tricky records
Hypnotic records which build very gradually (common in progressive house and techno) might give you very few clues as to where their phrases begin or end. Some records are so repetitive that nothing changes for ages. Here you can often wing it – forget about phrases and just mix bar on bar and no-one will notice.

How to be more like a musician

'DJing was our training and it still is. Learning the structure of songs, the bars, the breaks, is all through DJing.'

Masters at Work

65

10. **How to** cut

A cut is a sharp switch from one record to another, done without losing the beat. Cuts (sometimes called 'drop mixes') work like an edit – as if you've spliced the two songs together. They're used in most genres of music, but are key for breakbeat styles like hip hop, drum & bass and UK garage.

Record yourself

When you're practising cuts you should tape your efforts and listen back to them to see if they worked or not. Without recording things it's very hard to hear a cut the same way an audience would.

When to cut

'We're not fantastic mixers. We don't have the smooth, long, continuous mix. But what we get from DJing is a way of programming music. How you can shape a crowd, create ripples of energy and get people going crazy.'

Chemical Brothers,
DJ Times

Cuts work best for music with a lot of space in it, ie sparse, percussive music like hip hop. As a vague rule of thumb, the more continuous melody there is on both sides of the join, the less likely it is that a cut will sound good.

It helps to think of your cut as a musical transition.
- Does it sound like an edit you might hear on a record?
- Does it sound like something a real band might do?

You also need to consider where to place a cut.
- Is the outgoing record leading up to a place where a cut makes sense?

Cuts will generally work:
- from percussion to percussion
- from percussion to percussion and bassline
- from percussion and bassline to just percussion
- from full-on bassline and melody to just percussion.

Cuts only work in rare (but wonderful) instances:
- from full-on melody to full-on melody
- from percussion to full-on melody.

How to do a running cut

Once you can beatmatch, it's simply a question of getting the two records running together and then cutting the crossfader sharply from one side to the other.

1 Beatmatch the two records.
2 Wait until the right moment.
3 Quickly crossfade from record 1 to record 2.

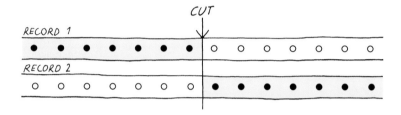

The actual mixing technique is very easy to learn. What takes skill and experience is timing it right and putting it in the right place.

Timing
Aim to move the fader across in the tiny silence between the beats – after the last beat of a bar in record 1 and before the first beat of a new bar in record 2.

Placing your cut
You need to anticipate things. Say you plan to make your cut four bars after starting record 2. In this case you need to have worked out that:

● in four bars' time record 1 will have reached a point you can cut out of
● in four bars' time record 2 will have reached a point you can cut into.

Exercises
Do lots of cuts, tape them and listen to see which work.

How to do a throw-in cut

This way there's no waiting. You start record 2 at the exact same time as you cut it in.

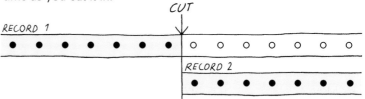

1 Cue up the first beat of record 2.
2 Wait until the right moment.
3 Start record 2.
4 At the same time quickly crossfade from record 1 to record 2.

This is harder to do but it requires less planning and anticipation. It also means you don't have to exactly beatmatch the two records. To prepare for this kind of cut, you need to get a really good feel for where that first beat is. Rock the beat back and forth in your headphones until you know where it is by touch.

Exercises
Do lots of cuts, tape them and listen to see which work.

Some different cutting styles

Cutting back and forth
If you have two records beatmatched you can cut back and forth between them at will and create a cut-up patchwork of the two tracks.

- This can be a good way of teasing an audience with snatches of an exciting new song.
- It can be a way of mixing two records for a long time without ever blending them.
- You could cut rhythmically on every half-bar, so it's like one record starts each bar and the other record finishes it.

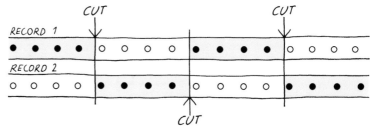

Scratch cuts

To build up some drama before a cut, you could scratch the first beat back and forth over the outgoing tune a little before you start it off. This is a good way of getting a feel for scratching.

Punching in

Here you use cuts to 'punch in' elements of one track into another.

- Maybe record 2 has a stab of horns every fourth bar. You might be playing record 1 but cut into record 2 for the bars with the horns.

Run-up beats

On some records there are notes or drum-beats ahead of the first beat of the 4/4 (ie ahead of the first kick-drum beat).

- Sometimes the bassline (or melody) starts ahead of the first beat.
- Sometimes there's an off-beat 'introducing' the first beat.

If you want the audience to hear these you have to cut in to that record a certain amount before its first beat, while still lining it up correctly. This is very hard. (You're used to doing things on the beat so this goes against your instincts.) Get a feel for the rhythm of the extra bit, then allow for it when you throw in the record and time your cut. Practise throwing it in in your headphones until you get it right.

69

How to get the levels right

Different records can have quite different volume levels (CDs too). In a cut it's important to match the volume of the two tunes. Most mixers have 'gain' controls to boost the input from your decks and correct any volume differences.

Level meters

The pretty lights on your mixer aren't just for show. You use these to compare the levels of your inputs. On most mixers the meters will switch between showing the overall output, and showing the PFL (Pre Fader Level) for the channel you're cueing.

- When you're cueing channel 1 the meter shows the input level of channel 1.
- When you're cueing channel 2 the meter shows the input level of channel 2.
- When you're not cueing anything (there's nothing in your headphones) the meter will show the master output level (what it's sending to your amp).

This is how most mixers work but yours may be different. Read the manual.

To match levels before a cut

1 Switch the cue to the record that's playing live and look at the level.

2 Switch the cue to the record you're cueing and look at the level.

3 If they look the same, great. If not, you need to adjust the gain on the record you're cueing.

Ideally your gains should be set so each channel is 0dB.

'One record coming in over another is a jolly for some folks because it's the anticipation of another great moment being born. If they trust the DJ then they know that next record is going to be something that takes them closer to the emotional rush they need.'

Derrick Carter

Faders vs gain

What's the difference? The gain controls are amplifiers so they actually make the electrical signal bigger (as does the master volume). The faders are attenuators which means they work like gates: they can't add anything to the signal, they just decide how much of it gets through. This is why the faders don't affect the input (cue) level but they do affect the output level.

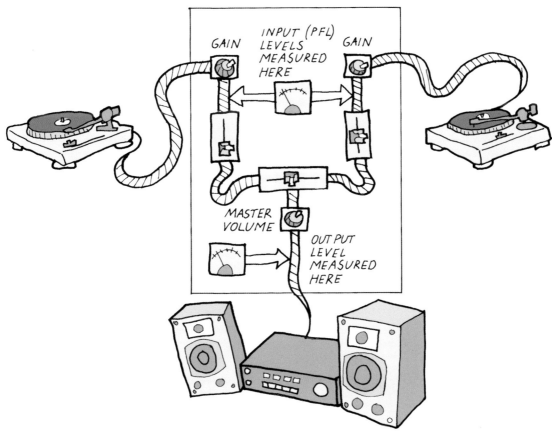

A JOURNEY THROUGH YOUR MIXER

The easy mistake

You need to match input vs input – cue level vs cue level. An easy mistake is to try and match an input level with the master output. This will result in your next song being much louder than you expected.

71

11. **How to** do stops and spinbacks

These are some of the most startling ways to go from one record to another. They're pretty easy to pull off but sound amateurish if you get the timing wrong.

How to do a power-off wind-down

If you turn off the power to your decks while a record's playing, the platter gradually slows to a stop but the music keeps on coming. This gives you a wonderful grinding-to-a-halt sound, like the record just couldn't keep its eyes open and fell asleep.

- This can be a nice way of ending a set. It's a bit like, 'Sorry, I'd love to carry on but they've pulled the plug on me.'
- Paul Oakenfold used to do it to his warm-up DJ's last record for an extra dramatic entrance (though we think that's a bit rude).
- Another way of using it is to have a really punchy tune waiting in the wings, and as the outgoing record dies, slam it in to explosive effect.
- If you have any control over the lights (or the nice person who controls the lights), you could synchronise a black-out. Just as everyone thinks there's a power problem, in comes your new tune and flash go the strobes.

How to stop with the brake

Decent decks have an electromagnetic brake, so when you hit the 'stop' button they'll halt more or less instantly. The sound it makes is a bit abrupt and not very elegant, but you can use it in a mix like this.

1. Beatmatch your two tunes and get record 2 synched and running in your headphones.
2. On the last beat of a phrase, hit stop on record 1. Time it so that the last beat plays.
3. Just before the next beat would be due to hit (the first beat of a new phrase), cut the fader quickly over to record 2.

A lot depends on your choice of tunes and where you place the mix. Get it right and it sounds like you slammed on the brakes but then screamed off again just in time.

72

Weak brakes
On some decks it's possible to boost your stopping power. See p39 *Fun with Technics*.

How to do a spinback

Spinbacks are when you suddenly put a record in reverse. You'll often hear ragga, drum & bass and hip hop DJs do them, but they're an exciting shock to the system in any genre of music. Rewind, mista selectah!

A spinback
1. Place your finger at 12 o'clock on the label of a record that's playing.
2. Catch the record quickly enough so it doesn't pause before it runs backwards.
3. Pull the record round backwards as fast as you can, spinning it on the slipmat.
4. Shout 'Bo! Bo!'

A cut with a spinback
1. Beatmatch your two tunes and get record 2 synched and running in your headphones.
2. Spinback record 1.
3. As record 1 comes to a halt (before it starts turning the right way again), fade over to record 2.
4. Time it so you do the spinback at the end of a phrase in record 1 and just before an exciting start in record 2.

This can be an escape hatch if you can't get two records to mix properly and you're running out of time.

A blend with a spinback
1. Bring record 2 in over record 1 with a blend.
2. Play the two tracks together and let record 2 build up to its moment of take-off (eg when the bassline comes in).
3. Just before this happens, spinback record 1.
4. As record 1 comes to a halt, fade it out and bring up record 2 to full volume just in time for its big moment.

Back in the dancehall

Spinbacks originated in Jamaica where DJs often played with just one deck and covered the gaps between songs with a big booming echo chamber. If a song was really popular they'd do a spinback, make it echo and then play the same record again.

73

12. **How to** place a mix

The most important things about your set are the records you choose and the order you play them in. But after that, your biggest decisions will be where to put the joins. *Where* you mix is more important than *how* you mix.

The basics

The simplest placement is to just tack the very end of one track onto the beginning of another. This can work fine; in fact, many producers structure their songs so this is all the DJ has to do. But with a bit of planning you can have much more control over the flow of your music. Placing a mix is about putting things exactly where you want them.

- Is this record leading up to a place where a mix makes sense?
- Will my next record start at a point that makes sense?

This means a lot of calculated guesswork – counting the length of intros, being aware of phrases, and anticipating the musical events in your tracks. To a good DJ it comes naturally. Once you have a feel for how songs are put together it can be quite intuitive. Most dance records today are so rigidly structured you'll soon pick up the formula.

Where to overlap your records

Imagine two very simple records. Each has a 16-bar percussion intro, a 16-bar percussion outro and some meaty music in between. Like this.

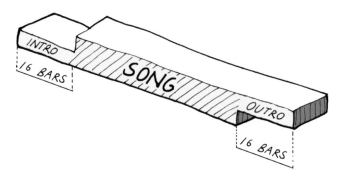

Simple intro to outro

The easiest way to mix these is to wait for the percussion outro of record 1. When this arrives, start record 2 going. You now have 16 bars where the two records overlap in which to do your mix (this could be a cut or a blend, it doesn't matter).

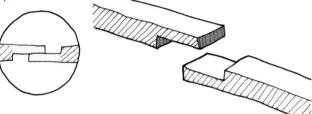

This style of mixing creates a kind of drum break in between the two songs. Some DJs might emphasise this further by playing a basic rhythm track as a 'bridge' record (maybe the 'bonus beats' of the song they're about to bring in). This style works well for deep, percussive genres like tribal or tech-house.

Tighter mixing

If you know where things happen in record 1, you can make the mix tighter. For example, maybe when the last chorus starts you know you have 16 bars until the start of the outro. Use this moment as a signal to start record 2. Blend it in and bingo – just as the meaty part of record 1 finishes, the meat of record 2 kicks in. This is 'couture mixing' – you can't see the stitching.

This style keeps the music at a peak and offers no chance for anyone to lose interest, so it works well for today's dancefloors (which have the attention span of a gnat). You'll hear someone like Roger Sanchez pull it off to perfection: bamm straight out of one song and straight into another. No pause for breath, no drop in energy.

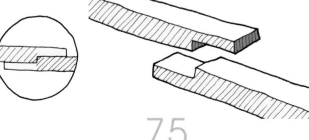

75

Even tighter

An even more energetic (or exhausting) method of mixing is to mix straight after a chorus. You time it so that the big opening moment in record 2 happens immediately after the chorus in record 1 shoots its shot.

This can be very effective with breakbeat genres (hip hop, two-step, etc) because it keeps the energy up in relatively mellow music. Here the mix would most likely be a cut. Done with house and trance (using sharp blends), it quickly becomes fever-pitch overkill – the DJ equivalent of a sledgehammer.

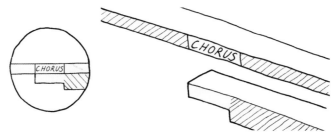

Long melodic blends

So far, our mixes have kept the meat of the songs separate. This is a safe bet because it avoids key clashes and prevents the full-on melodies getting tangled. However, if you have two songs which go together beautifully, you don't have to be so precise. Here you can quite happily bring record 2 in long before record 1 goes anywhere, let the melodies make love for a while and then fade out record 1.

This is how most progressive house DJs play. It works well for records which build slowly and are very repetitive.

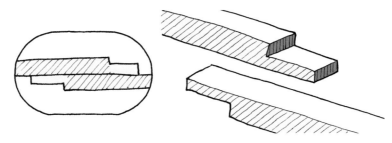

How to mix out of breaks

A break is where the song takes a breather, drops down to some exciting percussion and then comes storming back in again. It's a bit like a fake ending. This is great for a DJ because you don't have to wait for the real ending; you can use the break instead.

Most songs have some kind of break about two-thirds to three-quarters of the way through. On a record you can usually see where it is – it's that dark ring (quieter grooves are darker).

Mixing out of a break is more or less the same as mixing out of an outro. You time it so that as record 1 goes down into its break, record 2 is building up from its intro.

Of course, a lot depends on how record 1 breaks down and how record 2 builds up. You have to think about each pair of songs and how they might mix.

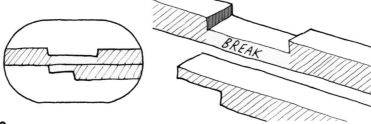

Breaks or breakdowns?

A break is where the song cuts into percussion; a breakdown is very different. This is where the song calms down and creates drama by stripping away its elements until there's nothing left (except perhaps a single string note, a German woman having an orgasm or the voice of God telling you to take drugs). Breaks are for the drummer; breakdowns are for hands in the air.

How to control energy levels

Mixing out of a break prevents the energy dropping. As soon as one record starts to chill out you're bringing in another rising star. This illustrates the power of carefully placed mixes – you can use the ups and downs of your tunes to create ups and downs in your set.

Placing mixes to give shape to your set

Imagine all your songs have this simplified shape.

Join them like this and you'd create a feeling that the energy was constantly rising. There's always something new arriving.

Join them like this and it would feel that the energy was constant. This might be a constant peak, or a really deep groove, depending on your style of records.

Join them like this and it would be a gentle up and down. Here you're letting the songs make all the decisions.

Song structure

Almost all songs follow a basic pattern, including songs without vocals. In fact even the weirdest, most experimental music will usually have a very traditional shape.

Listen to some of your favourite tracks with a piece of paper in front of you. Count the bars and make notes. Look for patterns. See how the song is made up of four-bar and eight-bar building blocks. If it's an instrumental track, listen for different hooks, samples and instruments coming and going.

Ol' Dirty Bastard 'Got Your Money'

Intro	8 bars	drums
Verse	16 bars	drums/bass/vox
Chorus	8 bars	drums/bass/vox
Verse	16 bars	drums/bass/vox
Chorus	8 bars	drums/bass/vox
Middle eight	8 bars	drums/bass/strings
Verse	16 bars	drums/bass/vox
Chorus	16 bars (and fade)	drums/bass/vox

Mousse T vs. Hot'n'Juicy 'Horny'

Intro	16 bars	beats/partial synth hook
Intro	8 bars	beats/bass/synth hook
Verse	16 bars	beats/bass/vox
Chorus	8 bars	beats/bass/synth hook/vox
Verse	16 bars	beats/bass/vox
Chorus	16 bars	beats/bass/synth hook/vox
Outro	8 bars	beats/bass

Darude 'Sandstorm'

Intro	8 bars	synth pad
Intro	8 bars	synth pad/partial synth hook
Main part	32 bars	beats/bass/synth pad/synth hook
Breakdown	34 bars	synth pad/partial synth hook
Outro	32 bars	beats/bass/synth pad/synth hook

How to find mix points

Every record has places you can mix out of and places you probably shouldn't. For example, you should always let a singer finish their verse or chorus. Apart from that there are a few simple dos and don'ts. The important thing is to have a feel for the rules that your kind of music plays by, and to do your mixes in the same way. Use song structure to your advantage; don't try to fight it.

Mix records so the join makes musical sense.

Try to create mixes that sound like something a producer or musician might have done in a studio – like the two records were recorded that way. It's like finding plugs and sockets which fit each other – the right mix points. In real life every record is different (they're those pesky foreign plugs), so get to know your tunes really well. See also p134 *How to choose the next record*. As you prepare your mix, think about:

- the structure of the two songs
- the type (and length) of mix you're planning
- the direction this mix will take things in
- the genre and style you're playing.

Cueing your mix

This is the most crucial time. Most young DJs jump the gun and get immediately engrossed in beatmatching. Calm down, pretty one. We know beatmatching's hard, but it's not as important as you think. There are plenty of other things to sort out first.

- Listen to the new record. Is it really the right choice? Are you sure it won't key-clash?
- Find a good place to start it off, bearing in mind where you might mix out of the current tune (think plugs and sockets).
- OK? Now you can think about your precious beatmatching.

'I'm dancing with this girl, trying to get my shit off but the DJ's fucking my groove up. The whole party'd be like "Yahhh what the fuck is that...? Why you took the record off there? The shit was about to explode. I was about to bust a nut."'

Kool Herc

How to know your records

Choosing the perfect next track, and finding the best place to mix it, is a matter of knowing your tunes inside out. You should know a record's mood, style and rough tempo just by looking at the sleeve, plus (even if you can't recall it exactly) have a feel for its rhythm pattern, bassline and melody.

Musical memory

The best DJs can remember every intro, breakdown, drop (micro-breakdown), bridge (linking bit), break and peak in each of their tracks. If you're not quite so superhuman, double-check things when you're cueing up the record. Musical memory is something great DJs (and musicians) are just born with. However, you can definitely improve this skill if you know what you're listening for.

- How does the record start? How long is the intro?
- How does it develop? How do the different elements come in?
- When does the bassline start?
- Where are the breaks, bridges and breakdowns? How long are they and how do they come back in?
- Which places are good to mix into?
- Which places are good to mix out of?
- Which places should you avoid mixing out of?

The good news is that a lot of this happens subconsciously. As you hear a record play, you'll just know what it's going to do next, eg 'the bassline's going to drop back in at the end of that rising organ noise', or 'there's a break after this chorus'. Great records some-how do everything at the exact moment you want them to.

Play your records as you pack your box to remind yourself how they're arranged. Familiarise yourself with new purchases by knocking up a tape to play in the car or on the Walkman.

81

13. **How to** match rhythms

Once you can beatmatch and you start mixing up your record collection, you'll notice how some tracks fit together better than others. It won't always be because their melodies are sweetly harmonious; often it's because their rhythms fit together like freshly greased puppies.

Beats and rhythms

It's helpful to understand the difference between a rhythm and a beat. A rhythm can be any pattern of sounds, but a beat is a very particular kind of rhythm – a constant pulse, a regular tick, tock, tick, tock, a heartbeat.

All modern dance music – house, hip hop, trance, techno, two-step, disco, funk – has the same 4/4 beat: four beats in a bar. Play any of your records and you should be able to count out '1, 2, 3, 4, 1, 2, 3, 4...' However, within this regular beat you might hear many different drum patterns – many different rhythms.

Think of the kick drum as the piston of the rhythm. It marks the beat and rarely messes around. It's so dependable you can leave it pumping away and forget about it. Meanwhile, swirling funkily around it in regular patterns are all kinds of other drums.

The most important of these is usually the snare drum, the tight, snappy *chip*, *chip* drum-beat. The hi-hat, the *tsst*, *tsst*, *tsst* cymbal sound which usually marks the off-beat, is also important. Listen to its snare pattern and you'll get a good idea of what makes a rhythm tick.

Two bars of a typical house beat

HI - HAT		o	o	o	o	o	o	o	o
SNARE DRUM		●		●		●		●	
KICK DRUM	○	○	○	○	○	○	○	○
COUNT	1	2	3	4	1	2	3	4

Two bars of a typical funk or hip hop beat (James Brown, 'Funky Drummer')

HI - HAT	oooooooooooooooo				oooooooooooooooo			
SNARE DRUM		●		● ●		● ●	●	●
KICK DRUM	○ ○		○	○	○ ○		○ ○	○
COUNT	1	2	3	4	1	2	3	4

What makes rhythms match?

As a general rule, rhythms mix together well when they have a similar pattern. You'll hear it in your records all the time. A good thing to listen for is whether their snares and hi-hats fall in the same places. Sometimes two very different rhythms will go together nicely, too. This is because even though they're different, their patterns are complementary – they are somehow pulling in the same direction.

There are no simple rules about all this (unless you want to get into some complicated music theory). A DJ will simply match rhythms by ear – by doing a test mix in the headphones and listening to whether it makes rhythmic sense. Does it sound solidly danceable or just confusing? We won't force you to take things any deeper than that. However it's good to understand what makes some mixes sound like a slinky six-armed drummer and some like a bag of clocks.

Off-beats
Tap out a beat on the table. When you hit the table that's a beat, but when you raise your hand each time, that's an *off-beat*. Count like this: 'A one & two & three & four & . . .' – every '&' is an off-beat. Drummers play off-beats to make things funkier.

Syncopation
Syncopation is playing a note either a little too early or a little too late to add a bit of spice to the rhythm – like rushing to the beat, or hanging back from it. Notes which are supposed to fall in one place surprise the ear by appearing somewhere else. If you clap on the off-beat you'll syncopate a rhythm.

For more, http://en.wikipedia.org/wiki/syncopation

Rests
The beat with no sound. Sometimes you'll come across a rhythm where there's an invisible beat. You should count it even though there's no drum played. Otherwise rests can throw you when mixing. Sneaky producers sometimes use a rest at the beginning of each bar, so what you thought was the first beat of the record turns out to have been the second.

Classic rhythms

Four on the floor

A kick drum on every beat. This is the classic house rhythm, originating with disco. So named because the kick drum (which sits on the floor) plays four beats in every bar.

On the one

A kick drum on the first beat of every bar, followed by whatever funky pattern the drummer feels like. This is the classic funk rhythm, the pattern you'll hear in hip hop and all other forms of breakbeat music. So named because all the rhythmic emphasis is on the first beat of the bar.

Four on the top

A snare drum on every beat. This is the classic sixties dance rhythm – the sound of all those Motown hits and northern soul stompers. These days you might hear indie bands using it, but four on the floor pretty much stole its thunder for dance music.

What makes rhythms not match?

When you mix two records you're forcing a couple of imaginary drummers to play together. Sometimes they get along fine. But what if one's playing a rhythm that's putting the other one off?

Syncopation is the main reason why two rhythms won't mix. Think of it as a force pulling the beat out of shape. Sometimes it will be pulling the beat forwards; sometimes backwards. Mix a forward-leaning rhythm with a backward-leaning rhythm and it will sound like a fight in a drum factory.

Another reason why a mix might not work is that it simply has too many drum-beats per square inch and your dancers get confused. If your imaginary drummers are hitting lots of their notes at the same time then the combined rhythm is reasonably simple. But if their rhythm patterns don't have much in common, when you add them together you'll end up with a machine gun battle.

A deliberate mismatch
For an extreme version of incompatible rhythms.
1 Beatmatch two similar records.
2 Start record 2 on an off-beat of record 1, so its kick drums sit over the other's hi-hats (count `1 & 2 & 3 & 4 & ... ' and start it off on an &).
3 Marvel at this complex yet undanceable rhythm.

84

Time signatures

Most dance music is in what's called '4/4 time'. This is a 'time signature'. The top 4 means there are four beats in a bar; the bottom 4 means each of these beats would be written like this as 'crotchets' ('quarter-notes' in American).

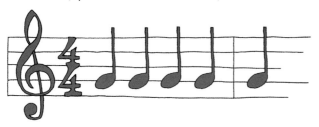

Other time signatures

Most DJs live in a 4/4 world, but classical, jazz, African and Latin musicians use a whole host of time signatures.

- Many Afro-Cuban and Haitian rhythms are in 6/8 time (although Latin styles like salsa, mambo and bossa nova are in 4/4). There's a form of Dominican Merengue which is in 12/8.
- 'Happy Birthday' and 'Roll Out The Barrel' are in 3/4 time, which is a waltz beat: boom, tap, tap, boom, tap, tap . . .
- The Mission Impossible theme is in 5/4 time, as is the Dave Brubeck Quartet's jazz hit 'Take Five'. This is on an album called Time Out on which every track has a weird time signature.
- Marches, sambas and polkas are in 2/4 time – left, right, left right.
- Power-rockers Rush have recorded several songs in 7/8 time.

Further information

Webthumper
http://216.103.111.115/perl/drums/index.cgi
A great site filled with free drum lessons and transcriptions of over 600 rhythm patterns.

Jaz Class
www.jazclass.aust.com/basicth/bt1.htm
Excellent (and simple) music theory site.

Dolmetsch
www.dolmetsch.com/theoryintro.htm
Another good music theory site.

Synthzone
www.synthzone.com/drums.htm
Loads of links to drum-based sites.

Ionline
www.ionline.net/~bmassel/index.html
Hippie site with lots about hand drumming.

14. How to avoid key clashes

Some records sound great separately, but when you mix them something sounds badly out of tune. This is because they contain incompatible notes – their keys clash. Ouch!

What's a key?

Keys are families of musical notes. They have a strangely emotional effect, and changing key can be very dramatic. There's more about using keys creatively on p176 *How to mix harmonically*.

- Notes from the same key sound nice and harmonious together.
- But if you add notes from outside that key they sound wrong, or 'off-key'

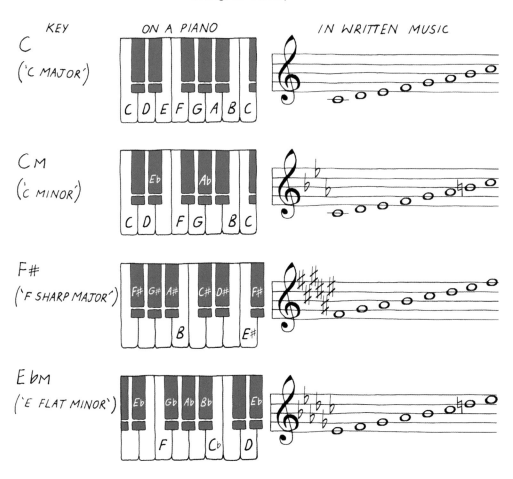

KEY — ON A PIANO — IN WRITTEN MUSIC

C ('C MAJOR')

Cm ('C MINOR')

F# ('F SHARP MAJOR')

Ebm ('E FLAT MINOR')

How to detect a key clash

The only practical way to detect a key clash is to listen to the two records together before you mix them. When cueing a record to one that's playing, as well as matching beats, pay attention to how the melodies, vocals and basslines sound together.

- Listen for a sour, off-key sound, as if there's an instrument playing out of tune.
- It's easiest to hear when you play the most melodic or vocal parts together.
- Hearing the two tunes mixed in your headphones (if your mixer allows it) is a great help.
- If two tunes sound weirdly out of time, even when they're perfectly beatmatched, it can be a sign that their keys clash.

Solo key clashes
Some records are actually out of tune with themselves. This is because the producer has sampled a bassline which is in a different key to the melody.

Perfect pitch
Some people's brains are so musical, when they hear a note they can tell what it is. These people have 'perfect pitch' (or 'absolute pitch'). You'll find really good DJs have this talent, which suggests they could also have been good musicians – if only they'd practised that xylophone more.

Tone deafness
Other people's brains just can't hear a key clash – they are 'tone deaf' and probably don't sound too good in the shower. However, scientists think it's all to do with training, so tone deafness is probably curable with practice.

'Fuck up. Make mistakes. The best bit of advice I ever got was from Jon Pleased at the Haçienda. I did this real car crash job, like a drag queen falling down the stairs in platforms. I said, "Aargh, I can't believe I did that!" And Jon went, "Well, at least they know you're here!"'

Boy George

87

How to mix tunes that clash

Don't mix them
This is the easiest way to deal with clashing records. There are lots of alternatives in your box.

Cut them, don't blend them
This way your dancefloor hears one tune and then the other, so they never hear any incompatible notes combined. You can be clever about this and use the cut to purposefully change key, just like a band. For more on this, see p176: *How to mix harmonically*.

Mix them when one (or both) is just percussion
You can safely mix clashing records if you wait for a part in one of them where there is no bassline, melody or vocals. Luckily, many records have percussion-only intros, outros and breaks.

Use the EQ to hide elements
This is a fudge, but it can work OK for certain mixes. It all depends on how well you can hide one of the elements that's clashing – and on how good the mix sounds after you've cut out those frequencies.

- If you're mixing two tunes at a point where each has just percussion and bass, you may be able to hide the incoming bassline by cutting the bass (although you'll also lose the kick drum).
- Trying to hide a melody is much harder because there won't be much left of the song after you've cut the midrange and treble. But if you really need to mix those records, you're welcome to try. If you're clever about it, you can make it sound like a natty bit of filtering.

Pitch-shift one of them
This is a feature available on some top-notch CD decks. It lets you change pitch separately from changing tempo. Most digital studio software lets you mess with this, too.

88

Tuneful drums

Drums are rarely melodic enough to create a key clash, but some (eg congas, bongos and kettle drums) might be.

Records that change key

Luckily, most dance records stick to a single key, but not all. A key change sounds like an engine shifting up a gear.

Large speed adjustments

When you change the tempo of a record (its speed) you also change its pitch (its notes and key). So if you're mixing records with quite different speeds, you may push them out of harmony. A change of +/-3% will definitely make a difference. Less than that and you might scrape by.

- Large speed adjustments may create a key clash.
- But they may sometimes correct one.

Some CD players let you change the tempo of a tune without affecting its pitch. They call this 'master tempo'. The Stanton STR8 100 turntables let you do it with records. In the studio this is known as 'timestretching'.

Things to look out for

'I just want to say to all those people out there who want to get involved in DJing to educate yourselves. Don't be afraid to try something different. Go for yours. There is always more to learn.'

Little Louie Vega, *Muzik*

89

15. How to mix CDs

These days all DJs should know their way around an adjustable-pitch CD player. CD DJing used to be the province of only the most commercial pop spinners, but since home CD recording became a fact of life and CDRs usurped acetates, the silver disc is pretty unavoidable.

The principles of DJing are the same whatever format you work in, so CD DJs need to read the rest of this book just like everyone else. For vinyl DJs it's not really about learning new skills, just doing the same things with new buttons.

CD vs vinyl

The idea of allegiance to a single format is fading away, since the best DJs are wise to the benefits of each. But anyone facing a large investment for their first set of equipment should weigh things up carefully (see p32 *How to buy equipment*).

Starting out
More and more first-timers are plumping for the CD option – mainly because the equipment costs can be lower. Cheap turntables are awful to learn on, but a cheaper CD player will work much the same as a pricey one. Also, thanks to compilations and CD burners, it's much cheaper to build a music collection on CD than on vinyl. And you'll probably learn beatmatching slightly quicker with CDs.

Switching formats
DJing is more about your listening skills than about what your hands are doing, so moving from CD to vinyl or vice versa is easier than is often claimed. CD DJs moving to vinyl will need to work on their physical dexterity (ie hand/ear coordination); vinyl DJs moving to CD will have to learn a whole set of fairly complex controls and think more explicitly about cue points.

'A lot of people say, "I'm not into CD players, they don't mix as well," and I totally try to convert them. Half the stuff I get now, I burn to CD because it's really an incredible tool. You can loop an intro, and extend it wherever you want, you can pitch things down or up and not lose the key – you have the master tempo feature. There's no reason to fear CDs.'

Danny Tenaglia

CD plus

+ The equipment takes up less room.

+ You can carry far more music.

+ You can afford more music.

+ If you've already got a CD collection, you can play it.

+ Major labels have started releasing certain mixes of tunes on CD only.

+ Most dance producers press up test CDs of their new tracks or work in progress (where in the past they would have made acetates).

+ You can burn tunes straight from your computer to a CD, including homemade tracks and downloaded MP3s.

CD minus

- The controls on CD players can vary wildly. You may have mastered your own, but if a club uses a different model, you can have considerable problems.

- Not all venues have full CD mixing facilities.

- On all but the most expensive models you can't see what's going on (where the breakdowns are, etc), so you have to really know your tunes.

- You can't instantly find a place on a song; you always have to scan through the whole track.

- You can't do many of the hip hop and scratch styles with CDs (although new equipment exists to let you try).

- Independent and underground labels still favour vinyl-only releases, though increasingly you can also buy their tracks as downloads (and you can always record vinyl or downloads to CD).

- Once you're bitten by the DJ bug you'll probably want to get into vinyl as well.

How to cue up a track

This is the biggest difference between CD and vinyl. You can't just stick your needle in the right place, so finding your cue point (where you want the track to start playing) is fairly involved.

❶ Find the track you want
Use the 'skip' or 'track search' buttons. The track number will appear in the display.

❷ Find the part of the track you want
Play the track and scan through it using the search buttons and/or the jog wheel (some models have a joystick) while listening to it in your headphones. As you zip through the tune the track counter will show you where you are. Some top models also have a pictorial display which shows you the loud and quiet parts of the song.

❸ Pause the track
Press 'pause'. Once it's paused the controls will change. The jog wheel (or the buttons/joystick) now becomes your fine-tuner. You can move very slowly, or frame by frame (even slower). A frame is usually 1/75th of a second.

❹ Find your exact cue point
Getting your cue points tight so you can start right on the beat every time is the essential skill of CD DJing. This is where you'll have to really get to know your particular machine and practise and practise. You can move backwards and forwards as slowly as you like, listening for the precise moment. It's usually the frame just before the drum-beat you want to start on. However, this varies between models, especially when you allow for the tiny fraction of a second most decks take to start.

❺ Lay down your cue point
When you've fine-tuned the track to the precise place, press 'cue'. This sets your cue point. This marks where the track will start from when you're ready to begin the mix.

❻ Check your cue point
Hit 'cue' while the track's playing and it will return to the cue point you just laid down and pause the track there ready to go. When you press 'play' it will start from there. This will be your cue point until you set a new one.

How to beatmatch CDs

We're just going to run through the basics here. If you're learning to beatmatch on CD decks you should spend time getting used to your controls and then read *How to beatmatch* on p48.

❶ Get ready to beatmatch

>> Use two tunes with clear, solid drum-beats.

>> Set the mixer so CD 1 is playing out loud and CD 2 is in your headphones.

>> Set a cue point on CD 2 as described above. The first kick drum on the track is probably your best bet.

>> Move your headphones so you have one song in each ear.

❷ Start the cued CD in time with the one that's playing

Hit 'play' on CD 2 in time with a kick drum of the song playing live. This should start the second song off in synch with the first. If you miss it slightly you can use the pitch bend controls to play catch-up (see below).

❸ Listen to the drum-beats and decide which track is faster

This is the crucial skill of beatmatching. It will take loads of practice before you can do it accurately. For lots more on this, see p48 *How to beatmatch*.

❹ Adjust the pitch control

Speed up or slow down CD 2 to match CD 1 using the pitch control slider.

❺ Go back and test it

Each time you make a pitch adjustment, go back and test whether the two tracks are now matched. Just hit 'cue' to go back to your cue point, then press 'play' in time with the live song. Keep repeating steps 4 and 5 until it's bang on.

❻ Use the pitch bend to exactly line up the tracks

Using the pitch bend controls (sometimes two buttons, some times the jog wheel) is like a quick burst of the accelerator or a tiny touch of the brakes. You use these to line up the beats exactly, both when you're beatmatching and then when you actually do the mix.

93

What to practise

- Putting your cue points in the right place (in relation to the drum-beat you're cueing).
- Starting the cued track bang on the beat. The 'instant start' is rarely completely instant. Get to know how big the tiny pause is.
- Getting the pitch bend functions to work how you want them to. Know how sensitive or brutal they are. Pitch bend buttons vary enormously in the amount of difference they make.

CD DJing is about knowing your controls intimately, so you can cue up tracks quickly and reliably. If you're playing a venue, get there early to figure out the equipment. Better yet, arrange a practice session before the club opens. We've seen people horribly thrown by unfamiliar hardware (especially pitch bend controls).

How to do clever stuff

Looping
Pick out a section of a track and have the player repeat it for as long as you want. This is great for extending intros or for making beat tracks to mix over. While the song's playing you hit a button to mark the start of your loop ('in') and hit another to mark the end ('out'). Once you've set a loop you can fine-tune these points. The loop will play until you hit 'exit', when it will carry on into the rest of the song.

Cueing on the fly
Some decks let you 'hot cue', which is simply laying down a cue point when the track is playing (eg if you want to mark a particular section of the song to come back to later). Some decks let you programme multiple cue points (to mark different sections of the track so you can do live re-edits) and some will hold them in the memory for every time you play that tune.

Master tempo
Decks with this feature let you adjust a track's tempo (its bpm) without changing its pitch (its notes), so you can speed up a song without it going all chipmunk on you. It's very handy for beat-matching because it hides any pitch bends you might have to do during a mix.

Instant reverse
Some decks let you flip from forward to reverse and back. A bit gimmicky, but fun for messing with people's heads.

Effects
Some decks throw in lots of effects buttons. Great for playing around with, but they can clutter up your controls. See p166 *How to add FX*.

BPM sync
BPM counters are common on CD decks, and some will even beat-match for you. This works fine for music with simple, clean kick drums. But try it with two drum & bass tunes and it'll sound like a machine gun.

Multiple tracks
Some decks let you play more than one track from the same CD. Very handy in theory, but utterly confusing in practice.

MP3-compatible
A lot of newer CD decks will also play CDs containing MP3s and this is becoming a popular way to DJ digitally without all the complications of a laptop.

Vinyl emulation

The best CD decks let you control CDs just like they were records. Put your hand on the turntable-like platter and you can rotate the track back and forth by hand, pause it, manually cue it, even scratch it or do a spinback. The Pioneer CDJ1000, launched in 2002, led the way and quickly became the CD deck of choice in clubs worldwide. Most manufacturers have their own versions.

www.pioneer.co.uk

16. **How to** DJ digitally

Music started as a living form which no-one could own. Around AD 1000 we figured how to write it down, and a century ago we worked out how to lock it into objects like records. Now music is no longer physical – it just whizzes around in a mist of ones and zeros.

Why DJ digitally?

It's the future, kiddo. Vinyl and CDs will be around for some years yet, but increasingly you're going to see DJs turning up for a gig with nothing more than a laptop. You can argue against it all you like, but digital DJing is here to stay, and one day someone will kick your ass using it.

If you're a clever producer-type it lets you wow the crowd with all the trickery you normally save for the studio; if you're more the respectful connoisseur it puts the whole breadth of your collection at your fingertips; and if you're simply a beginner, it lets you get cracking on the cheap with a load of dodgy downloads.

- Bring your whole collection
- Use playlists to super-organise your tunes
- Access a universe of music online
- Use studio software for live edits and remixes
- Your spine will last longer

The downside is that it can be a steep learning curve to move to digital. There will be heartaches, and possibly tears, before you feel completely at ease with your software/hardware set-up. And until that happens there's a danger you'll be spending too much time staring at the screen rather than the dancefloor. But if you're prepared to put in the effort, digital DJing can offer you the creative flexibility you always dreamed of.

What format?

A soundfile is a piece of music that's been cleverly coded ('compressed') so you can store it on a computer without using tons of memory, and send it across the internet without it taking forever. The less a track is compressed the more musical information is left – this is its 'bit rate' or 'sample rate' measured in kbps (kilobits per second). A higher bit rate means better sound quality but a bigger file size. Downloads typically range from 128kbps to 320kbps. For comparison, CDs are encoded at 1411.2kbps (44kHz 16-bit stereo). Whatever format, the sound quality is only as good as the source.

If the file was ripped from an ancient cassette or a scratchy record it might be a big fat WAV and still sound like a bag of crisps.

Choosing your format

It's basically down to three questions: what software will you be using (not all formats work in all programs); where will you get your music; and how much do you care about sound quality? You can usually convert from one format into another, but this can sometimes leave a mess.

WAV

(WAVeform audio format) The biggest and best. WAV is a 'lossless' format. That means no information is lost during encoding, so your tracks will be CD quality. (In fact, if you're making your own tracks or ripping from vinyl you can encode at double the usual 44.1Hz and have near-vinyl quality). The down side of WAV is that file sizes are larger and tracks are not as easy to come by commercially. Increasingly though, online music stores, especially those aimed at DJs, offer downloads in WAV.

AIFF

(Audio Interchange File Format) Essentially the Mac version of WAV, with the same top-of-the-range sound quality. Should work anywhere that WAVs do.

MP3

The most popular soundfile format, MP3s are all over the place – extremely easy to buy legally or download on the sly. They're a great option for the bedroom and there's tons of software for playing and mixing them. And many DJs happily play MP3s in public, arguing that ones encoded at 320kbps sound fine. We'll leave the choice to you but we don't really agree. MP3 encoding works by chopping off as much musical information as it can get away with, and the first things to go are any frequencies beyond human hearing, which means there's no sub-bass to hit your dancers in the chest. You can get away with MP3s in a bar, but they sound crap on a decent club system – anywhere with sub-woofers will sound thin and lifeless.

AAC (MP4)

(Advanced Audio Codec) This is Apple's standard iTunes format. Plays on most MP3 players. Uses .m4a file extension.

Other formats

It's a jungle out there, and there are scores of 'codecs' competing for attention, many developed for gaming and telephones rather than music. Of most interest to DJs are the lossless formats, such as **FLAC** (similar to WAV and AIFF, but with smaller file sizes and available from some DJ download sites), as well as **Apple Lossless** (another iTunes format, also used in Quicktime), **AU** and **Monkey's Audio** (APE). **TTA** and **WavPack** were made for compressing WAVs without losing info. There are old stalwarts like **Real Audio** (RA) and Microsoft's **Windows Media Audio** (WMA). **ATRAC** was Sony's (largely failed) attempt to fight MP3 with their own exclusive format. Lesser-used music formats include MP3 competitors like the open-source **Ogg Vorbis** and **VQF**, and **MOD**, for making music on ancient Amiga computers.

Where to get digital music

There are basically two ways to get digital soundfiles – either you pay to download them legally from a commercial site, or you network your computer with millions of others using peer-to-peer (P2P) file-sharing and download tracks for free. Some sites look like commercial music services but are actually selling you file-sharing software (which you could get for free, anyway). Basically anywhere that charges you money for tracks (a subscription or a per-download fee) is probably legal and anything that promises you millions of tracks for free (or a one-off payment) is file-sharing.

Legal downloads

From the giants like **iTunes**, **Napster** and **MP3.com**, new contenders like **Wippit, HMV** and **Virgin Megastore**, to sites run by tiny independent labels, there are thousands of places you can buy and download music online. For more, just google the track, label or genre, eg 'MP3 Ninjatune'.

File-sharing

Peer-to-peer file-sharing puts your computer in a mind-meld with lots of others so it can suck out tasty music from them. On the one hand, this is a great way of grabbing tracks for free, on the other, it's illegal and it chokes the livelihood of producers and musicians.

First you install the file-sharing software in your computer. Whenever the program is running you have access to millions of

DJ download sites

www.addictech.com
Breakbeat mission control.

www.beatport.com
The big boy, started by Ritchie Hawtin.

www.bleep.com
Strong on alternative electronica.

www.clickgroove.com
Discerning soulful grooves.

www.djdownload.com
The UK's largest, courtesy of DJmag.

www.nufonix.com
Broad dance-based site.

www.playittonight.com
Straight outta Canada.

www.traxsource.com
House central, with hot promos.

music files stored in the computers of everyone else who is running it. A search tool finds the tracks you're looking for, using filters for particular artists, albums and file formats. You can choose which of your own folders are open to the public, and if you open up your music collection for sharing you'll be given access to more people's music.

File-sharing makes you more vulnerable to hackers and viruses, so get security software. And remember: although owning and using the software is OK, sharing copyrighted material is 100% illegal and you can be severely punished. And it's not a victimless crime – if you get your tunes free, you are contributing to a world where making underground dance records is no longer profitable.

File-sharing software

www.acquisitionx.com
www.gnutella.com
www.imesh.com
www.kazaa.com
www.limewire.com
www.morpheus.com
www.slsknet.org

How to record to a computer

'Ripping' is simply recording something – a track from vinyl, a mix you're going to burn to CD, an old cassette, your cat miaowing – so it ends up as a soundfile on your hard drive.

Connecting your computer
In most cases you connect the two phono (RCA) sockets on your mixer's RECORD outputs to your computer's single 3.5mm stereo input jack (this normally has a microphone icon next to it). You'll need either:

- A double phono to phono cable plus a 3.5mm Y adapter.
- A double phono to single 3.5mm stereo cable. If you have the cash there are some high-quality versions of this (pictured).

Get the best leads you can afford, as these are the main thing affecting sound quality. If you're using an external sound card or any other interface, your connections may be different. Other possibilities include:

- A phono to USB interface. For about £90 this lets you plug a deck or mixer directly into your computer or hard disc via USB or firewire.
- Some mixers now have USB output so you can connect them to your PC with a simple USB cable.

99

'You give these new technologies to an 18-year-old kid who's going to approach it from a completely new mindset, that's when fireworks will happen. That's when we'll see the next generation of what a DJ performance can be.'

Sasha

Preparing your computer

You will be using a lot of memory and processing power. Disconnect from the net and switch off screensavers, power-saving programs, and any applications you don't need, especially virus software, so your computer can concentrate on the job in hand. Slow or old PCs may cause problems, especially if you're recording a long mix.

Software

You need a program that will record from an external source to WAV.

- If you've bought a separate soundcard, the drivers for this will do the job.
- Otherwise, use an editing package. This lets you import and save your track, show it onscreen as a waveform, and then edit it.

Recording/editing software

Expensive

Ableton (Mac/PC) www.ableton.com

Logic (Mac-only) www.apple.com/logic

Peak (Mac-only) www.bias-inc.com

Pro Tools (Mac/PC) www.avid.com/products/xpressStudio/proToolsLE

£50-£100

Sony CD Architect (PC-only) www.sonymediasoftware.com

Soundforge (PC-only) www.sonicfoundry.com

Sound Studio (Mac-only) www.freeverse.com/soundstudio/

Free-£30

Audacity (PC/Mac freeware) http://audacity.sourceforge.net/

Amadeus II (Mac-only) www.hairersoft.com/Amadeus.html

Final Vinyl (Mac-only freeware) www.griffintechnology.com/support/imic/

GoldWave (PC-only) www.goldwave.com

Spin Doctor (Mac/PC) www.roxio.com/eng/products/spindoctor/

Settings

Decide the sound quality you want to end up with.

- If you're recording a mix to burn to CD use 44.1kHz 16-bit stereo (CD quality). At these settings each minute will take up about 10MB in WAV format.
- If you're going to stream the file online, use 16-bit mono at 22.05kHz and you'll get a file a quarter of the size. (Don't try recording at 8-bit – it will always sound rubbish.)

Levels

Mixer

Your mixer channels should be set to peak around 0dB, which means no red lights. Play something in each channel and check.

Computer

Check your computer's audio input controls. Make sure the line input channel is the only one active, it isn't set to mute, and the balance is centred. Adjust the input volume so it's nice in your PC's speakers without any distortion.

- Mac OSX – Go to System Preferences/Sound/Input.
- Windows – Click the loudspeaker icon in the system strip.

Software

recording software will have level meters. Make sure they aren't going into the red. If they are, you need to adjust the input volume, and then maybe the mixer levels.

Recording

Click 'record' and play your music. Don't worry if there's a gap at the start – you can edit it out later. If you're making a mix, don't let the levels creep up, and keep an eye on the clock. Once the track is imported, save it as a WAV file. If you're going to change or edit it in any way, make a back-up copy first (hard disc space allowing).

Top-and-tailing

You might want to edit out any dead sound or unnecessary intros before and after the track.

Editing

Here's when you can get busy and cut up your own unique version. (see p244, *How to make a re-edit*).

Normalising
This makes your recording as loud as possible without distortion.

Adding track marks
If you've recorded a long mix, you might want to add track marks so listeners can flick through it easily.

- Some editing software lets you do this by simply marking places on the waveform.
- If not, you have to chop the mix into separate tracks and renumber them accordingly, before you burn them to CD. To minimise strain on your PC, start with the last track and work backwards. Number tracks 01, 02, 03... rather than 1, 2, 3... or they'll end up in the wrong order. Make sure your burning program is set to leave no gaps between tracks.

Importing into your music library
If you're ripping vinyl, the final thing is to import each track into iTunes or whatever library program you use, remembering to put it in at least one playlist (eg 'latest tunes') so it doesn't get lost.

Further information

Read the manuals of whatever programs you're using. And try:

www.djmandrick.com/htmlpctutorials/
pctutorials-recording-decks-to-pc.htm
www.djrecess.co.uk/How2recmix.html

How to choose DJing software

How do you play? How do you *want* to play? DJing software is a tool to get a job done, and like any equipment choice, you have to discover which tools work best for you and your particular style. You will almost definitely find yourself experimenting with different set-ups and tweaking things until you feel completely comfortable.

No two laptop DJs will have exactly the same rig – they may use a different library system, a different interface, a different mixing program, a different computer, different socks even. Talk to other DJs about what they use, read reviews and check out DJ forums for bitching, especially the ones on the manufacturers' sites.

- What formats will it play?
- How easy is it to use?
- What else will you need?
- What hardware/software is it compatible with?
- What problems do people complain about?
- What features do people rave about?
- How good is the support if things go wrong?

All these programs give you decks and mixer on-screen on your laptop. The better ones let you switch to just decks so you can use an external (ie a real) mixer. Most programs come in various strengths, and there are often trial versions to use before you buy. Cheaper packages may only play MP3s.

Traktor
(Mac/PC; £190) www.native-instruments.com
When it comes to a serious program for straightforward laptop DJing, Traktor is the front-runner. Up to four decks, loops, filters, delays, jumping between cue points, play two copies of same tune. If you want a vinyl interface it integrates with Final Scratch, and it's also a snug fit with Beatport.com so you can buy new tracks even while you're DJing. On the downside it is known for plenty of bugs (especially on a Mac) and support can be less than helpful.

PCDJ (PC-only; £100–£170) www.pcdj.com
One of the first digital DJing programs, and much-loved, especially in the States. Its fans like the track navigation and dedicated hardware controllers.

Alcatech BPM studio (PC-only; £150–£600) www.alcatech.com
Atomix (PC-only; £50) www.atomixmp3.com
DJ-1800 (Mac-only; £50) www.dj1800.com
DJ Mix Station (PC-only; £10–£20) www.ejay.co.uk)
DSS DJ (PC-only; £35) www.myxoft.com
Jackson (PC-only; £50) www.jacksondj.com
Megaseg (Mac-only; £130) www.megaseg.com
Mixmeister (PC-only; £30–£200) www.mixmeister.com
MixVibes (PC-only; £60–£175) www.mixvibes.com)
Pioneer DJS (PC-only; £130) www.pioneer.co.uk
Virtual DJ (PC-only; £20–£170) www.virtualdj.com
Virtual turntables (PC-only; £30) www.carrot.prohosting.com)

DJing software

Luddite Lament

The most important objection to digital DJing is not about how you control your music ('It's not sexy and tactile') or even what it sounds like ("We've lost that warm analogue sound"); it is that music is now so overflowingly *available*. When everything is easy to find, nothing can be rare or special.

A never-released Fluke mix? An impossible-to-buy Pharoah Sanders live set? Just tap into a search engine and before you can say Limewire it's sitting in your hard disk. It's great that music is becoming so democratic, but not if it means we start taking it for granted.

A vinyl collector might spend years on the trail of a rare record, all the time building up its importance and learning about its creator. By the time he finally owns it, he has the respect and understanding to go with it.

Don't let digital music kill connoisseurship. Learn about the tracks you're rabidly downloading. Get into their history. Pay tribute to their makers. Especially since you're probably not paying them.

DJing with a vinyl interface

'The undertaker is coming to measure up my vinyl.'

Nicky Holloway

If you scratch, or if you like the physical nature and the showiness of playing vinyl, then these packages are the answer. Designed for hip hop-style DJs, they let you use standard turntables to control soundfiles in your computer. You use two time-coded 12-inches which tell the computer every little move you make, so whatever you do on the decks, the computer does to the track.

Final Scratch (Mac/PC; £500) www.stantondj.com
Stanton Final Scratch is the original and most well-known system, and has many loyal users, but is known for its instability. Integrates with Traktor.

Serato Scratch Live (Mac/PC; £440)
www.rane.com/scratch.html
Many prefer Serato because it's simpler than Final Scratch. It's also reckoned to be more stable, and benefits from regular updates and bug fixes.

Miss Pinky (Mac/PC; £60)
www.cycling74.com/products/mspinky
Control anything you like using a vinyl interface. Made by maverick developers keen on sharing their baby with similarly creative techies.

Alcatech Digiscratch (PC-only, £400) www.alcatech.com
MixVibes DVS (PC-only, £160) www.mixvibes.com
Numark Virtual Vinyl (PC-only, £430) www.numark.com
PCDJ Scratch (PC-only, £100)
www.pcdj.com/products/scratch.asp

DJing and live remixing

Many of the programs above let you arrange simple loops and edits, but for those who really want to get busy splicing and dicing...

Ableton Live (Mac/PC; £270) www.ableton.com
Live is studio software designed for production and remixing, but its interface is so clear and simple, DJs found they could happily bring it into the booth. When Sasha started raving about it, the future was clear. Live's claim to fame is that it will beatmatch for you, leaving you free to do other, more creative things – like layer ten different tracks over each other or divide a track into several

sections and re-edit it while you're playing. This multilayered style is perfect for the progressive house scene, which has given it a hearty seal of approval. Critics point out that to use it to the full takes a lot of preparation time marking tracks and preparing loops, and so it pushes you into playing largely pre-planned sets. However, Ableton Live is undoubtedly a dramatic change in the way DJs can play music.

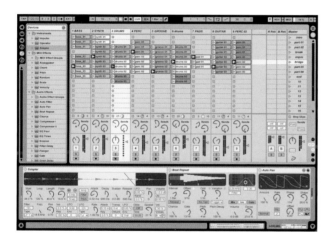

Which hardware?

Laptop
Mac or PC? Techies like PCs in the same way mechanics like tractors; creative people like Macs in the same way creative people like BMWs. Other than price, performance and personal preference, consider the software you plan to use – what platform was it originally written for? Because Macs all come from the same manufacturer, software written for them is generally considered more stable.

Hard drive
If you have all your tunes on the same drive as your DJing software, its little needle will be frantically zipping all over the place and it will wear out about a hundred times faster than normal. So invest in an external drive for your music and leave the laptop free to run everything else. It's worth having a second drive synched to the first as a back-up you can leave safely at home. And of course a third to lock in a fireproof, climate-controlled bank vault under armed guard.

Audio interface (sound card)

An audio interface (also known as a sound card) turns your computer's digital signals into analogue ones that traditional sound equipment can understand. Anyone working with music should invest in one – it vastly improves the sound quality of whatever you're doing, and gives you a full range of audio inputs and outputs rather than just a single 3.5mm headphone socket. Usually a small box, a soundcard connects to your laptop via a USB or firewire socket; they range from about £60 right up to £700 or more. Some new digital-compatible mixers and controllers (see below) have built-in sound cards, as do systems like Final Scratch and Serato.

M-Audio Audiophile 2496 (Mac/PC; £55) www.m-audio.com
Echo Indigo DJ (Mac/PC; £115) www.echoaudio.com
Edirol FA66 (Mac/PC; £200) www.edirol.com
Edirol Firewire FA-101 (Mac/PC; £300) www.edirol.com

Controller

Mixing onscreen with a mouse can get tedious, so there are MIDI hardware units to make life less fiddly. You transfer functions from your on-screen controls to physical buttons, dials and sliders. Most useful is a slider to work your pitch controls. Some controllers also include an audio interface; some even include a full mixer.

EKS XP10 (PC-only; £200) http://eks.fi
Hercules DJ Console MkII (Mac/PC; £180) www.hercules.com
Evolution X-Session (Mac/PC; £75) www.m-audio.com
Behringer BCD-2000 (PC-only; £125) www.behringer.com
PCDJ DAC-2, DAC-3 (PC-only; £200, £330) www.pcdj.co.uk
Peavey DAI (Mac/PC; £650) www.peavey.com
Kontrol DJ (Mac/PC; £210) www.kontrol-dj.com

Mixer-controller

Some mixers are digital-compatible, meaning you can plug your laptop into them directly via USB or firewire. Some units (like the Behringer BCD2000) are controller, interface and mixer all rolled into one. And the latest top-of-the-range mixers come with built-in MIDI controls for DJing software: Pioneer DJM-800 at £1,100 or the Allen & Heath Xone:3D at a massive £1,550.

106

Other ways to play soundfiles

On CD decks
Many of the newer decks will play MP3s as well as standard CDs, so instead of bringing a laptop and worrying about all that software, you can just burn your MP3s onto CDs and play them through the regular set-up. You'll get nine hours of music on a single disc. But you can only do this where you're sure the CD decks are MP3 compatible.

On dedicated hardware
Always keen to sell you a gimmick, the equipment manufacturers have dreamt up gadgets that let you dispense with a laptop. These cut the cost and the complexity of digital DJing, but you will find yourself trapped by their limitations.

On iPods
Get it out of your pocket and stick it in. If you can bear the embarrassment, there are now units like Gemini's iTrax (£230) and Numark's iDJ2 (£430) that let you mix from a single iPod.

How to organise your tunes

Ironically, one of the hardest things about digital DJing is all the choice you have. Where a box of scruffy sleeves might contain plenty of emotional hints, an endless alphabetical list of song titles isn't very inspiring. Here's how you can make navigation easier.

Make lots of playlists
We'd never find anything if our creaking record shelves weren't organised into different sections. Do the same with your soundfiles. Put them all into playlists and you can find them much more easily. For example 'End-of-the-night stormers', 'Mid-tempo madness', 'Frosty the snowman', 'Songs about rain' – you get the idea.

Pack your box
The physical act of packing records into a box gives you the chance to think about what you're going to play that night. Try doing the same with the tracks in your laptop – build a custom playlist for each gig. You can throw in plenty of others from your wider collection, but this gives you a handy starting point for the evening.

Problems with playlists
If, like many digital DJs, you use one program to DJ with and a different one to hold your music library, you may encounter

107

compatibility issues. Most programs let you label each track in a number of ways, so as well as the title you can tag it with its BPM, genre, 'feeling', its waveform, its cue points, even the year and the producer, but tags made in one program can fail to show up in another.

How to set up

Bigger clubs are getting used to laptops, but in some places they'll look at you like you just brought a wet goat into the booth. Always give plenty of thought to setting up; it might take as much as 30 minutes to get fully functional and iron out any problems. No two sound systems are the same, there are a lot of wires to connect, and it can be hard to find room for your hardware.

- Visit the venue ahead of time to check the equipment, connections and power supply.
- Try to set up at the beginning of the night, before the other DJs are playing, ideally before the place opens.
- It's worth buying some longish leads so you can be more flexible about where you put your gear. Get shielded ones.
- A common problem is lower volume when playing from laptop. Check with the sound engineer/bar manager about compensating for this.

How to follow someone
This can be tricky. No DJ wants you plugging in wires and testing connections through the climax of his set.

- Set up at the start of the night so everything's in place (except perhaps the last couple of connections).
- To avoid a gap in the music, plug in to a spare channel. On mixers with fewer channels you might have to wait till the outgoing DJ's last song.
- Begin with CDs or vinyl so you can finish setting up while you're playing your first tunes.

How to deal with crashes
Always have standby music in another format. Carry some reliable tunes on a CD or vinyl in case the worst happens and your computer crashes. (Make sure it's easy to switch quickly to the turntables or CD decks if you have to).

PPL digital DJing licence

In 2006 the PPL (Phonographic Performance Ltd) introduced a new 'Digital DJ' licence at a cost of £200 per year. Immediately there was an outcry. Why should digital DJs have to pay more for simply playing a newer format? We think the licence is a cheeky opportunist tactic to increase the PPL's revenue, it's based on uncertainty and fear, and it's pretty unworkable. Are they really going to check whether your soundfiles were bought online or ripped from a CD? Are they going to force every iPod user to get one? Sure, artists should be paid when their music gets played, but through the existing system of PPL licences, not by picking on laptop DJs. Here are the facts:

- An old-style PPL licence is paid for by the venue, not the DJ. The only time a DJ needs one is if he's playing somewhere the PPL haven't licensed, like an office party or a sports club.
- The Digital DJ Licence is not specifically about *playing* soundfiles – it's actually a licence to make digital copies of music you own in other formats.
- You don't need one if you only play soundfiles you've downloaded from pay sites.
- You don't need one if someone else has done the copying.
- You don't need one for bedroom DJing.
- It only applies in the UK.

We hope the PPL rethinks this. Personally, we're going to fight the power and ignore the licence, but don't take our word for it because they may choose to bust some heads (though we think they'd have a tough time getting any convictions).

File-sharing

As we've said, file-sharing is only legal when you download or share material with the copyright owner's permission, ie not very often.

Digital rights management

There are various DRM technologies, all with the aim of making sure producers and musicians get paid for their work. Essentially, these are bits of computer code that prevent anyone copying tracks without permission. Rumour has it there are some very sinister types, which let you download the track illegally but then report back to teacher.

How to stay legal

109

17. **How to** add a mic

So the decks are at your house and you're cutting up a storm, but your best mate's sick of sitting on the bed listening to your dodgy mixes (although he quite likes your sister). To keep your friendship intact you say, 'Hey, why don't you MC?'

Buying a microphone

'Silence is as important as sound.'

Richie Hawtin, *Looking For The Perfect Beat*

Prices for a vocal mic start at £50 and climb up to £225 (£200–£400 for a decent cordless radio mic). A cheap mic will make rattling noises when you move it, its lead will be about two feet long, it will scream with feedback even at fairly low volumes and will pick up interference from low-flying aircraft and your mum's mobile. Worst of all, a cheap mic will be knackered the first time you drop it (and you will drop it). So get the best you can afford. Try some out and see which one makes your voice sound sexiest. For vocals you should get a low-impedance, dynamic, cardioid mic.

Dynamic
You need a dynamic or 'moving coil' mic. These are nice and rugged and because of the way they're made (with a coil of wire attached to the diaphragm, science fans) they have lower impedance. This means you get more noise out of them with less interference, you can stick a long lead on them with no problems, and they don't need a battery.

Condenser
These are the kind you *don't* want. They're very fragile, designed to pick up the detailed sound of instruments like acoustic guitars.

Cardioid
An 'omnidirectional' mic picks up sounds from all directions. You want a 'unidirectional' mic, which only picks up what's pointing right into it (ie vocals). There are different types of unidirectional mics – 'cardioid', 'supercardioid' and 'hypercardioid' – depending on exactly how they pick up sound ('cardioid' means heart-shaped). For more about mics, www.dpamicrophones.com

Omnidirectional

Cardioid

Super-cardioid

hypercardioid

Plugging in a microphone

Some mixers have a separate mic volume control; others automatically feed it into a particular channel. Set the volume carefully or a shout might blow your speakers. If the mic channel has EQ controls, use them. As a rule, it's better to reduce EQ than to increase it. You might then add a touch of volume to make up for it. Add some reverb (if you've got it) to beef up the voice.

- If it sounds too boomy, turn the bass down rather than adding treble.
- If it sounds too skinny, turn the treble down rather than adding bass.

Feedback

That's the squealing noise which can burst cats. It happens when the mic is picking up sound from the speakers. Move the microphone or turn the volume down. Alternatively, find the frequency which is causing trouble. Try turning the treble down a bit. If you have a graphic equaliser you might find killing one particular frequency does the trick.

Playing for an MC

The best DJ-MC duos have a really good understanding of each other's style, so each can anticipate what the other might do next. The key thing is to respect each other's skills and to give some time to each other.

- The DJ should choose a nice simple rhythm track and give the MC a chance to go off now and again.
- Equally, the MC should give the DJ some space occasionally. Don't rhyme over mixes, don't rhyme over vocals, don't rhyme over really exciting parts of the record. And just plain shut up occasionally – it makes it more interesting.

Getting on the mic

Like many DJs, Snowboy believes 'Using a mic is the quickest way to break down the barrier between DJ and audience'. For certain gigs, including mobile DJing and playing in commercial clubs, talking on the mic is important. Some places won't hire you unless you can do it. Just be yourself and be as relaxed as you can. Try to avoid putting on some kind of fake style.

18. **How to** pack your box

Leaving your house with a box full of records is one of the most crucial moments in your set. Before you lock the door, ask yourself: have I got the right tools for the job?

How to organise your box

Most DJs we know are ridiculously disorganised. Their record box has a mysterious life-force of its own. Fresh choices go in one end and fully digested tunes come out the other in some weird biological process.

Can you afford to be so laid back? A bit of effort here will reduce the pressure you feel in the booth and give you more freedom to be creative. For example, for each record in your box you should have five others you could play after it. Take the right tunes and you'll have nothing but fun. See p116 *How to play out*.

Finding what you want

Give some thought to how you organise your box. When you're in the zone trying to choose the next record, you don't want to waste a second scrambling around for something. A DJ never pre-plans a set, but most put their tunes in a rough order, ie warm-up at the front, peak-time in the middle and cool-down at the back. Junior Vasquez used to have labelled bins in his booth at the Sound Factory with each one containing a particular part of his evening's set. Other ways to organise things include.

- by mood
- by style
- by tempo
- by key

Some DJs keep their box in the same order as their record shelves, so it's easy to pack and unpack. Some with librarian tendencies actually make it alphabetical. And some keep their box as random as possible so they can improvise freely without the box forcing choices on them. Find whatever system works best for you.

'I'd say to anyone trying to make it as a DJ to collect some records, play at home until you're confident, and then put on a party for some friends. That's how I did it. One of your friends will eventually bring somebody along who owns a club.'

Harvey, *Muzik*

How to look after your records

Other jocks may call you a sissy, but you really should take good care of your records. Every tiny scratch or piece of dust will make a difference to the sound. If a record jumps when you're playing out, or starts snap, crackle and popping like breakfast, you'll sound very amateur. And if your favourite tune becomes unplayable, it will be difficult (and expensive) to find a replacement.

- Put them back in the sleeves right after playing them.
- Keep them upright. Stored flat they're more likely to warp.
- Keep them out of the sun and away from heaters.
- Wipe any dust off them before you play them.

A plumber takes care of his tools because they're his livelihood. Likewise you should keep your records in tip-top condition. Remember, this is music we're talking about – something magical and beautiful that can transport you to a higher place. Can a monkey wrench do that?

Cleaning products

Get yourself a decent dustpad (we like the Stanton) and some cleaning fluid. Don't waste your money on fancy record store liquids; for a fraction of the price, neat vodka, isopropyl (from the chemist) or lighter fuel do the trick, though some collectors claim lighter fuel damages certain vinyl compounds.

CD DJs

CDs were supposed to be indestructible – *Tomorrow's World* presenters spread jam on them to prove it. In fact the tiniest scratch can make them stutter like Gareth from *Pop Idol*. Get in the habit of replacing them in the box as soon as they come out of the machine. You can usually fix jumps with repair fluid (from a good record shop) which magically fills in scratches. When finding a scratch, remember: CDs play from the middle outwards.

Go get 'em

Your box's packed and you're ready to leave your bedroom for the excitement of a club. We're so proud. When we met you were just an overenthusiastic young thing, full of ambition, bursting with hopes for the future. Now you're going to be a real DJ playing for real dancing people. Have a blast!

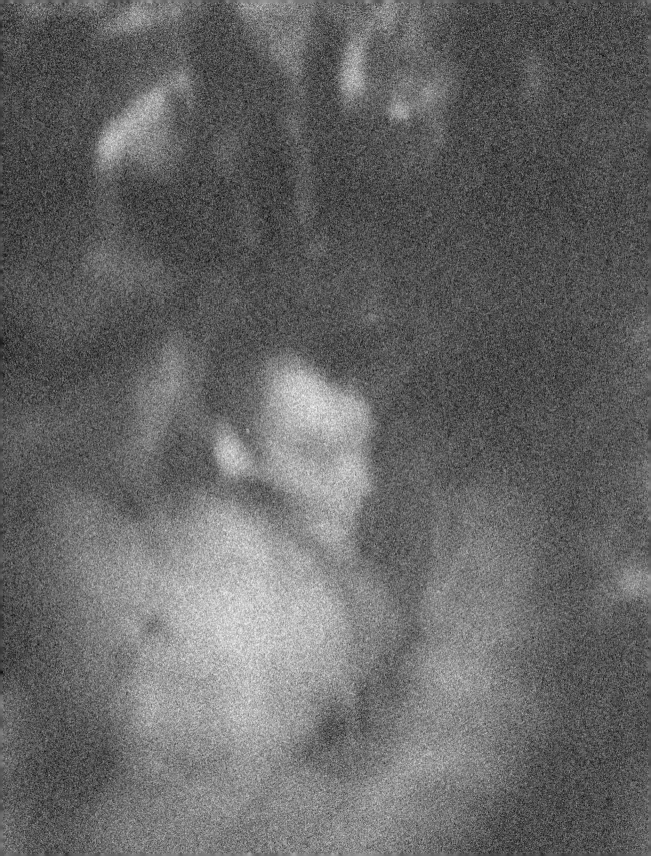

The dancefloor

19. **How to** play out

By now you're wearing a pallid disco tan, your neighbour's got a noise abatement order out on you and you've stopped eating properly, convinced that every minute spent practising on those sleek steel babies brings you closer to dating J-Lo. Now your big break is here – a chance to play in public.

Bedroom DJing is a lot like masturbation: there's no risk of upsetting your audience, but there's no-one to cheer and scream when you get it right. So what's it like playing for a crowd for the first time? Well, imagine being given the chance to have sex with loads of people when up till now you've been locked in your room wanking away on your own.

How to prepare your set

The most important part of playing out happens before you leave your home. Choose the right records and you'll be well ahead of the game. Make the wrong decisions filling your box and you'll be guaranteed a few hours of misery in the club. It's a very lonely experience playing records that no-one wants to dance to. Most of it is common sense. For instance, don't turn up to play a wedding armed only with the entire Underground Resistance catalogue. For your first gig it's wise to take as wide a variety of music as you can possibly carry. It will be the first time you've really had to consider other people's tastes, so give yourself lots of room for manoeuvre.

Don't just grab the last 100 records you bought. Every gig (especially your first) is a chance to show who you are musically. Look for old favourites that deserve an airing, tracks that didn't get the attention they deserved at the time, or some killer secret weapon you've been keeping in cold storage – anything that will mark your set out as unique. You should be aiming for a box of records that includes different moods, styles and tempos, and also represents your personality and your take on DJing. It's your chance to be original and daring – even if you bottle out of playing that Tonto's Expanding Headband track once you get in the club.

'Everything sounds great in the bedroom. Then you go out and it's a whole new world. Everything's that much further away and that much louder.'

Barry Ashworth, *Looking For The Perfect Beat*

How to research the gig

The best way to get a firm idea of the type of music to bring is to visit the same club night ahead of time. See what the DJ's playing and whether the crowd is responding. Don't, however, go into a blind panic if he's caning Bulgarian trance and you don't have any. Maybe the promoter's given you the slot so you can rescue the night with your Ugandan hip hop.

Ask the bar staff what it's usually like, what type of crowd they generally get in. Have a chat with the owner or promoter (beware – the promoter's idea of what his crowd wants and what the dance-floor actually likes are often two different things). Your visit is also a good opportunity to get a sneaky peek at the facilities (or lack of them) in the DJ booth. If you can't get down to check it out, ask some of your DJ friends who have.

How to defeat nerves

Your first time playing out can be pretty frightening. It's like learning to drive in a Mini and then being given the keys to an articulated lorry. There are many ways to deal with nerves, including taking Valium, throwing glasses at the wall and getting extremely pissed. We'd caution against all of them. A beginner is one thing; a barely conscious beginner is quite another. If your hands are shaky you need to get rid of some adrenalin – jump around on the dancefloor before you're due to come on.

- Don't panic, breathe deeply, concentrate on your job.
- Pick records you know well and that will get the crowd on your side.
- Forget about what anyone's thinking; have a laugh.

It's like coming on as a substitute in a football match – once you've had a few touches, you'll be ready to steam in at the near post for that last-minute winner. Really experienced DJs get nervous too, you know.

117

Don't overprepare

Don't plan too much. Have lots of options. Fight the temptation to prepare a whole set in your head. Be ready to respond to the crowd and make sure you have a few records that suit each direction they might lead you in. You'll be surprised how much easier it is to improvise when you have real-life dancing bodies in front of you. Have some fun. It's not an exam. No-one's judging you on your trendiness or your amazing pyrotechnical mixing gymnastics. They just want to dance.

The shock of a club system

Your housemates may disagree, but there's an enormous difference in volume between your bedroom and a nightclub. It's a real shock the first time you try to mix records on a booming club system.

Records sound very different
The first thing you'll notice is how big a record sounds. The clarity of your home hi-fi is lost amongst all this crashing, reverberating bass.

Some sound amazing
Remember that this music was specifically created to be played on large systems.

But some won't work
You've probably never thought much about the dynamics of your records, but a big system will highlight any weaknesses: I could have sworn that track had a stronger kick drum.

It smooths some of your mistakes
What sounds like a train wreck to you is often barely noticeable to the crowd. A big sound system can be surprisingly forgiving on your hiccups and mistakes.

self portrait by mr.scruff

'In DJing, the preparation is work, the execution is play.'
Mr Scruff

118

How to get ready

Run through the equipment with the previous DJ. Are there any problems or things you should know about (mixer channels not working, jumping decks, dodgy needles, guy who keeps asking for Eminem, etc)? Ask about anything you're not sure of – there's no shame in this (we've spent many a fraught minute with our headphones plugged into the mic socket wondering why we can't hear anything).

Check the monitoring
Check there is some and that it does its job. If not, try to remedy things.

Check how the mixer is adjusted
Especially things like the crossfader assign.

Check what it sounds like on the floor
Before you arrive in the booth, stand in the middle of the floor and give things a listen. How's the volume? How's the EQ? Most inexperienced DJs will have too much of everything. If the bass is distorting you should notch it down. Likewise if there's too much treble. There's more on getting good sound on p158 *How to improve your sound*.

How to adjust your monitors

Monitor speakers sharpen up the sound in the booth. They play the same music as the speakers on the dancefloor but because they're close to you they don't have all that echo and audio delay (a baby version of the sound-lag you get when you yodel across a valley). Find out how to control the monitors (ask the previous DJ). There may only be a volume control, but some let you adjust the EQ as well. Ideally they should be:

- loud enough to be heard over the main sound system
- crisp enough for you to hear everything clearly
- not so loud you'll need a hearing aid after your gig

Turn them down when you don't need them. You should turn them down occasionally in any case – to hear what the dancefloor really sounds like.

119

How to deal with no monitors

'I was in a really naff school heavy metal band. Then I clocked the DJ at a school disco and I just thought, "Forget all this drumming nonsense. It's too much of a racket. I'll play other people's records. They sound great".'

Pete Tong, *DJ Times*

Although club owners are starting to spend money on the things that matter rather than on the design of the toilets, monitoring is still not always great. Sometimes it's non-existent. Without monitors you'll be hearing a muddy and slightly delayed version of what's playing in the speakers. It's far from ideal but not impossible to mix like this.

Use the headphone mix (if the mixer has one)

- This lets you do a test mix in your headphones. It's very useful for beatmatching without monitors. See p48 *How to beatmatch.*

Use the split-cue (if the mixer has one)

- This lets you hear one record in each ear of the headphones, so in theory you could use it to monitor your mix. One ear is always too loud, though.

Mix off the speakers

The delay means the speakers are telling you a slightly different story to your headphones. So you're going to turn off your headphones.

1. Beatmatch the next record.
2. Bring it up into the mix as low as possible so you can just hear it without headphones. It will be a tiny bit out of synch because of the delay.
3. Turn your headphones off.
4. Listen closely to the dancefloor speakers and readjust the record to bring it in synch with the song already playing.

It's not easy, but once you've done a few mixes you do get used to it. If you practise at home mixing without headphones it will prepare you.

How to learn from your experience

The best thing about playing out is that it makes you better, stronger and far wiser for next time. Hopefully you'll have seen how much easier it is to choose records when there's a crowd in front of you. You'll have seen some records go down worse than you thought, and seen some you thought were only average blow up the dancefloor.

As you play out more, this accumulated experience will feed back into your record-buying habits and help you narrow down which types of records work best for you. We'd love to give you some rules about how and why certain records work but the truth is there aren't any. The only real test is to play them in front of an audience.

After your set, head to the bar and have a self-congratulatory drink. DJing will never be this nerve-wracking again – at least not until the first time you play a stadium supporting U2. You've popped your cherry and now you know a little of what DJing is really about – the smiles and shouts and human interaction of playing for other people.

DJ checklist

Don't leave home without these (and don't leave the club without them either).

>> **Record boxes** The right ones. If you have a lock on them make sure you've got the key.

>> **Headphones** Buy good ones. See p35 *How to buy equipment*.

>> **Penlight** eg a MagLight torch. It's always nice to be able to see which record you're putting on next.

>> **Dust pad and cleaning fluid** Look after your records and they'll look after you. See p112 *How to pack your box*.

>> **Ear plugs** See p43 *How to cue*. Get the best. It's a small investment if you still want to be listening to gabber when you're 60.

>> **Business cards** (or pen and paper). You never know who might be there listening to you play. This is how you build up bookings; you can't beat this kind of word of mouth.

>> **Flask of tea** and cheese and piccalilli sandwiches. Only joking.

Optional extras

>> **Cartridges** Some DJs like to bring their own (for the well-being of their precious records).

>> **Slipmats** If you're a bit hip hop you might want your own special mats.

>> **A 45 adapter** If you're going to play 7-inch singles with those big holes. Bring a plastic one, not the shiny one off your Technics, 'cos you'll lose it.

20. **How to** warm up

If one thing's been lost in the explosion of DJ mania over the past 15 years, it's the art of warming up. Before house music arrived in the UK and devoured our noble club traditions, the DJ turned up at the start of the night along with the bar staff and played until the club closed.

Warming up is a real skill

Guest DJs used to be a rarity, so playing all night on your own was the norm. Apart from creating a generation of DJs with aching legs and back problems, this forced a young jock to learn the subtle art of atmosphere – the delicate skill of guiding an evening through many moods, from an empty dancefloor to peak hour, and back again.

Nowadays most young DJs toil away in their bedroom with nothing in mind but a two-hour peak-time set. Yet ironically the first break any DJ will get is warming up. So when you arrive early at most clubs, you'll see DJ Wet-Behind-The-Ears banging away at an empty dancefloor with peak-hour anthems. The music's at fever pitch and you haven't even checked your jacket into the cloakroom. Meanwhile, the few DJs experienced enough to start a night in style are the star names who only ever get booked for peak hour.

Warming up is hard. It takes sensitivity, talent and really good records. Approach it right and it's the best arena for improving your skills. What's more of a challenge – playing some big tunes to a drunk and raucous 1am dancefloor, or creating an unforgettable atmosphere for people to step into, and gently building up the mood and the tempo until you can coax them onto the dancefloor?

'For me, it's creating a vibe in a room, when you know something's coming, and you're slowly sucking the crowd into the night,' says Danny Howells, who spent nine years as warm-up for John Digweed at Bedrock. 'A warm-up DJ should know that when people walk into a club they don't automatically jump straight into larging it on the dancefloor. What you're there for is to get the crowd geared up – creating an atmosphere in the room and creating an atmosphere of anticipation, without resorting to banging it out or overshadowing the DJ who is following you.'

'In bigger clubs, if someone gives me an option, I'd rather play early on than main time in the back room,' says BBC London's Ross Allen, whose subtlety and eclecticism make him a true expert at starting a night right. 'I love watching the floor gradually fill up, so by the time you've finished it's heaving. You haven't battered the fuck out of it, you've just left it at the point where the next DJ can take it wherever he wants to go. That's setting the whole night up. It's full. It's primed.'

Ross thinks of an empty dancefloor as a chance to be selfish. 'If there's no-one in the club I put on whatever I want. Just really chilled, then pace it. I used to do these little house parties and you'd start off chilled and build it gradually and save your big records till later.' He too cautions against playing uptempo music too early. 'You don't jump on a merry-go-round if someone's spun it round fast. You get on it when it starts slowly and builds up momentum.'

How to choose warm-up music

A room full of people needs some gentle coaxing before they'll venture onto the dancefloor. Your music should suck people in, get them tapping their toes or nodding their head, and continue to work its funky seduction until they can resist no longer. The best music for building this kind of 'dance pressure' is:

- Melodic
- Familiar
- Slower tempo

Weirder tracks
Provided they fit the atmosphere, it's also a chance to play your more 'interesting' tunes. Not to mention those quiet songs you've always wanted to hear loud.

Old favourites
It doesn't have to be last year's Christmas number one – just a club classic, something that'll strike a chord with the majority of people there.

'It feels weird when you've got a room that's empty and someone's playing really fast.'
Danny Howells

123

How to set the mood

Your two jobs as a warm-up DJ:

- To (eventually) fill the dancefloor for the next DJ.
- To play a soundtrack that sets the mood for the night.

At the beginning of the night tell yourself, quite literally, that you don't want to make anyone dance. Instead you're going to play an hour or so of wonderful music – the soundtrack to this evening's slowly developing movie. The climax of your movie will be a full and super-excited dancefloor just before the next DJ comes on, but for now it's all about collecting the characters, following each of their stories, and setting the scene for the action that's ahead.

Remember all the times you've walked into a club. We bet you haven't often run straight onto the dancefloor. People need time to find their bearings, put their coat in the cloakroom, order a drink, rendezvous with their friends... They want time to wander about. Have a natter. Smoke a fag. Chat up a boy or girl. Fall in love...

You should give them the perfect soundtrack for this. You're using music to welcome people into your home, to ease them into the evening, and to get them excited about what's going to follow. The best DJs will gently engage the audience, and gradually seduce them onto the dancefloor. The amateurs will rape them with peak-hour tunes three hours too early. It's the difference between inviting someone into a bubble bath with soft lights and scented candles, or forcing them to get stuck in with a cold shower and a cross-country run. There's nothing more uninviting than an empty dancefloor pumping out demonically fast beats.

Remind yourself: at the start of an evening you're playing music for meeting, drinking, chatting and hovering round edges. No one's passing comment on your music by not dancing. Relax, they're not going anywhere – an hour or so of your charms and you'll have their arms in the air.

'Lead, don't follow. Believe in what you feel. Do what you love, not what you think people might want. Don't take no for an answer and be prepared to work your ass off, 'cos it won't fall into your lap.'

Adam Freeland, Breaksworld.com

Lost in the loft

As well as inspiring many of the world's most legendary DJs, the Loft, David Mancuso's groundbreaking New York club, was famous for the way it seduced people onto the floor. 'Some of my favourite music was David's early records,' remembers writer Vince Aletti. 'He would make this whole atmosphere when people were coming in. Before people started dancing. He would play these oddball things that he would discover, that were mostly like jazz-fusion records or world music. Things that didn't have any lyrics for the most part, but were just cool-out or warm-up records. It was great to see the mood getting set. Little by little, they would get more rhythmic and more and more danceable and people would start dancing. I loved seeing the whole theatre get underway. It was like being at a play before the actors had started performing.'

How to turn up the heat

If you think of your set graphically, it should have a steady upward curve. Aim to build the mood slowly and have the dancefloor full and primed by the time you hand over to the next DJ (and not much before).

Look at the crowd

Interaction is crucial at this early stage. Once the club's crowded no-one cares if you ignore them, but early on it's more one-to-one so make sure you look up and read the reactions on people's faces. Give them a smile; show you're as friendly and up-for-it as they are. This is the best way to work out which course of action to take next, which record to choose. Let their faces be your guide.

Get the girls on the floor

Girls are far less scared of an empty dancefloor than boys, so when it's time to start the dancing, aim some tracks firmly at the females. Girls respond to good vocal songs and tunes with nice basslines. (Don't argue with genetics.)

Build it slowly

Increase the tempo slowly and avoid the temptation to go mad too early. There's no rush – wait until the later part of your set to really kick things off. Great DJing is about teasing and holding back.

125

Nought to 130 in two hours

1. You're on your own, kid

The barstaff are still doing things with boxes. It's time to relax and play some great tunes you'd never hear otherwise (and check the equipment, etc). As people start arriving, try guessing which song might make them go, 'Oh my god, I haven't heard this in years.' Gently increase the tempo with each track until you're playing things that might entice a few pioneers out onto the floor.

2. Pioneer time

Soon, some brave souls will venture out to enjoy a particular song or two. Don't worry if they go back to the bar at the end of the track they liked. They've shown their colours and they'll return. Don't bother finding a tune to keep them dancing unless you're approaching stage three.

3. Your entrance

Yes, we know you've been on for ages, but now there's enough people for the dancing to start properly. The signs? A sprinkling of dancers. Plenty of people round the edges. Lots of people looking at the dancefloor and nodding or tapping something. It's time to say hello. Play a 'let's go' record and get this show on the road.

4. Get the stragglers aboard

Once you have a healthy-looking dancefloor, you should find ways to draw those on the edges into the fray. Why are those boys standing at the side when they should be dancing? What are those people doing chatting at the bar? How can I get them all to dance on my floor?

5. Ready for take off

The dancefloor has a momentum of its own. People aren't going anywhere for a while. They're excited and expectant, looking towards the booth to see what's going to happen. Keep it like this until a couple of songs before you're due to hand over.

6. Bingo

When you think the room is primed and ready, drop that one tune you just know is going to finally trigger the floor; the one that will take them from warm to hot. You'll know when it is. The rising hum of people has almost become a shout. It's as if they've been waiting for you to play it, as though their impatience has forced your hand. It's like a bursting dam: it's the only way to relieve that pressure.

Warming up is invaluable for learning about pacing and for developing confidence in your DJing. It can be liberating, too. If you normally only play one style of music, this is your chance to experiment with different styles, slower tempos, weirder, less obviously dancefloor-friendly records.

How to get some experience

Play in bars
There are hundreds of club-oriented bars these days and most of them will be happy to give you a chance on their decks (the manager might need to hear a fairly mellow tape first). Since you're not judged on how well you can fill a dancefloor (most bars don't even have one), it's a chance to have fun with the music in your collection and be more daring with your programming. This is a great way to learn about mood setting – the *raison d'être* of a bar DJ.

Watch the pros
Check out either mobile DJs or experienced pop DJs (the ones who play at your local Ritzy). They may like the sound of their own voice too much; they may play the most predictable array of pop records; but they also know how to take an evening from an empty room to peak hour and back again. Effortlessly! They know how to work a crowd of people, how to interpret what they want and how to give it to them. Even if they do it using Steps records. Forget the music they're playing and watch their mastery of crowd psychology.

'Warming up is the most important role of the night; the warm-up DJ makes the night. But I reckon clubs should have speed limits! No going over 125bpm before midnight. If you do you're off and we'll suspend your pay for two weeks.'
Anthony Pappa

127

21. How to read a crowd

Crikey, I can barely read a book, never mind a crowd. Well, actually, yes you can – the signs and clues are all there. The whole point of DJing is that you interact with the people on the dancefloor – otherwise you might as well just put on a tape. Your job is to get inside their heads and figure out what makes them dance.

How a dancefloor works

Study the dynamics of the dancefloor whenever you're in a club. If you're a regular clubber this should be instinctive. If you've never been on a dancefloor, leave this book immediately.

One happy monster
Think of your dancefloor as a single organism. How much energy does it have? What mood is it in? What's it trying to do tonight – get sweaty or pose and look beautiful? What drink or drugs has it taken? What's its number, where did it get that top and didn't you see it in *Mixmag* last month? Think in terms of the total energy in the room – your job is to maximise it and point it in the right direction.

The party starters
You've got a mass of average people but sprinkled among them are little islands of energy: great dancers, big show-offs, people with infectious smiles, a group of really excited girls, someone who seems to know all your tracks... They generate energy and it spreads out from them like ripples on a pond. If you work on the party people they'll bring up the energy levels of the rest.

The party poopers
You've also got the dross: the sharking boys and the bystanders who can't decide whether they're dancing or just having a fag. These people are sucking out valuable energy. Ideally the dancefloor police would cattle-prod them into a taxi. In the real world you have to either make them dance, or get everyone else so excited that they feel out of place and shark off to the bar.

How to figure out what they want

Your mission is to learn enough about the lovely bodies and souls in front of you to accurately choose the records they'll really like. The most obvious clues are: on the one hand a full and excited dancefloor, and on the other an empty floor with disgruntled dancers banging their glowsticks on the door of the DJ booth.

Instant clues
Provided you're not too politically correct, you can judge a lot just from appearances.

- Which country/city/club you're in.
- How gay/straight/male/female/black/white the crowd is.
- What they were dancing to earlier.
- What they're wearing.
- How old they are.
- What year it is (wake up at the back).

How do they respond to your music?
Once you start playing tunes you can conduct experiments to find out more. Gently probe the crowd with a range of different records. Do they like it faster or slower; do they prefer big breakdowns or tracks which stay in a groove? Make a mental note of these reactions.

- People leaving the floor (which people?)
- People arriving to dance (which people?)
- People going bonkers (which people? How bonkers?)
- People looking at the booth/dancefloor expectantly.

Be observant and responsive and every tune you play will teach you more about their likes and dislikes.

'A good DJ is always looking at the crowd, seeing what they're like, seeing whether it's working; communicating with them. Smiling at them. And a bad DJ is always looking down at what they're doing all the time and just doing their thing that they practised in their bedroom...'

Norman Cook

129

How to approach your crowd

'A DJ is there to participate. He should have one foot in the booth and the other on the dancefloor.'

David Mancuso

It's about teamwork. Never forget you're in this together – dancers and DJ on a joint mission. While the crowd might not know you, they are not against you.

Make eye contact
They're dancing to your music; the least you can do is look at them. Eye contact can tell you volumes about the mood of the floor and how your songs are going down. This is especially important at the start of the night or when the floor is thin.

Win their trust
You're their team leader but they won't follow you blindly. You have to give them enough of what they want to win their trust. Then you can lead them in the more interesting directions you want to go in.

Find a friend
One DJ trick is to pick out a single person who you think represents the overall energy and tastes of the dancefloor, see what turns them on and play for them. You might pick out several people at once or choose different people as the night progresses.

Keep charge
Just because you know exactly what the crowd wants, you don't have to give them an endless supply. Don't get suckered into delivering crowd-pleaser after crowd-pleaser without really thinking about the bigger picture. Our advice is this: don't let them *lead* you, let them *guide* you.

Ring the changes
Experiment with different styles and sounds and see how they react. It might seem that they're loving every minute of the Chinese gabber you're playing, but throw on some jazzy techno and they might go crazy. Never underestimate the willingness of your audience to accept surprises and changes.

Factors to consider

Each crowd is unique, but there are a few general rules about mob behaviour.

Crowd size
Smaller crowds are more sensitive and easier to throw off. A big crowd has more momentum so it's harder to mess up.

Drugs
We don't approve of them, being strict Methodists, but drugs have a powerful effect on a crowd. They change how people perceive music, making them want it faster (or slower if they've taken Horlicks). Drugs change people's energy levels – how long and hard they want to dance. And they affect people's moods, which changes the room's energy (smiles or stares have a strong effect on the people dancing next to them). What's the mong factor?

Alcohol
We're not just talking about illegal drugs. There's nothing like alcohol for getting a dancefloor going (although a floor fuelled by booze will burn itself out pretty quickly). How pissed are they?

Pose factor
There's a scale of showing-off-ness, from fashion-crowd-inertia to tops-off-and-proud-of-it. Are people here to dance or stand still and be seen?

Attention span
Is there a lot of wandering on and off the floor or are people pretty much rooted? Are they willing to stick with your super-deep, ultra-repetitive house or will they lose interest before you get to the vocal reward at the end? Are they so lazy they need a snare roll every two minutes to stop them going to the bar?

Musical knowledge
Look for people who react to a new song – they're the ones who are most into the records; the ones who actually listen to what you're playing and possibly know what it is.

Alternative environments
Where can they escape to? Is your music too similar to the guy playing in the other room? Are they waiting on the sidelines for you to kick in with something a little zippier, or has everyone gone to chill out because you're driving them too fast?

131

How to
learn more

Play out as often as possible. For audience interaction, experience is the only thing that counts. Every time you play out you learn more about other people's musical tastes and about the psychology of a dancefloor. Once you have a feel for the basics, you can do homework whenever you go clubbing – just watch the crowd with your new DJ's perspective.

Weddings and bar mitzvahs

The best man won't pay you because you haven't got anything from *Grease*; the bride is drunk and quietly sobbing; her father is trying to start a fight with the groom; and the page-boys keep nicking your headphones. Weddings can be psychopathic events, and it's rare for the DJ to come anywhere near to enjoying the experience, but they are also amazing occasions for learning about dancefloor behaviour. In fact, if you can swallow your pride, and if you have enough disco favourites, golden oldies and commercial pop-dance records, the tackier the event, the more you'll learn.

You'll see how easily a familiar tune can get people rushing to the floor, and how after going loopy to three records they know, you have enough momentum to slip in one they don't. You'll see how the crowd divides up into little dancing groups, how one enthusiastic dancer (the wacky uncle) can liven things up a bit, how drunken girls are the key to starting things off. And given the simple, obvious tastes on display, you'll gain real confidence about predicting which records will work for which people.

Perhaps it's because there's usually a real psychodrama lurking. Perhaps it's because dancing isn't the only reason they're there. Perhaps it's because there's such a weird cross-section of people. Whatever the reason, at a wedding the quirks of dancefloor psychology are writ large. And when you raise the roof with 'We Are Family' and the mad auntie starts squeezing your bum, you might even have a great time.

132

How to deal with requests

'Got any Tygers Of Pan Tang?' In the course of your DJ career you can expect requests from boggle-eyed punters, ranging from the annoying to the unfathomable. Don't kid yourself that because you play in the most underground drum & bass club in Weston Super Mare you'll be free from this. No matter where you play, the one thing you can guarantee is that you will get requests.

The first thing is to be nice. This person, however musically clueless, has bothered to ask you for a particular record. Forget about guessing what the dancefloor likes. Part of it just told you directly. We're constantly amazed at how snotty some DJs can get over requests. If that record's in your box it doesn't hurt to play it (when the time is right). After all, why did you bring it in the first place?

However, for every perfectly sane request, there are several demented ones. Here are three of the most common.

- Can you play something with a beat?
- Can you play something we can dance to? (As though the packed dancefloor in front of us is busy knitting sweaters . . .)
- I've lost my friend Mandy. Can you get on the mic and ask her to meet me by the DJ booth?

Be polite, stand firm, and resist taking it to heart as an attack on your DJing abilities. It doesn't take much to humour someone, even if you have no intention of playing that Black Sabbath record they've been screaming for. Take a deep breath and say . . .

'I do have it but, unfortunately, I don't have it with me.'

And remember: some people will never be happy. The exchange below took place a few years ago and is reproduced word-for-word.

Punter: Can you play some Roy Ayers?
DJ: This *is* Roy Ayers.
Punter: Yes, well, not this one.

22. **How to** choose the next record

This is the single most essential skill of DJing. Programming, or sequencing – choosing the order in which you play your records – is a DJ's core talent. We don't care what bullshit you've been told about clever mixing; putting records in the right order is much more important.

The essence of programming

You could be the smoothest, most technically perfect mixer, but if you can't choose the right record for a particular moment, you can't DJ yet. Unlike beatmatching, which you can pick up in a few weeks or months, programming takes years to perfect, because it is more art than science. Programming is about developing a sensitive understanding of how people react to music. The more you play out, the more of the necessary experience you accumulate.

You are creating a flow, rhythmically, melodically or lyrically, so that the tunes you play make complete sense to the dancefloor. This flow is not something you can plan ahead of time, it's an improvisation based on the mood of the crowd. Often this is entirely instinctive: a record just sounds right. Some nights, when everything is going perfectly, it can be so natural it feels as though someone else is telling you exactly which records to play. Your aim is to be really good at saying:

'This is totally the right record for this precise moment.'

Each time you pull out a track it should hold memories as powerful as your first kiss/pill/marriage/arrest. You should be able to remember every time you've played this tune and the reactions to it on each occasion. Did it clear the floor or have their arms in the air? Some records work in any context, any club, any country, while others will inspire a variable response. It's up to you to mentally tabulate all of this information, so you know how best to use your records to work your dancefloor.

How to choose by mood

Forgive us for being poncy, but each record in your collection has a 'mood' and you should figure out what it is. This isn't just what mood it gives you personally; it's what mood it gives a dancefloor. Programming is essentially choosing records with the right mood.

- The energy level each generates.
- The emotional feelings each creates.

When you start out, you'll find you can only envisage a few different mood groups for your records (eg 'warm-up', 'peak hour', 'cool-down'). But with more experience you'll be able to subdivide these categories into subtler ones (eg 'gentle-optimistic-climbers', 'steady-but-energetic', 'full-on-toffee-flavoured-bonkers'). You don't actually have to think of names – unless it helps – because most of this will be subconscious. The more you play out the more sensitive you'll become at deciding which records fit which moments. Your record collection will become an enormous library of moods, with you as its librarian.

Watch and learn

Dancefloor feedback is key. Watch how people react to the music you play, and use this to collate your mood library. As you play out regularly you'll start to connect your records with different parts of a night and different requirements of your set. Some will become fail-safes, some groovers, some stormers. Some will have a particular resonance for a certain audience or a certain occasion. One or two might turn out to be 'secret weapons' – killer obscure tracks that get the crowd screaming for more every time you play them. Once you start thinking about records in terms of their effect on an audience (and not just their effect on you), you'll be able to continue your mood cataloguing whenever you see people dancing to records.

'There is no approach other than play what you feel. You can't have any preconceived notions about what you're going to play.'

Grooverider, *DJ Times*

135

How to choose by musical features

A record's mood is quite subjective, but there are some more concrete factors you must consider. These depend on really knowing your records.

Tempo

Unless you're planning a sudden change, you'll need to follow one record with another of similar tempo. Make sure you know (roughly) the tempo of each of your records. You don't have to memorise their bpms, but you should mentally fit each record into one of maybe four or five personal tempo categories.

Style

Obviously you should consider the genre of a record, but you can take matters of style a little deeper. Is it melodic, percussive, dubby, jazzy, rocky, annoyingly filtered . . . ? What instruments does it use? (Or what instruments do its synthesisers and samples sound like?)

Structure

This is extremely important (there's more on this on p74 *How to place a mix*). However, don't select a record purely because it mixes easily with the one playing. There has to be more to your choice than that.

Musical association

It's not just about scientific musical matches. Let the record that's playing remind you of others that you have available. 'This rhythm pattern sounds just like the one in that Luciano track', or 'Isn't that a similar bassline to that Masters At Work remix?' Like moods, musical associations are things that just occur to you. Of course, the better you know your records the more associations will come to mind and the more possibilities you'll have.

Tried and tested mixes

A record might remind you of another one simply because you remember mixing them successfully in a previous set. Be careful, though – rely on this too much and you can easily fall into the trap of playing pre-planned sequences and ignoring what's happening on the dancefloor.

How to choose by meaning

Some records actually say something and this is another weapon in your armoury. Even though much of today's dance music is instrumental, your music can still reflect your feelings or comment on the world outside.

Whether it's playing a track as a tribute to a singer who recently died, or dropping 'It Should Have Been Me' at a wedding, never forget the emotional power that words and meanings can have. Even if only a few people pick up on your message it can dramatically change the feelings and energy of the room.

When the Body & Soul parties resumed after the terror of September 11th their soundtrack reflected the city's need for solace. The music of that first evening included such songs as 'Why Can't We Live Together', 'Love To The World' and 'What Will Tomorrow Bring?' These records might be old, but they were made newly poignant by the context.

Telling tales

In the days of disco, when the majority of songs had lyrics, DJs would often weave together records that shared a similar theme. 'I used to try to tell stories, that was my gig,' said Steve D'Acquisto, one of the first DJs to mix records, back in the early seventies. 'I used to try and talk with the music: I love you; I need you; You're hurting me; I'm going to leave; But I want you back again.'

'Nicky Siano knew how to talk with music,' said Kenny Carpenter, recalling another disco pioneer. 'He used lyrics to send a message: I love you, I hate you, I miss you. Freddy Prinze was an actor in a famous sitcom here. He died and that night Nicky played "Freddie's Dead" from the *Superfly* soundtrack. Those kind of things.'

'There is actually a message in the dance, the way you feel, the muscles you use,' said post-disco legend Larry Levan. 'Say I was playing songs about music – "I Love Music" by The O'Jays, "Music" by Al Hudson and the next record is Phreek's "Weekend", that's about getting laid, a whole other thing. If I was dancing and truly into the words and the feeling and it came on, it might be a good record, but it makes no sense because it doesn't have anything to do with the others. So a slight pause, a sound effect, something else to let you know it's a new paragraph rather than one continuous sentence.'

137

How to go in a certain direction

'Bringing in other genres of music – making people connect them to dance music – is a really good thing. When I first started playing Nirvana's "Smells Like Teen Spirit" people would boo – it made me so happy. I thought this is great. It really got a reaction.'

Jeremy Healy,
Mixmag

Programming is not just about *responding* to your dancefloor, because you're also leading the way. Like a chess grandmaster you should be thinking several moves ahead. Perhaps you have a storming vocal you want to play in about half an hour. Maybe you want to bring things down a little so that in three records' time you can play a real 'climber' to best effect. Most DJs think of their set in terms of these kinds of goals. So each record has to be:

- perfect for now
- pointing in the right direction.

As you put a new tune on, think of five records you might follow it with, and five records you could play after each of those. In your mind you should see a network of records and their possible connections.

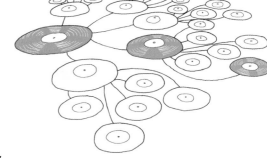

It's a journey
Your records are towns and cities on a road map of possibilities, and there are hundreds of scenic routes to your destination. But please make sure it's a trip through the Himalayas, not a coach tour of the Netherlands.

It's a story
You have a tale to tell. Some of your tunes are bold chapter openings, some are full stops, paragraph endings or even exclamation marks. Make sure you have the readers' attention and don't forget a beginning, a middle and an end.

Other considerations
In choosing a direction to head for you should also consider the musical policy of the club and the style of the DJ following you (up to a point).

Never ever plan a set

You can plan the next couple of records, you can plan a rough strategy for the next 30 minutes or plan the overall shape of your set, but *never start a gig with a firm running order already in your mind*. We've come across a lot of bedroom DJs bragging on bulletin boards about how they have their set perfectly worked out before they leave the house. These are the kinds of DJs who will wank away on their own without once thinking about what the crowd wants. Perish the thought that something like an empty dancefloor should scupper their plans for world domination.

The practicalities of programming

Only by being properly organised will you have enough headspace to be sensitive, emotional and spontaneous when choosing tunes. You need to have the right records to maximise your options, and you need to organise your box so you can find things as easily as possible. See p112 *How to pack your box*.

On the diagonal
Most DJs think about where their set is going and stick possible records up diagonally in the box. The idea is to separate all the records which might work next (the diagonal ones) from the ones which definitely wouldn't. Some DJs reshuffle this selection every time they put on a record; others do it at strategic intervals during their set.

How to be brave

There are some rare occasions (especially with radically new styles of music) when it's OK to ignore the audience reaction. This is like making them eat their greens instead of just letting them go mad for ice cream. If you're right, and you're sure you're right, sometimes you have to let the crowd know they're wrong. Veteran DJ Dave Dorrell remembers the first time he played Chicago house in London. 'I played those records back to back as soon as I could get my hands on the decks.' The dancefloor cleared and stayed empty for 30 minutes. For Dave, such a powerful negative reaction was proof that house would be huge. 'I thought, boy, those records are going to do something.' We're all in favour of this kind of bravery. You can't be a great DJ without taking risks. But if the dancefloor stays empty week after week, maybe you'd better take notice.

139

23. **How to** pace the night

Your job as a DJ is to encourage and control the energy in the room. And that means thinking of the whole night and not just going hell-for-leather from the moment you hit the booth.

Shaping the night

Play too hard and fast early on and you'll shag out the dancefloor long before the end, however many Red Bulls they've injected. Even hard house DJs should vary their levels of boshness. Treat your dancers with care and respect and they'll last all night.

Pacing the night is about programming your music to create a shape for the evening – in mood and, crucially, in tempo. Looking at your set graphically: it should be full of undulations, peaks and troughs. If you play trance or progressive house, be aware that much of its appeal rests on the illusion that the music is continually peaking. This is persuasive and effective, but since all the ups and downs are already built in to the records it can be very limiting for a DJ. When each track is an epic six-minute rollercoaster, you have much fewer true pacing possibilities.

Good DJing is about keeping a constant groove while throwing in plenty of changes – balancing the expected with the surprising. A lot depends on your dancefloor's stamina (whether natural or chemically assisted) and their attention span (how long they're willing to be teased before a pay-off). A sports coach knows that an extended flat-out sprint will wear out an athlete much quicker than a series of sprints and jogs. Whatever style you play, if you vary the pace, ultimately you'll get more from your dancefloor.

'Start out with a slow groove, the way it used to be and the way it should be. I call it the appetiser, the entrée and then the dessert. The end of the night I come back with the classics. The last hour I'll pull out all those surprises.'

Danny Tenaglia

Up, up and away

This is the norm today, largely because every DJ wants their little two-hour set to peak the night. Crowds respond to it, but only because they're rarely offered anything different. Start off fairly quickly and continue in an upward curve until the dancefloor is banging away so fast that everyone's running on the spot. Not for the faint of heart.

The rollercoaster

Good pop DJs programme sets that are almost Pavlovian in their effectiveness, and you'll see this style in most carpet-and-chrome nightspots (it lets the DJ run through all the genres and it's good for alcohol sales). Take the tempo gradually up until you reach a frenetic peak, and then drop down dramatically to reggae pace. Repeat. Then repeat again.

The work-out

This is how most long-set DJs play – they treat the evening as an aerobics lesson. Start out slow with warm-up exercises to let the dancers acclimatise. Gradually shift it up a few gears until you reach a peak, and then hold it there (allowing a few breathers along the way). Finally, gently drop the tempo at the end of the evening to allow for cool-out stretching exercises.

Riding the waves

David Mancuso started the world DJing with his Loft parties in Manhattan. Pleasingly, he is still doing them over 30 years later. David eases people into his evenings with slower tunes – ambient, jazz, world music – before gradually upping the tempo and making the music more dancefloor friendly. As the evening progresses, he's not afraid to occasionally slow things down, creating a gently undulating night.

Shaping your set

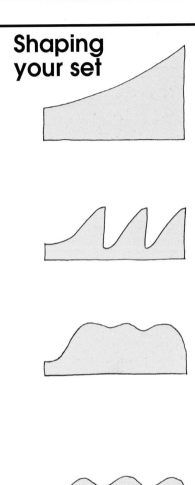

How to keep them dancing

'You've got to want them to go mad, but they've got to show a willingness to go with you. Sometimes you can do it by building up the energy of the music without having to resort to silly break-downs and big moments and drum rolls. Anything that increases the tension and lets them know something is about to happen.'

Pete Heller

Your aim is to keep the dancefloor full, happy and engaged while satisfying your lust for introducing new sounds and styles. Play too many obvious hits and you'll wear everyone out (and, eventually, bore them to death). Play too much minimal German techno and you'll soon drive them to the bar. The trick is to hypnotise and seduce them, balancing the expected and the unexpected, the familiar and the unfamiliar. Your job is to build rock solid grooves so unmissable they can't leave the floor even if they're dying for a pee.

It's all about suspense

You are controlling a room full of emotion. That's a powerful thing. To keep a crowd under your spell you need to generate anticipation and suspense. It's like watching a good thriller. You know something's going to happen, but you're not sure when, so you can't tear yourself away for even a second. Alfred Hitchcock was the master of suspense because he knew, 'There is no terror in the bang, only in the *anticipation*.' To keep a dancefloor entranced you have to show them you are totally confident, and are taking them somewhere they want to go.

It's all about drama

Drama is life with the dull bits left out. Think about the '3D-ness' of your set. Is it a dramatic landscape or an endless flatland? Do you choose the next record because it really goes somewhere or because it mixes well with what's playing? Of course you want your set to fit together as a whole, but within that you have to include some ups and downs, otherwise you'll be boring and repetitive. So vary the tempo, change the mood, and contrast the sounds and the styles of the records you play.

It's all about sex

Dancing is just thinly disguised sex. And you can't make love with just one stroke. Like sex, you should make your music as exciting and varied as possible (at least you should if you want to keep getting laid). Get in a steady groove, then change positions, try something else, have a smoke and do it all again.

How to make them go mad

You make a crowd go mad by building up tension and then releasing it. Simple as that. Let everyone know what's coming, make sure they realise it, warn them again, and then... only when they're totally desperate... let them have it. The longer you hold back, the bigger the release will be. Great DJs, like great lovers, are expert teases. They work up a fever of expectation, and only when they've toyed with their lover for as long as possible do they let loose with a gigantic orgasm... er, epic vocal.

Build tension and expectation

- Play a steadily rising series of records which is obviously going somewhere.
- Play hints of a big song long before you play the whole thing.
- Play something repetitive and hypnotic.
- Take something away (the bass, the volume, the song...) so they're desperate for it to return.

Is it you or your records?

A build-up used to take careful programming and might last as long as an hour. Nowadays records are filled with snappy musical tricks (drum rolls, long breakdowns, phasing, filter effects...) that do it all in a matter of minutes. Lots of DJs are happy to sit back and let their records do all the work. But this is the fast-food version of what a DJ can achieve, and if you really want to master your craft we think you should try a bit harder. Feel free to use a tune that builds tension then makes the crowd go insane, but remember: this is the record being clever, not you.

'For me it's sex. Absolutely. It's classic, spiritual sex. A great night, man, sometimes I'm on my *knees* in the middle of a mix, just feeling it. And you can bring it down, you can just turn everything off and the people going nuts. And you stand back, you just wipe your forehead and, *shit*! Just knowing that you're right there, you could play whatever you want. *Whatever you want*. You got 'em from there.'

David Morales

143

Avoid big tune syndrome

It's extremely seductive to be in control of a room full of people who are all going nuts to your music. This is why young and inexperienced DJs get drawn into playing an endless succession of hits (usually straight from the Sasha playlist). These people are just too eager to get their rocks off; sex with them would be over in a couple of minutes (if they're lucky). Whoa! Hold on, fella. You might only have two hours to play, but these dancers are going to be here all night and you're wearing them out. By all means pull out your heavy hitters, but ration them – build up to them and make them really count. We don't want to hear Pete Tong's Greatest Hits in a 30-minute flurry.

How to create punctuation

Use stops, starts, changes and pauses to break up your set into different sections. Instead of always mixing one record into the next, in one long monotonous splurge, why not create some 'moments'. A good DJ can change styles, tempos – even drop into complete silence – without losing any dancers. The reason no-one leaves the floor is that they know it's just a pause for breath, and that something fantastic is going to happen next.

Fresh starts

If a film is just the same damn thing all the way through, you soon get bored. But if the action shifts to a fresh scene, it wins back your attention. Having brought the music to a climax, it can be a useful device to slow it right down to a totally different tempo. This gives you a new starting point to work up from, as well as creating a bit of space and movement on the dancefloor.

Cleansing the floor

If you're brave enough, you can purposefully thin out the crowd. Let the lads go for a beer while you play something more girly. Or simply lose the half-hearted bystanders. 'Sometimes we decide to sort out the men from the boys,' says Matt Black from Coldcut. 'We put on something incredibly difficult and give the more "into it" element a little more space to wig out in. We don't clear dance-floors, we cleanse them!'

144

How to play all night

Bring lots more records
Obviously. In a short set you express your musical essence; here you can dig deep and show your very soul. With space to expand into, you can let records play their full length and air things you might not have risked otherwise.

Divide the night into sections
Imagine you're three different DJs (eg warm-up, peak hour, wind-down). When the evening reaches a certain stage (watch the crowd and decide), you kick yourself off the decks and let yourself come on for a new set. Some long-set DJs bring different boxes for different stages. Others have a complete reshuffle of their records.

Go to the toilet
And watch your beer intake. For stamina, have a decent meal three or four hours before your gig (eating too late will send you to sleep). Plus a disco nap.

All night long

The reason why Danny Tenaglia's marathon 18-hour sets at the Winter Music Conference became so legendary is not only because he's a brilliant DJ, but also because one DJ playing the whole night is now sadly a rarity.

Prior to the acid house explosion, the accent was on residencies, and DJs played extended sets, usually for the same crowd, week after week. This let them gain a deep understanding of their dancefloor's tastes and quirks, and it taught them how to pace the night – how to play a set which had a shape to it.

But today, thanks to an emphasis on guest spots, we have a culture based entirely around two-hour sprints. This has narrowed the scope of the music (with DJs playing the same or similar records throughout the night) and it has pushed tempos to ridiculous heights (as each DJ tries to go faster than the last one). Rather than bring dancers up and then down gently, most young clubbers now expect a DJ to simply 'bang it out', whatever time it is.

To master your craft you should aim to play for as long as you can – if possible all night. It will teach you things you can't learn any other way. Of course no-one's going to offer you a gig like that straight off the bat, so your best move is to throw your own parties, build your own following and give yourself the freedom to develop your own individual style.

'Give most DJs an eight-hour set these days and they'd shit themselves.'

Laurent Garnier, BurnItBlue

24. How to come on after someone

Coming on after someone is much more nerve-wracking than warming up – you're starting cold but you're playing for a floor full of dancers who are already in a groove. And if the previous DJ was playing a different style, you can't help worrying that your music might empty the floor. Nerves aren't necessarily a bad thing, though. All that adrenalin heightens your awareness; makes you feel things more keenly. Your task is to channel it into the music.

DJ etiquette

'Don't be big-headed! Stop bigging up your chest. Big ego DJs have lost it a bit, I always find.'

Mr C, *Mixmag*

Show some respect to the outgoing DJ
Be friendly and polite (no trying to cop off with his wife while he's playing).

Let the DJ's last record run its course
It's very rude to suddenly stop a record in the middle or mix out of it prematurely (even if you think it's crap). Think about the flow of the dancefloor more than your own ego.

Discuss when you're coming on
Don't be too hung up on the clock, but have a word well ahead of time to confirm when you're expected on, and then be in the booth a couple of records ahead of your slot.

Discuss what you're going to play
He probably won't care, but a real pro might take your style into consideration and finish with something that leads neatly into your set.

Don't talk to the DJ during a mix
You wouldn't like it, would you?

Be thoughtful when setting up your box
In a cramped space co-operation is key.

How to get ready

Get there early

Despite all that extra time to bite your nails, it's worth it because you can watch how the night builds and get a good idea of the crowd and the music they like. By the time you're on you'll know exactly which direction you can take things in. It also prevents you repeating records. No-one wants to hear the same song twice in quick succession because the incoming DJ has only just turned up and doesn't realise that big vocal anthem was played ten minutes ago.

Check things out thoroughly

Your first job is to get into the booth and check things through with the outgoing DJ. How's the crowd tonight? How does the mixer work? How is the monitoring? Which promoter has the drinks tickets? Give yourself enough time to go through everything. There's full details on getting ready on p116 *How to play out*.

When Gilles followed Carl

Radio 1 once thought it would be 'really Balearic' for Gilles Peterson to come on straight after Carl Cox and close their Ibiza weekend. 'As we arrived he was still on and we could hear people cheering,' recalls Gilles. 'I've got to do a radio show, live to the UK and I've got to follow this. I'm freaking out. The closest record I've got is the Herbert remix of Moloko's "Sing It Back"! Carl saw me coming and he was, like, "You can't be serious?!" But there was no escaping. So I had to go on.'

Gilles dealt with this hilarious mismatch the only way he could. 'I let his record play out and then played the most mad record that I had. A weird, tripped out future jazz tune with a long intro. And I watched people's faces just drop. Suddenly, they're like "What's happening?". I got on the mic, but I sounded nervous; like I was shitting it. And the reaction was basically "Fuck off. You cunt".'

The crowd dwindled from 800 to 150. But Gilles soldiered on and turned things right round. 'In the end we had a really good party. It taught me as a DJ that you don't need to be frightened. I dealt with that situation. Not particularly well, but I dealt with it and I didn't die. It was probably my most freaky experience as a disc jockey and a real turning point. Ever since then, I've been far more confident.'

How to make an entrance

If you're not sure of yourself, you can choose to mix seamlessly out of the last DJ, but this is a bit like creeping in unannounced. Why not show confidence and let people know there's a new gunslinger in town? This doesn't mean arriving on a throne carried by well-oiled bodybuilders (though don't rule that out), but with the right record you can do the musical equivalent. Play something that announces your arrival. Make an impression. Cause a stir. Be bold. Say hello with a tune that's defiantly *yours*.

Let the last record play out

If you let things come to an end before starting your set, it's a statement about how confident you are. Leave it a few moments before putting your first record on. It builds dramatic tension and lets the crowd show their appreciation of the last DJ.

Turn the volume down

Most experienced DJs do this, either as the other guy's record is playing out, or just before they put on their first record. It's important to have some 'headroom' so you can notch things up later. Give yourself somewhere to go.

Play something noticeable

A different style from what's been playing, a record with a weird intro, a piece of spoken word, a sound effect, some white noise, an orchestral piece, a local favourite, a timely classic, a signature record... It's completely up to you, your imagination and the level of drama you want to create.

'I'll have 1,500 people in front of me and I'll turn off the turntables and just stand there. Everyone's looking, thinking, "What the fuck's going on?" I want all the attention on me, so everyone knows – now we're going to start something *different*. The first record sets the pace, the rhythm, the direction. Now I'm going to take you where *I* want to take you.'

Paul Oakenfold

Seeing the crowd going nuts to music you don't even possess is a scary thing, but don't let it push you into playing like someone else.

How to follow a different style
If you have a 'bridging' record that's close to what's been playing, you can gradually work your way into more comfortable territory. Otherwise it's better to have a pause and start fresh.

How to follow a slower DJ
Rarely too much of a problem. Simply build up the tempo with a few well-chosen tracks and a bit of pitch control.

How to follow a faster DJ
Following a speed demon can be difficult, since audiences have been trained to expect a constant upwards curve. But don't get suckered into pitching up your records to match. Few tracks sound good beyond +4, and you'll only be backing yourself into a corner.

>> Start from scratch
Let their last tune finish, have a pause and then play something with a dramatic opening and a strong upward energy curve – it may be very different, but if it feels like it's accelerating, the crowd will stick with it. If you're less confident, start with a safe bet – either a classic or something you know will definitely work in that club.

>> Throw a curveball
Play something brilliant but completely weird, leftfield and unexpected. The crowd will either agree that it's brilliant or clear the floor. Leaving you to either bask in glory or start again from fresh.

>> Slow the previous DJ's last tune down
If you take your time and do it gradually enough you can bring the previous DJ's last record down by maybe 3% without the crowd really noticing. This is a much better idea than pitching your records up. It calms the crowd down a bit as well.

Have confidence in yourself
A dramatic change of music is usually better than trying to fudge things – it shows confidence. Remember: losing a few dancers or even clearing the floor is not necessarily a disaster. You're letting the last DJ's crowd have a break and rebuilding the floor with people who are into *your* music. If the worst happens and they hate everything you play, try not to be too hard on yourself. You're in the wrong club and it's the promoter's problem, not yours.

How to deal with a clash of styles

149

The masterclass

25. **How to** build a collection

Many of the best DJs were record collectors first and DJs second. Ever since northern soul, DJs have known that owning hidden treasures is a sure-fire way to beat the competition. Even the most upfront DJ will occasionally use a carefully placed classic to bring a dancefloor to its knees. You already know how to buy music that anyone can get hold of. Now get ready to dig deep.

The philosophy of collecting

It's going to be a mystical apprenticeship. As you trail rare and wonderful records you'll soak up their history, you'll see how today's tunes are part of a long dance music tradition, and you'll add no end of secret weapons to your box. Collecting is about being more than just a consumer – it's about getting truly involved with music.

- Find music your competitors don't know about.
- Gain a far better understanding of current music.
- Get loads of ideas for samples, re-edits and tracks.
- Become a better DJ.

Look further, young Jedi

Lots of young DJs call a six-month-old record a classic. It's not a classic, it's a six-month-old record. You could go back 40 years and still find tracks which could be played today, so broaden your horizons. A good collection should encompass much more than house records made since you took your first pill. Great records don't stop being great because they're old. In fact, as their context changes, some of them manage to sound more relevant now than they did when they were released.

'You must be prepared to search through all the shit, and that might mean waking up at five in the morning and trekking off to some car-boot sale in Epping.'

Pete Heller, *Muzik*

No one wakes up with an encyclopaedic knowledge of seventies jazz-fusion or early nineties breakbeat. Here are some jump-off points.

Compilations
There are few better sources for learning about music of a different time or place. Retro compilations are everywhere these days and most come complete with nicely educational sleevenotes.

Specialist radio
Those late-night and weekend shows can be goldmines.

Veteran DJs
Hang out with the older generation. It'll make you look younger and more handsome, and like London cabbies, they have The Knowledge.

Magazines
Fact and *Wax Poetics* can be goldmines of great old tunes. *Record Collector*, *Mojo*, *Uncut* and *Q* also cover music you might be curious about.

Online forums
Where DJs and clubbers reminisce about old classics and where trainspotters use musical chat to avoid work.

DJs' all-time charts
And magazine features profiling a lost era or classic label.

Buying blind
Follow your hunches and you'll strike charity shop gold.

Old music magazines
Head to the library and improve your set. We can auction you a full set of *Melting Pot* magazine. Bidding starts at ten grand.

Samples
New records often point back to old records (beware, though: they might have sampled the only good bars in the whole tune).

Your records themselves
Every record you acquire should add to your knowledge. Got a great tune? Note its drummers, percussionists, singers, songwriters and producers. Next time you come across their names in a dusty basement, you'll know what to do.

How to gather information

'I look for hair styles and beards on a band. If they've got long hair and beards they're likely to make better records. Especially those big seventies bands with eight of them in – half white, half black and they look like they all take acid.'

Norman Cook

153

How to maintain a collection

It's a lot like gardening. You can leave your collection to sprout in all sorts of directions, but it needs a fair amount of attention to stop it becoming a chaotic, overgrown mess.

Structure it
Put your records into some sort of order: by genre, by date, by label, by alphabet. Whatever lets you find things quickest.

Cultivate it
Maybe you'd love to own more nineties hip hop. In that case you need to spend time finding out about it and planting a few key tunes on your shelves.

Prune it
If you lose sight of the best bits under lots of foliage it's time for some weeding. Careful, though – don't throw out records you might want back one day.

How to buy secondhand

Once they've left their original owners, records enjoy all sorts of adventures. And once you start searching for them, so will you.

Rarity
Don't be fooled. A rare record is not necessarily a good record. Some people collect things for the sake of it, while others are only interested in tunes they'll actually play. It might be valuable, but is it valuable to you? Think about why you're about to give that badly dressed man £30.

Condition
It's hard (but not impossible) to find completely unplayed vinyl. Scratches you can see but not feel will usually play OK. Most dealers use the *Record Collector* categories: M (Mint), VG+ (near-mint), VG (Very Good), G (Good), OK (OK!) . . . Good dealers don't usually trade in anything below VG, and neither should you.

Price

It's usually a toss-up between money and digging time. You might find the occasional £25 record in a 50p car-boot sale, but you'll have spent hours looking through thousands of Tchaikovsky LPs to find it. The same record may well be sitting in a neatly organised website where you can zip straight to it, but here it'll cost you... £25. Yet paying full price all the time is lazy and you'll never get to join our club with that attitude.

Charity shops

You've probably spent your whole life avoiding charity shops, with their attractive displays of clothes designed for Polish shipyard workers. But only the lazy and complacent would ignore the treasures buried deep in their bowels. So head in and boot up your sampler – both Bent and The Avalanches created their debut albums from charity vinyl.

Admittedly, most of the records are by Klaus Wunderlich, Ray Conniff or Mantovani (and every charity shop has at least one copy of Phil Collins' *Face Value*). However, dig a bit further and you'll be surprised at what you find. Best of all, because the records are so cheap (eg '20p for the big 'uns, 10p for the little 'uns...') you can afford to take chances with interesting-looking records you've never heard of. The same goes for car-boot sales.

- Buy records by producers you know to be good.
- Buy any record featuring good drummers or percussionists.
- Buy any cover versions of good songs.
- Buy any rock record with song titles that include 'Africa' (except Toto), 'rhythm', 'space', 'drum' or 'funky'.
- Buy any record that has band members standing in front of a spaceship.

Secondhand dealers

Most cities have at least one secondhand dealer, plus the occasional record fair in the church hall. And of course there's the glorious internet. Venture capitalists have been bled dry by daft ideas that were never going to work online, but selling secondhand records is the perfect internet industry and has created a global village of hungry record collectors and DJs.

Crazy Beat www.crazybeat.co.uk
Long-established black music specialists with a store in Upminster.

Music & Video Exchange www.nottinghillexchanges.com
Several great shops, including the soul and dance exchange.

Reckless www.reckless.co.uk
A clutch of London stores and an extensive online database.

Vinyl Exchange www.vinylexchange.co.uk
Manchester's biggest secondhand store.

Hard To Find Records www.htfr.co.uk
Birmingham-based. Very good for classic house and techno.

Online mega-dealers

These guys use clever internet know-how to bring lots of dealers and individual vendors into one big online record fair.

GEMM www.gemm.com
A huge database of records available from a long list of dealers (mainly US-based but some are in Europe). GEMM lists the records and takes the money, but you're actually buying from a particular store. It's reliable and simple to use, sells every conceivable style of music and has over 16 million items on sale.

Netsounds www.netsoundsmusic.com
Netsounds is the UK equivalent of GEMM. Though not as comprehensive, it's still an excellent resource for all styles of music. Nearly 3 million items on sale.

Music Stack www.musicstack.com
An American rival to Gemm.

eBay www.ebay.com or www.ebay.co.uk
Great for finding records you thought you'd never see again, but it's very easy to get suckered into bidding wars. Set your limit before making bids and stick to it, otherwise bankruptcy is imminent. It's also responsible for ludicrous price hikes of sought-after records among dealers.

Other Resources

Some more great sites for vinyl junkies.

The Breaks (formerly Sample FAQ) www.the-breaks.com
A vast and fantastic database of who sampled what.

Bumrocks www.bumrocks.com
A new MP3 posted every day. Available as RSS feed or podcast, too.

Discogs www.discogs.com
Every electronic release ever is the aim. Indispensable reference tool.

Funk 45 www.funk45.com
The world's funk 45s gathered on to one site, with sound clips and comments.

Waxidermy www.waxidermy.com
Brilliant site, with MP3s, covering everything from Children's school bands
to soul and funk.

Track Listings www.essentialmix.nu
Radio One Essential Mix track-listings back to the eighteenth century.

Tune ID www.tuneid.com
Got an unidentified tune? Ask' em here. Great for '90s rave, techno and house.

Record detectives

When you've exhausted every other option these guys are the musical equivalent of crack dealers. They only deal with collectors, but if you've got a serious habit, a tasty wants list and the wedge to finance the deal, they'll be able to supply the tunes.

DJ Friendly www.djfriendly.co.uk
Run by the legendary Nick The Record. Specialises in hip hop, disco, breaks.

Resolution www.resolutionrecords.co.uk
Pricey, but popular with producers looking for unused samples and breaks.

John Manship Records www.raresoulman.co.uk
Northern soul DJ and dealer. Also sells funk, soul and disco.

Jazzman Gerald www.jazzmanrecords.co.uk
Longstanding UK dealer Gerald specialises in rare funk, soul, Latin and library music.

Pure Pleasure Music www.purepleasuremusic.com
Good for weird dance offshoots, like early eighties UK leftfield.

26. **How to** improve your sound

It's strange how few DJs make any real effort to improve the sound quality of their sets. Yet if you show some love to the sound equipment you can make a huge difference on even the roughest system.

How to reduce distortion

Your ears are ringing, the speakers are bottoming out with nasty crumping noises and your tunes sound like grunge rock played in a bucket. Yet somehow it doesn't feel very loud. What can you do to boost the sound? DJ Clueless will keep turning things up, but you know better...

Try turning things down!

Amazingly, turning things down will often make the music louder because you're reducing distortion. Turn down the gain and the mixer will be able to deal with the signal from the decks better. Turn down the master volume and the amplifier will be able to deal with the signal from the mixer better. Turn the bass down and the speakers will actually be able to reproduce those kick drums with some punch, rather than flapping around pointlessly because they're just about to burst. Distortion happens whenever sound equipment is pushed beyond its optimum range. There's a reason those lights on your mixer are red – it's because you shouldn't let them light up too much.

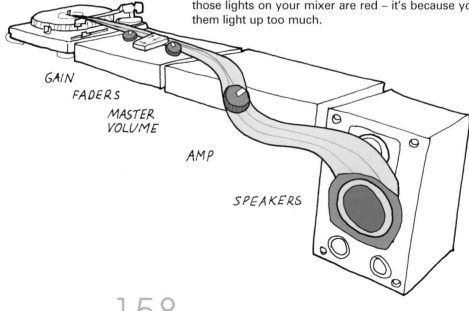

GAIN
FADERS
MASTER VOLUME
AMP
SPEAKERS

How sound behaves

Sound bounces off hard things (like walls and empty dancefloors) and is absorbed by soft things (like curtains, sofas and people). As the room fills up your sound will change dramatically. It's best to have the volume lower when the room is empty or you'll have nasty booming echoes bouncing everywhere.

- Bass speakers ('woofers', 'subwoofers') are best on the floor, where they can make more things vibrate. Bass noises are not very directional (you can't really tell where they're coming from).
- Treble speakers ('tweeters') are best above head height where they can be nice and loud without piercing eardrums. Treble and midrange is much more directional.

How to get your levels right

To fight distortion, smooth out the journey of your sound signal. See also p70 *How to cut*.

Get the input level right
Cue the channel the music's coming through and your mixer's meter will display the input (PFL) level for that channel. Measure the most musically dense part of the song (the loudest bit). Adjust it with the gain control. Set it so it occasionally touches but never stays in the red. This will be at around 0dB.

Get the output level right
When you're not cueing anything (there's nothing in your head-phones) the meter will show the master output level – the level the mixer is sending to the amp. This is affected by the faders and the master volume. Again set it so it occasionally touches but never stays in the red. This will be at around 0dB.

Adjust the amplifier to suit
You now have the best possible signal going into your amp, and can increase the volume as necessary using the amplifier. 'No I can't,' you say – in real life the bar manager won't let you near the amplifier. In that case, your compromise is to turn up the mixer's master volume a bit, but not the gain. This will distort the signal as it leaves the mixer but at least it will go through the mixer in good shape.

159

How to deal with feedback

Bass feedback
A low rumbling roar, usually your decks picking up vibrations from the speakers. Move them away or turn down the bass on the monitor. Sometimes it's the table that's vibrating – try putting a blanket under the decks (or half a tennis ball under each foot).

Treble feedback
An ear-splitting squeal, usually caused by a microphone, rarely by turntables. You cure it either by moving the mic or by turning down the frequency that's causing problems (the frequency of the squeal).

Earth those decks
If you get an electrical hum it could be that your decks aren't earthed properly. Look for the tiny single wire coming out of each turntable. Connect this to the earth screw on the back of the mixer or amplifier.

'If you're playing somewhere where you know the people, you know what type of things they like. So once you get a grip on what people are feeling, if it's a really great night you get to that magic little moment when you instinctively know that whatever you play next they're going to go mental to it.'

Rocky (on the right) (X-Press 2)

How to EQ the room

Before you start playing the mixer's EQ controls like a whirling dervish, you should figure out their 'normal' setting. This will be different on every system and every occasion (so there's no point in remembering your favourite EQ settings).

Diagnosis

- Start with the bass, mids and treble at zero or 'flat'. This should let you hear the record exactly as it was recorded before the room's acoustics affect it.
- Play a record fairly loud that you know is mastered well (good and punchy, with a broad range of frequencies).
- Listen to the sound system, ideally from the middle of the floor, and decide how it sounds.

Treatment

Make all your adjustments in small steps. With EQ it's better to reduce what there's too much of (and then increase the volume) rather than increase what's lacking.

- If the room sounds thin and trebly, it's soaking up bass. Remove a little treble and turn the volume up slightly. If that doesn't do the trick, add some bass (turn the volume back down and the treble back up first).
- If the room sounds booming and bassy, it's soaking up treble. Remove a little bass and turn the volume up slightly. If that doesn't do the trick add some treble (turn the volume back down and the bass back up first).

If there's a graphic equaliser

If the system has a proper graphic equaliser (plugged in between the mixer and the amplifier) then this is what is used to EQ the room. Chances are it's been set by someone who knows more than you and you should leave it alone. If this is the case they will have set it so your mixer EQs should all be at zero for normal use. If you do have access to the equaliser the drill is the same as above, except each control has a much smaller bandwidth.

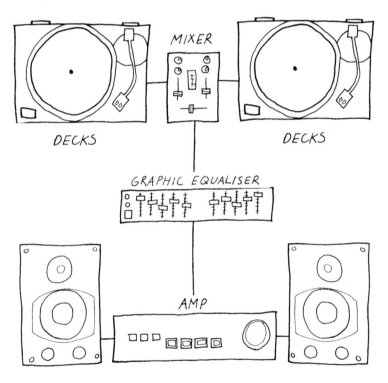

What DJs do wrong

In a big club the DJ's best friend is the house sound engineer. We asked the guys at Fabric – Dave, Sanjay and Fly – what bad DJs do to annoy them.

Playing too loud

'The sound system's set so that if you're just hitting the red it's perfect,' says Dave. 'If you take it beyond that it's going to sound worse.' Most big systems have compression circuits to protect the speakers. Once the volume starts peaking, the louder a DJ tries to make it the quieter it will get. 'You can tell the DJs who give us the most hassle,' adds Sanjay, 'because we're in the booth every ten minutes telling them to turn it down. That's the wrong way to run a night.'

Not anticipating volume rises in tracks

'It's called gain structure,' says Sanjay, explaining how lots of DJs turn up the quieter start of a track, but don't turn levels back down as the track builds in volume, leaving themselves nowhere to go. 'They can't build a set properly, they can't get the dynamics right,' adds Fly. 'They build, build, build, till you get to a point where you're really pushing the system.'

Relying on the monitors too much

Holed up in their cosy booth, too few DJs give any thought to what it sounds like on the floor. The bass could be distorting badly but they'd never know because all they can hear are those nice crisp booth monitors.

Not turning the monitors down between mixes

'DJs have got to turn the monitors off in between mixes,' says Fly. 'They'll deafen themselves. The more you expose your ears to music at that level, they get tired. After two hours it won't seem as loud as you had it before, even if it's actually louder, so you'll turn it up even more.'

Basic ignorance

'Anything goes wrong, they're clueless,' says Dave. 'They should know how to connect a mixer. They've got this stuff at home. You should know some of this. Start learning about things.'

Not respecting the equipment

Fag butts on the turntables, ash on the mixer. Jeez – these Fabric DJs sound like animals.

27. How to EQ

EQ is short for 'EQualisation'. It's about picking out different frequencies in the music – bass, midrange and treble. Sound engineers use the EQ controls to boost particular elements (eg to make weedy vocals richer) and smooth out harsh spikes (eg to soften a too-loud hi-hat). A DJ uses the EQ any damn way he feels like to make the crowd go crazy.

How EQing works

Most decent mixers let you play around separately with the bass, midrange and treble, using rotary controls. Some have 'kill switches' as well, which turn a frequency range off. The killing ability of these can vary a lot from mixer to mixer, however.

	Typical frequency range	Elements/instruments
treble ('highs', 'tops')	3,000–20,000Hz	strings, hi-hats, top half of vocals
midrange ('mids')	250–3,000Hz	melodies, lower half of vocals, snares and other percussion
bass ('lows', 'bottom')	20–250Hz	basslines, kick drums

EQing for better sound
You can use EQ controls creatively, but first you should set them to get the best sound from the room. See p158 *How to improve your sound*.

EQing to clean up mixes
Cutting or lowering frequencies tidies up blends.

- Mix with the bass out and then 'swap' basslines.
- Cut the treble on a song which is 'brighter' (eg with more piercing hi-hats) than the one you're mixing it with.

'It's not a tricky thing to do – it's to do with frequencies and dynamics and building tension and drama into a track. If you're rolling along with the lower range of the spectrum, a kick drum and a bassline, that tends to keep people rooted to the floor. Then, if you add the really high frequencies and remove the bass – for some reason – people just put their hands in the air.'

Tom Middleton

How to EQ creatively

EQing lets you add drama and contrast to a song. If you know there's a big change coming up in the music, exaggerate it by making a simultaneous change to the EQ. You're putting certain parts of the song in italics to make the dancefloor notice them. How you use the EQ is up to you, but here are some starting points.

>> Cut the mids and bass for a tinny, anxious sound
'All highs' messes with people's heads and makes them desperate for their nice, comforting bass to come back.

>> Cut the mids and treble for a dark, booming sound
'No highs' makes the music sound ominous, as though the sound is hiding in wait, ready to jump out at you.

Slam in the bass
The most basic EQ trick is to cut the bass for a few bars during a build-up in the music and then return it, bamm, at exactly the right moment (eg at the same time the bassline comes back in).

Push the treble
Turning up the mid and treble creates an unsettling, almost painful effect. If you cut the bass for a build-up, try also boosting the treble.

Highlight elements
Tweak the EQs and you can pick out some elements or instruments of a song and dampen others.

Mix different elements
Blend a vocal or a melody from one track over the kicks and bassline of another.

Be careful

Don't cut too much
Remember that most instruments and vocals are spread over a fairly wide frequency range. Cutting too much of their EQ will take away a lot of their texture. That's why you can't make a convincing acappella by killing the bass and treble.

Steady on
If a record is properly mastered, it is designed to be played with no EQ changes, so go easy. Too much brash EQing can become tiresome.

165

28. **How to** add FX

You've had the bread and butter. Effects are the disco jam. Some DJs' idea of fancy equipment is a stainless steel centre for their crackly 7-inch singles. But you're young, beautiful and technically minded; you can wire a plug without looking at the diagram; you saw X-Press 2 twisting a favourite tune to within an inch of its life last week and you want to know how they did it. Welcome to the world of FX.

What are effects?

Effects units are 'signal processors'. They take a signal from your mixer and, scientifically speaking, fuck with it creatively. They used to require acres of pricey analogue circuitry and had to be carried on the backs of elephants; now they're digital and tiny. Most importantly they are also cheap, putting them within reach of every budding DJ. In the hands of a beginner, effects are used to cover up dodgy mixes and dodgier records. In the hands of an expert like you they are exciting sonic tools, adding a whole new dimension to your performance. Allegedly.

How to use effects

Like the age-old trick of dropping the bass then slamming it back in, digital effects let you highlight and exaggerate selected places in a record. Add extra drama to a build-up, make a peak moment even peakier, or turn a familiar tune into a swirling, disorienting monster. And when you get into mixing looped, phased or reverbed versions of one tune back into the same tune (or another) you'll really start to see the possibilities. No two DJs will use effects in the same way so we're not about to start lecturing you. They're toys you need to just mess around with.

Moderation, please
There is one great rule, however: moderation. Effects should be your secret weapon not your constant companion. Bash every tune through your Kaoss pad and your crowd will soon be sick of it. Save it for a special moment and they'll worship at your feet.

How to connect effects

Mixers (or CD players) with built-in effects connect in the same way as normal ones, so just get on with hitting those buttons. If you have an external effects box there are two ways of connecting it.

In series between mixer and amp
This means the entire output of your mixer will go through the FX box. This considerably reduces the sound quality of your music because it has to squeeze through another set of circuits even when you're not using the effects. It's also less flexible because you can't mix the mutated sounds back in with anything else. You'll be forced to connect like this if you have a basic mixer with only one output.

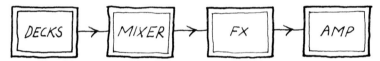

In a send and return loop
This takes the PFL signal from a chosen channel of your mixer, adds effects and then feeds it back into another channel. This means you can mix the coloured signal with the clean one, or with anything else that's going into your mixer.

- Connect the 'send' output on your mixer to the FX box's 'line in'.
- Connect the FX box's 'line out' back into a channel of the mixer (in a 'line' input not a 'phono' one).

There'll be a 'send' button for each channel. Press this and that channel will be sent to your FX box.

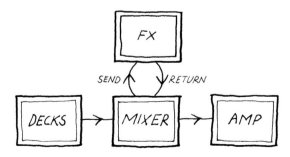

167

The effects

Here are the standard effects. You'll also see lots of custom ones with weird names. These are essentially combination effects based on the classics. Hang on and we'll hum them.

Delay

I'm a bit late... late. This puts in a time-delay (anything from milliseconds to several seconds) so the sound repeats itself for added depth. Delay is the mother of all effects, since most others are just different ways of combining delayed signals with the original.

Echo

Echo, echo, echo... A kind of multiple delay where the sound repeats itself several times, getting fainter and fainter until it dies out. Made in the old days with a loop of tape, it's a staple of reggae and other booming bouncy music.

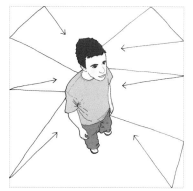

Reverb

Reverb

Clap your hands in a room and you'll hear reverb(eration) – lots of different echoes happening at once. Reverb takes a flat audio signal and fattens it up into the 3D-sound which our ears are used to (because of all the audio reflections around us). It's most famously used by vocalists and radio DJs to hide their puny voices. It dramatically changes drums, too.

Phasing

When you add sound waves together just out of synch (phase-shifted) you get a weird ocean-like effect – with a kind of in-and-out wobble where parts of the sound have partially cancelled themselves out. You can do manual phasing on your turntables (see p182 *How to do deck effects*) Good for build-ups, where it boosts the crowd's sense of 'what's going on?'

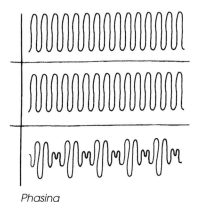

Phasing

Flanging

A more extreme kind of phasing where again a delayed version of the sound is mixed with the original. The difference is that here the delay is greater and changes in size. Adds a whooshing aeroplane effect, to make a sound that's rushing to get somewhere. Flanging was invented by The Beatles. While double-tracking Lennon's voice an engineer accidentally rubbed the flange (rim) of the tape reel.

Chorus

The effects equivalent of inviting some mates over. To make one voice or instrument sound like lots together you knock it slightly out of tune and move it slightly. A bit of delay and a pitch shift later and Britney sounds like the Boys Choir of Harlem.

Tremolo

Like someone moving the volume level up and down very quickly to make a wavering effect. Tremolo is what gave Buddy Holly (and every other fifties guitar player) his shimmery golden sound.

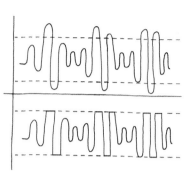

Distortion

Distortion

The Hell's Angel of FX noises. Think dirty, gritty, buzzy guitar players. Hendrix made it famous with his Fuzz Face FX pedal. It's made by clipping the sound, ie snipping off the highest highs and the lowest lows, which is what an overloaded amp will do. You'll get distortion for free if you turn things up too high.

Panning

A stereo balance effect where the mids and trebles move back and forth between the left and right speakers. The bass tends to stay put. At Chicago's Warehouse, Frankie Knuckles used to confuse the hell out of his dancers by panning in a sound effects record of a train thundering through.

Filters

They let the water through but keep the coffee grounds in the... Oh, sorry, they let certain parts of a signal through and not others. A low-pass filter will let the bass through and cut the mids and highs; an all-pass filter will let everything through (but it might slow it down a bit). And so on.

http://en.wikipedia.org
Detailed explanations of all the individual effects we've covered.

www.harmony-central.com/Effects/effects-explained.html
Utterly techie explanations of signal processing.

Buying effects units

There's always a compromise with effects. The studio-quality stuff isn't very DJ-friendly, but the stuff aimed at DJs is (on the whole) of pretty poor sound quality.

What to look for

- Does it actually add something extra? There are a lot of gimmicky products on the market.
- Is it easy to use? It should enhance your performance, not cause nervous breakdowns.
- Is it easily transportable? You might have successfully recreated Pink Floyd Live at Pompeii in your bedroom, but you want equipment that can be carried on a bus not a fleet of lorries.
- Is it compatible with the clubs you play in (ask the sound engineer)?

Mixers with built-in FX

You can now choose between scores of cheap units containing FX – too many to list here. Our advice, though, is that if you're buying budget, a boring mixer without FX will sound better and last longer (cheap FX are largely a marketing tool to jazz up shoddy equipment). Only a couple of FX mixers reach professional standards (at professional prices!). But like Technics decks, you get what you pay for.

Pioneer DJM-600 www.pioneer.co.uk
(DJM-600 – around £630) Mr. C and Rocky of X-Press 2 use this brilliant mixer to stunning effect. If you measure quality against price this is better value than stand-alone FX units.

Denon DN-X 1500 www.denon.dj
(around £600) A serious rival to the Pioneer and clearly inspired by it, too. Clear digital displays, assignable channels and an onboard sampler are all here; installable upgrades are available via your computer. Users say it sounds far superior to the Pioneer.

Stand-alone FX

There are presently four main pretenders to the FX throne.

Kaoss Pad 2 www.korg.com

(around £220) Produced by Korg, the latest Kaoss Pad has nearly 30 effects, including delay, filter, phaser, wah, tremolo, reverb and also percussion synthesiser, vocoder and analogue modelling synthesiser. It's operated by rubbing the finger on a square pad that looks like the *Saturday Night Fever* dancefloor. Although at first this looks very gimmicky, once you mastert the technique it's actually a very handy piece of portable kit.

Alesis AirFX www.alesis.com

(around £100) Even more sci-fi in appearance than a Kaoss Pad. Alesis AirFX has a very simple layout and is operated in a similar way to a Theremin, by moving your hands above four beams that project from the unit. Again, very gimmicky, though we quite like the names of some of the effects (Big Bottom, Gender Bender...). Don't be fooled, though: they are merely variations of the classic effects.

EFX-500/EFX1000 www.pioneer.co.uk

(500 around £275; 1000 around £650) A stand-alone sister unit to Pioneer's excellent DJ and mixer series. As well as having an array of effects (flange, delay, echo, auto pan...), you can isolate the effect to different frequencies (so it only affects the lows mids or highs). It also has a three-band isolator (sound silencer) which makes the average EQ look effete. More controllable that the Kaoss Pad or Alessi AirFX, but pricier too. The new addition to the range, the 1000 is the first DJ unit to deliver 24bit/96khz sampling, among many other things.

171

29. **How to** hot-mix

Hot-mixing is a flashy term for mixing in anything that isn't recorded music, eg drum machines, samplers, grooveboxes and more. Don't get Emerson, Lake & Palmer ideas of building a stack of synths the size of Swindon. Let's just blur the lines a little between DJing and studio production.

How to add instruments

Non-electronic instruments need a microphone, but feel free to experiment with plugging things into your mixer: a keyboard, a violin, your computer... DJs with production experience have long been dragging studio hardware into their live performances. It gives them something big to hide behind when they play Glastonbury. Manufacturers have responded with a few bits of kit tailored especially for the DJ booth.

Drum machines
Used live by DJs since Chicago invented house. Plug into a line input on your mixer (set the level carefully) and synch it up to what you're playing (it's easier to match records to a drum machine than vice versa). Use your own rhythms as bridging tracks or beef up otherwise wimpy songs.

MIDI synchroniser
Electronic instruments speak MIDI; records speak funk. For around £150 here's the translator. It calculates the tempo of the tune you're playing and produces a MIDI signal to synch it with a drum machine, synth or sampler. It can be slow to react to pitch changes, though.

Micro Sync www.redsound.com

Groove boxes
Drum machines with knobs on. They have a whole lot of other sounds as well, plus effects and a sequencer.

Workstations
More than a Groovebox, less than a nation state.

Roland Groovebox series
(MC-808, MC909) www.roland.co.uk
(£400-£700) Introduced with an eye on home studio and live performance.

Korg Electribe Series
(ES1, E-SX1, E-MX1) www.korg.com
(£250-£600) Korg's Electribe series are Roland's main rivals in the field.

Yamaha RS-7000 www.yamaha.co.uk
(around £600) A sequencer, FX box and sampler all in one. With a large memory and versatile programming options. This is one of the best machines for live use and it fits into an SL-1200 flight case.

Yamaha QY70 www.yamaha.co.uk
(around £260) Smaller, more basic version of the Yamaha.

Akai MPC-2000/3000/4000 www.akai.com
(£800-£1,600) Extremely popular multi-purpose workhorse (sequencer, beat generator, sampler, etc). Good editing capabilities as well.

How to use a sampler

As well as stand-alone units like Cycloops many CD players and mixers have effective samplers and loop features. You need a 20-second capacity to sample eight bars of house; more for slower music.

SoundBite (formerly Cycloops) www.redsound.com
(around £180) This fiendish bit of kit will sample something and automatically loop it and match its tempo to another piece of music. It takes a signal off a headphone socket so you can use it with even the most basic mixer.

Live re-edits
By sampling and looping certain sections of a song as you get to them, you can extend intros, breaks and breakdowns as long as you like and meanwhile move the needle to another bit of the record for a live re-edit.

Make sound-beds
If you loop a particular section (eg a bass and percussion part) you then have a solid, unchanging sound-bed. Leave this running in one channel of your mixer for as long as you like and mix other parts of the song (or other songs) in over the top.

Drop a sample in
Here you play a sample more as icing on the cake, maybe dropping in a little acapella or a snatch of another song.

Add FX
Use EQ and effects to create changes in your loop, so there's some progression in the music (eg create a build-up before you drop back into the main song).

173

30. **How to** mix harmonically

Sasha does it. Oakey does it. Norwegian producer DJ Prince has a whole website devoted to it and thinks DJs who don't do it are plain lazy. We're talking about harmonic mixing – knowing the keys of all your records and mixing them accordingly.

What's harmonic mixing?

Harmonic mixing gives a DJ the same understanding of notes, keys and harmonies as a musician. A good DJ has a strong ear for harmonies – they can hear when two records' keys are clashing and when they fit together beautifully (although we've heard several big names scrape their way through the sourest key clashes). Harmonic mixing takes away the guesswork, using a little bit of music theory to unlock the full emotional power of your records' keys.

Harmonic blends
We all stumble on tunes whose melodies fit together like a choir of angels. If you know the keys of your records, finding harmonious mixes is no longer just trial and error.

Changing key
Mix from a record in one key to a record in the next key up and you can create a powerful feeling of renewed energy. Some DJs change key (or 'modulate') with each new tune, creating the illusion of ever-rising energy.

What's a key?

A key is a family of compatible musical notes. Notes from the same key usually sound nice and harmonious together, so you can play them simultaneously to make tunes and chords. But if you add notes from outside that key they can sound wrong, or 'off-key'. See p86 *How to avoid key clashes*.

- Notes from the same key go together.
- Some keys will complement other keys; some won't.
- Most chords uses notes from a single key.

'Keys are very important because they fuck with your feelings.'
Paul Oakenfold

174

Minor and major

Keys are named after their first note. They are 'minor' or 'major' depending on the distance between their notes (the 'intervals').

- A minor key has smaller intervals and sounds more mournful. (eg George Michael's 'Careless Whisper' – D minor)
- A major key has larger intervals and sounds more confident. (eg Wham's 'Wake Me Up Before You Go Go' – C major)

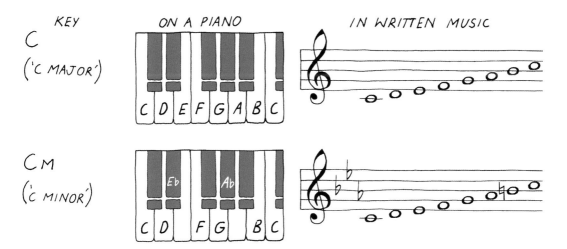

The majority of dance records are in minor keys. This is probably because they come from a black music background and blues scales tend to be in minor keys. A lot of people think they're more soulful.

Blue notes

A 'blue' note is one which is deliberately off-key. These are used in jazz and blues to get your attention – they create a sad or jarring effect.

How to find the keys of your records

Camelot Sound
www.harmonic-mixing.com
A subscription service giving the keys (and bpms) of thousands of records, including new releases.

DJ Prince www.djprince.no
A champion of harmonic mixing, DJ Prince has a database of keys, as well as other DJ hints and tips, on his fine site.

Look them up
There are various nice people who compile lists of which keys records are in, including Camelot Sound and DJ Prince.

Work them out
You'll need a keyboard, plus either some musical experience or a lot of practice. Play the record and doodle around on the keyboard until you find the one note which seems to blend into it the best. This is the 'root'. Put your right thumb on this and move your middle finger and little finger to play different three-note chords based on this note until you find one that fits perfectly. From the chord you can then work out the key. DJ Prince's site goes into more detail on this (with lots of chord diagrams), and even has a little PC piano program you can download.

Pitch and tempo
When you change the tempo of a record (its speed) you also change its pitch (its notes and key). So if you're mixing records with quite different speeds, you may push them out of harmony. A change of +/-3% will definitely make a difference. Less than that and you might scrape by.

How to mix harmonically

Once you've 'keyed' your records you'll know whether they'll sound good together without having to listen to them. Finding harmonious mixes is no longer a matter of trial and error.

- Do imperceptible blends.
- Mix a melody or vocal from one track over the bassline of another.
- Play an acappella of one track over a dub of another.
- Make one of those annoying two-for-one bootlegs.

In most cases a record in a certain key will . . .
- mix perfectly with another record in the same key (its 'tonic')
- mix really well with one in a minor key three steps down (this is its 'relative minor', which shares almost all the same notes)
- mix well with one in a key five steps up (its 'sub-dominant')
- mix well with one in a key seven steps up (its 'dominant').

176

(The 'steps' we're talking about are 'semitones' – the distance between the notes on a piano keyboard (or in the 'chromatic scale').

A key in the left column should mix with the three to its right, plus itself of course. In the table m means 'minor'. Some keys, as you can see, have two names.

A record in this key	...should mix with a record in these keys		
	relative minor	five steps up	seven steps up
C	Am	F	G
D♭/C#	B♭m/A#m	G♭/F#	A♭/G#
D	Bm	G	A
E♭/D#	Cm	A♭/G#	B♭/A#
E	D♭m/C#m	A	B
F	Dm	B♭/A#	C
G♭/F#	E♭m/D#m	B	D♭/C#
G	Em	C	D
A♭/G#	Fm	D♭/C#	E♭/D#
A	G♭m/F#m	D	E
B♭	Gm	E♭/D#	F
B	A♭m/G#m	E	G♭/F#
Cm	E♭/D#	Fm	Gm
D♭m/C#m	E	G♭m/F#m	A♭m/G#m
Dm	F	Gm	Am
E♭m/D#m	G♭/F#	A♭m/G#m	B♭m/A#m
Em	G	Am	Bm
Fm	A♭/G#	B♭m/A#m	Cm
G♭m/F#m	A	Bm	D♭m/C#m
Gm	B♭/A#	Cm	Dm
A♭m/G#m	B	D♭m/C#m	E♭m/D#m
Am	C	Dm	Em
B♭m/A#m	D♭/C#	E♭m/D#m	Fm
Bm	D	Em	G♭m/F#m

(m = minor).

177

Marking your records

Some musically trained DJs just write in the key (eg 'C#' or 'E♭m' etc). Camelot's Easymix™ system offers an alternative. Instead of keys, mark your records with their code numbers. Then use the wheel below to see which keys will fit together.

Your next record can have any keycode that's the same or next to the keycode of the record playing (not including diagonally). For example 6A should mix with 5A, 7A and 6B. Or 2B should mix with 1B, 3B and 2A.

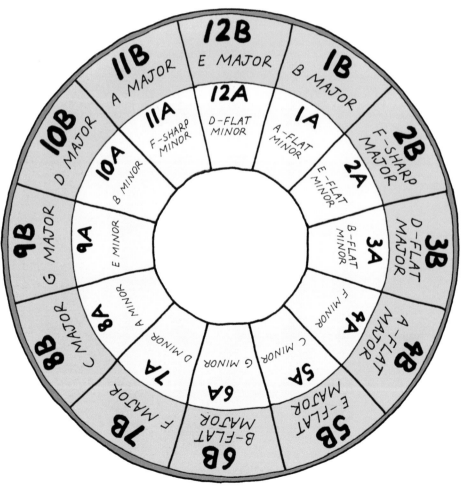

How to change key

Musicians sometimes change key part-way through a song. This gives the illusion of renewed energy and excitement (it sounds a bit like a car changing gear). Eurovision songs usually change key for the last chorus (when the singers whip off their dresses to reveal miniskirts). Changing key is also called 'modulating'.

Changing key with records

If you move up one step (eg from C to C#, or from D to E♭, etc) the new record will use a completely different set of notes to the one you were just playing and so the change will be very dramatic. To be honest, most DJs who key their records are only interested in this one thing. This is a mixing style most closely associated with trance and progressive house.

As Anthony Pappa explains, 'Say you're playing a record in a certain key, and it goes down to just drums. Then if you bring in another record in the right key, when the bassline comes in, it gives an energy lift because it acts like a key change.'

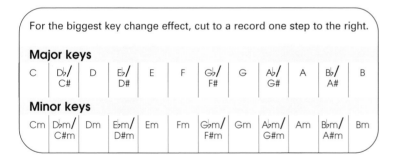

For the biggest key change effect, cut to a record one step to the right.

Major keys

C	D♭/ C#	D	E♭/ D#	E	F	G♭/ F#	G	A♭/ G#	A	B♭/ A#	B

Minor keys

Cm	D♭m/ C#m	Dm	E♭m/ D#m	Em	Fm	G♭m/ F#m	Gm	A♭m/ G#m	Am	B♭m/ A#m	Bm

The same table with Camelot code numbers.

Major keys

8B	3B	10B	5B	12B	7B	2B	9B	4B	11B	6B	1B

Minor keys

5A	12A	7A	2A	9A	4A	11A	6A	1A	8A	3A	10A

179

How to use this in a mix

The two songs are in different keys so they would clash if you did a gradual blend. You need to mix so the melodies and basslines are kept apart. Most DJs who pull off these kinds of mixes do some kind of cut or try to exactly match the end of one melody with the start of the new one.

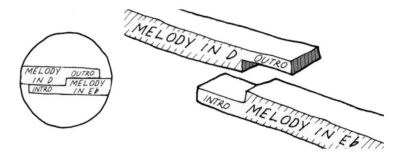

With the right records you'd get a melodic build-up as record 1 went into its outro, followed immediately by the exciting arrival of record 2's melody in a higher key.

'When I started, DJs weren't in the media, electronic music wasn't in the sales charts and a DJ was the freak in the corner who provided the music while other people had fun. So to do it, you must have been a freak and a music lover. And I still am: this is still the engine which drives me.'

Paul Van Dyk, *DJmag*

Some more music theory

Arpeggio

A series of notes in the same key which would make a chord if you played them together.

Chord

More than one note played simultaneously, eg on a guitar or a piano. Chords and keys are closely connected because a chord will be made up of notes from a certain key.

Chromatic scale

The full set of 12 notes found on a piano. Go from one note to another on a piano keyboard and you're playing a chromatic scale. These are the 'steps' we've been talking about.

Interval

The distance between two notes. These could be in a key, a chord or a scale, eg a 'major third', a 'perfect fourth', a 'diminished fifth'. How many notes apart they are on a piano.

Scales

When musicians practise scales they play all the notes from a particular key in sequence. It's all about getting from one note to another friendly note. Remember 'do-re-mi-fa-so-la-ti-do' from *The Sound of Music*? That's a scale. You can choose any note to sing the first 'do' and the tune will guide you up through a scale in the key of that note.

Octave

Do-re-mi-fa-so-la-ti-do. The eight-note distance of a scale. The distance from one note to the same note higher up the scale (eg C to C, or F# to F#).

Further information

Camelot Sound
www.harmonic-mixing.com

DJ Prince www.djprince.no
Both sites explain harmonic mixing in some detail.

http://orion.neiu.edu/~jalucas/mus con/lectures/chords/index.htm
This site has a nice explanation of major and minor chords.

www.jazclass.aust.com/basicth/bt 1.htm
Excellent (and simple) music theory site

www.dolmetsch.com/ theoryintro.htm
Another good music theory site.

Still getting higher

By overlapping records in rising keys, a DJ can create the illusion that the energy is constantly rising and never falling. For a scientific illustration of the principles behind this, listen to the sonic illusion known as the 'rising tone'. This is a sound generated by computer, which uses complex harmonies to give the impression that it's always rising in pitch. You could listen to it for days and it would still sound like it's getting higher and higher. You can download it from www.exploratorium.edu/ exhibits/highest_note/fr.continuous.html

181

31. **How to** do deck effects

We don't really approve of technical skills for their own sake (even scratch DJs should be forced to play for a dancefloor now and then), but to get you competitive types ready for the turntablist chapters which follow, here are a few ways to show off.

How to play on three decks

Slamming it on the ones, twos *and threes*! That'll really impress, er, somebody. Now just start saving for that third deck. Is there really enough space on your dressing table?

It's possible, it's not actually that hard, and it's been done for as long as DJs have been mixing records (Terry Noel claims he did it way back in 1969; Nicky Siano was certainly trying it in the early seventies; and Carl Cox was tagged the king of three decks in the nineties). The thing is, it's kind of like having three legs. When a DJ can completely wow you with two turntables, why would they really need three?

That third deck?

A DJ will mostly use a third deck simply to cue something up well ahead of time. Line up your first record while the other guy still has two decks spinning, or cue up the next two records because you're only going to play one for ten seconds. Plus, if you insist, you could actually *mix* three records.

- Mix two beat tracks and an acappella.
- Mix a track with its dub with another track.
- Mix three beat tracks and EQ them so you take different elements from each.

Beatmatching three tracks

If you can beatmatch to a high standard – blend two tracks for as long as you feel like – then all you do is mix in a third. Monitoring is the hardest part, but if you keep your wits about you, you should be able to keep track of which tune is where in the mix, especially if one is an acappella.

How to do repeat tricks

Slightly mismatching two copies of the same song lets you repeat a beat, a bar, or half a bar, for some dramatic effects. Beatmatch the two records but cue record 2 a certain amount behind record 1. Then cut to record 2 and everyone will hear the last bar, half bar or beat repeated.

- Create a tiny bit of tease before a payoff.
- Repeat the last part of a verse.

How to phase-shift

You've probably got a phasing button on your FX box. In the spirit of showing off, here's how you phase a record manually. This is great in a big build-up.

1 Get two copies of the same record, beatmatched and exactly synchronised, same tempo, same position in the song, playing at equal volume with equal EQ.
2 Now drop the pitch of one very slightly and listen to the weird whooshy effect as it falls back from the other.
3 Before they go out of synch completely, shift the pitch so it's now slightly faster. Listen to it do the same effect as it plays catch-up.
4 Fade between playing both and just one of the records.

Exercises
- Get to know how much pitch shift you need relative to how fast the records will go out of synch.
- For static phasing (where the records stay the same amount apart), just synch up two identical records and instead of changing pitch, brush the platter briefly to knock one a tiny bit out of synch.

183

32. **How to** back-cue

Back-cueing, looping or 'the Quick Mix', as its creator Grandmaster Flash called it, is the foundation of hip hop. By cutting between two copies of the same record you take a chunk of a song and manually loop it into a new and unshakeable rhythm track. Armed with a sampler you could do this by pushing a button, but any hip hop DJ worth a damn does it by hand on the one and twos.

How to back-cue with headphones

We're going to start with headphones to get you used to the idea of back-cueing. You're aiming to cut between two copies of the same record, continually repeating the first eight bars.

1 Find a record which starts with a breakbeat that carries on for at least eight bars. Get two copies.

2 Use two decks, with headphones.

3 Play record 1.

4 While 1 is playing, cue up record 2.

5 After eight bars cut on-beat from 1 to 2.

6 While 2 is playing, cue up record 1.

7 After eight bars cut on-beat from 2 to 1.

8 Keep going until you mess up.

Exercises

● Practise making your cuts seamless.

● Tape yourself so you can hear how well you're doing.

● When you've mastered it, practise cutting every four bars.

'I said to myself: if I take the most climactic part of these records and just string 'em together and play 'em on time, back-to-back-to-back, I'm going to have the crowd totally excited.'

Grandmaster Flash

How to mark your records

If you want to back-cue faster than every four bars, there's no time to lift the needle and cue up with headphones. You need to be able to find the exact position by sight. Hip hop DJs stick paper marks all over their records and rewind the record to the right place using the marks as guides.

What to use
Use non-gummy stickers like cassette labels or the sticky part of cut-up Rizlas. Some DJs use a line like a hand on a clock; others use a dot. If you need to remove the stickers, lighter fluid should clean up any marks.

Where to put them
For back-cueing you need a mark that works like a clock hand so you can count how many times it goes round.

Some DJs put the line level with the start of the break, so it starts to play when the mark goes past the needle.

Others put the mark so it's at 12 o'clock when the break starts to play.

185

Cue marks

With steady hands you can also mark the start of the break itself. This is a useful way of marking things you're going to scratch.

Use tape with a hard, shiny surface (splicing tape is great if you can get it). Have the needle in the groove at the exact start of the break. Cut a piece of tape about 20mm x 10mm. Stick it on the edge of a credit card and slide it up to the needle.

Position it like this, lift the needle, stick the tape down and pull the card away.

To cue the break, place the needle on the tape, wind the record very slightly and the needle should drop into the groove at the right place.

How to cue by sight

Now you've marked your records you should be able to cue up your chosen break without having to find it in your headphones. Your clock-hand mark shows the start of the break. To return to this, leave the needle in the groove and rewind the record the right number of revolutions.

The following is an exercise to get you ready for proper back-cueing.

1 Use just one deck, playing out loud.

2 Cue up the break on the record you've marked. Play it for four bars and count how many times your mark goes round.

3 Cue up the break and play it again.

4 After four bars, cut the volume with the crossfader and rewind the record the correct number of times (you counted), as fast and as smoothly as possible.

5 Use the mark to find where the break starts and play it again.

6 Cut the crossfader, rewind and play again. And again.

Exercises

- Practise speed and accuracy.
- Make sure the needle doesn't jump when you're rewinding.

This is the quickest way to rewind a record – use your finger as though you were dialling an old-fashioned telephone.

187

How to back-cue by sight

Once you can cue up a record by sight fairly quickly, you should be able to back-cue a four-bar section without headphones. Remember: the aim is to play four bars from one record, then the same four bars from the other, and so on in an endless loop.

1. Use two decks, no headphones.
2. Get two copies of the same record with the break marked.
3. Play record 1.
4. After four bars cut on-beat from 1 to 2.
5. While 2 is playing, rewind 1 to the break mark.
6. After four bars cut on-beat from 2 to 1.
7. While 1 is playing, rewind 2 to the break mark. And so on.

Exercises

- Practise speed and accuracy. When you've mastered it every four bars, try it every two. A year without leaving your room and you'll be cutting on every bar...
- Tape yourself so you can hear how clean your cuts are.

Back-cueing, together with scratching, is the basis for turntablism, and the reason why hip hop DJs buy two copies of each record. Done extremely fast it is an important part of beat-juggling.

CD DJs

can do this at the touch of a button by using the loop function. Just hit 'loop in' at the point you want your loop to start and then 'loop out' where you want it to end. It's the same if you have a sampler. Not quite as exciting, though.

'I love to go there and see these guys at these new DJ battles, 'cos now it's off the hook. I look at these guys and I think, "We started that shit." It's incredible what they took from us and there's no end to it. Me and Flash at the DMC, we was sitting there going, "Yo man, look what we did. Look at this, man, this is ridiculous".'

**Grandmixer D.ST
(now DXT)**

Adventures on the Wheels of Steel

Back-cueing is where the concept of a breakbeat comes from – it's a beat made by looping part of a break. In the mid-seventies DJs in the Bronx started highlighting the breaks of old funk records – the bits in the middle where the musicians take a rest and the drummer cuts loose. This was first done by Kool Herc, who would play two copies of a record back-to-back. Grandmaster Flash took Herc's idea and cleaned it up – by cutting on time and keeping the beat – and hip hop as a style of music was born. The first record to showcase the power of back-cueing was 1981's 'Adventures of Grandmaster Flash on the Wheels of Steel', where Flash mixed together about a dozen records live to make a single monster jam. 'It took three turntables, two mixers and between ten and fifteen takes to get it right,' he recalls. This was the very first record made by a DJ from nothing more than other records.

33. **How to** scratch

Scratch DJs don't just play records, they play sounds. Scratching, or turntablism as it's now known, uses the decks as actual instruments, playing tiny chunks of records and using the mixer to cut these noises up even smaller.

How to approach scratching

There's no test, no exam, no rules. This is about artistry and musicianship. These tutorials are starting points, not rigid techniques. They should give you a feel for the basic moves and grooves, but no way is this the whole story. Turntablism is a martial art. If you're serious about it you'll wave goodbye to normal life and become a scratch monk, watching endless battle videos and practising 24 hours a day (at least) until you've developed your own unique style.

One request, though – can you make it funky? The best turntablists can actually make people dance, as well as doing an 800-click flare with their eyes shut. If you watch the originators – Flash, Theodore, DXT – you'll see something missing in a lot of younger kids. These pioneers might not have the lightning technical speed that wins battles today, but they do know how to rock a dancefloor, so everything they do has an incredible expressiveness. The noises they steal from their records are fluid, sexy and full of feeling. That, young Jedi, is your goal.

How to adjust your decks

You need powerful decks for scratching. Technics are still the favourite, though Vestax is winning a lot of friends for its straight tone-arms. These reduce lateral forces, so reducing needle jump. See p36 *How to set up*.

Adjusting your decks
Turntablists love to share adjustments. These usually boil down to: lots of tracking force on the needle (the counterweight screwed all the way in, often screwed on backwards); a high tone-arm (so it slopes down); and the anti-skate turned to zero. These things prevent jumping but really wear out your records.

Adjusting your cartridges
Go for a spherical needle – it stays in the groove better. A cartridge with a headshell lets you make more adjustments. Many DJs move the cartridge further forwards to put more weight on the needle. Another trick is to twist the cartridge round about 23° so your S-shaped tone-arm behaves like a straight one.

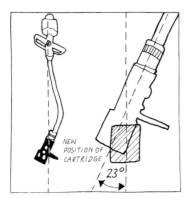

NEW POSITION OF CARTRIDGE

23°

Long, continuous noises are best, eg *oooh* or *aaaw* type vocals, sirens or long notes from an instrument.

Battle breaks
Compilations of hundreds of samples and beats all pressed up onto a single 12-inch. 'Bionic Boogie Breaks', 'Animal Crackers', 'Snuff Breaks', 'Toasted Marshmellow Feet Breaks' are just a few examples. Buy them in specialist hip hop record shops.

Breakbeat collections
Compilation albums of complete songs which have great breaks. The many volumes of Ultimate Breaks & Beats are still available – many a US deckmaster started with these. Newer compilations from labels like Strut and Harmless are great, too.

Ordinary 12-inches
'I like people just cutting up two twelves,' says Mark Rae, 'because you know the records so you know how the DJ is deconstructing it. That's what made the original guys so exciting – they were cutting up pop hits like "Good Times" which everyone knew. Nowadays the best way to get people to really understand what a DJ is doing would be to cut up Kylie's "Can't Get You Out of My Head".'

Records to scratch with

CD DJs
Don't feel left out of all this turntablist fun. Scratching beyond vinyl has arrived. For a lively forum about scratching CDs and MP3s, scratch samples on CD for sale, and endless hints and tips, try www.digitalscratch.com

---

Make sure you don't buy warped records – they'll be useless. Most DJs 'wear in' a new record by playing it a few times. This makes it less jumpy. You will also want to mark your records so you can find the right parts quickly. For this, see p184 *How to back-cue*.

Tighten your hole
A too-big centre hole can cause dangerous side-to-side wobble. Add a slither of sticky label through the hole.

Loosen your hole
If the centre hole is too small the record won't turn freely. Enlarge it very slightly with a rolled up piece of sandpaper.

Slippy slipmats
Your slipmats better move like ice. Soft felt ones with little or no printing are the slippiest. You can add a layer of cut-out shiny paper or plastic underneath (eg a plastic inner sleeve). There are specialist ones too, like Technics' Speed Slipmats or ISP's Butter Rugs.

Preparing your records

191

Where to put your hands

Whether left- or right-handed, you have to choose which hand moves the record and which moves the fader. This decision has a serious impact on your scratching style because you're choosing which skill – record control or fader control – to give the most emphasis to.

Most DJs these days use their strongest hand on the fader, but we think you'll be more expressive if you use your strongest hand on the record (our humble opinion). Try both and decide which feels more natural, or force yourself to learn a certain way from the start. In any case, you should always put lots of effort into improving the skills of your weaker hand.

Where to hold the record

There are no rules about where you put your hand on the record. Make sure your hands are clean, though.

Pushing the centre gives you more power.

Holding the edge gives you more sensitivity.

Dextrous

The best DJs are 'dextrous' (short for 'ambidextrous') – they can do all the scratches on the left deck that they can on the right. This is very useful for battling. You can develop this – just practise everything both ways.

Setting up your decks

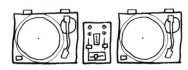

Most clubs will have the decks like this.

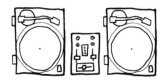

'Battle-style' keeps the tone-arms out of the way.

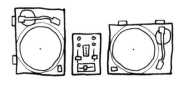

Some DJs prefer 'L-style'.

192

Baby scratch

We're going to start you off with some scratches which don't use the fader. Find a part of a record with a long, continuous sound, use one deck, no headphones and leave the mixer alone.

❶ Find your chosen sound and hold the record still while the platter spins underneath.

❷ Move the record back and forth smoothly with your hand to make the unmistakable *zig-zag, zig-zag* scratch noise.

❸ In between pushing and pulling the record, let the sound play normally as well.

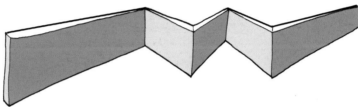

Exercises

- Scratch faster and slower. Notice how this changes the note of the scratch.
- Practise starting it exactly when you want to.
- Play around. Get more control. Try to be smooth.

Tear

Let the sample play forwards normally, and then pull it back, but while you're pulling it back make it stop dead for a split-second – so you divide (tear) the back-stroke into two (or more) pieces. You can divide the back-stroke up any way you like, but the classic tear has the first part fast then the second part slower: *ziiig*, *zag-zaaag*.

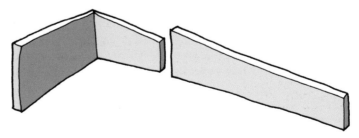

193

Adding the faders

With the faders on your mixer you can start cutting those simple scratches into something a bit more complex.

Cut-in point
Scratch faders are designed so you only need a small movement to bring in the other channel at full volume. This lets you use the crossfader like an on-off switch. Where it goes from on to off is called the 'cut-in point' and you should get a feel for where this is. Don't worry if your mixer has a smoother 'beatmix curve' crossfader; it just means you'll have to move it further for the same effect. For more on crossfaders, see p47 *How to fade*.

Upfaders or crossfader
Most DJs use the crossfader to control their scratches. But you can use the upfaders to get the same results. The only major difference is that your hand is zipping up and down instead of left and right. It's good to practise both methods – you'll be more flexible when you get to the tricky stuff.

 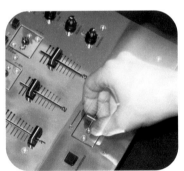

Hamster-style
If you scratch hamster-style, you've got the left and right channels reversed on your crossfader. This lets you do the same tricks using different fingers and is handy for combining certain moves. In the old days you'd switch the input cables round (in which case your upfaders would be reversed, too); today lots of mixers have a hamster switch ('X-fader control' or 'X-fader assign') which swaps the crossfader round internally. Named after the Bulletproof Scratch Hamsters, apparently.

The following scratches are the simplest ones that use the fader. They should give you a feel for the possibilities ahead.

Mom on the groove
Grand Wizard Theodore recalls the day he first encountered the scratch. Home from school, he was practising in his bedroom trying to get new ideas. 'This particular day I was playing music a little bit too loud,' he remembers, 'and my mom came and she's banging on the door. "If you don't cut that music down..." While she was cursing me out in the doorway, I was still holding the record – "Jam On The Groove" by Ralph McDonald – and my hand was still going back and forth with the record. And when she left I was like, "What is this?" It was a scratch.' So the truth of the scratch is that Theodore's mum invented it. 'Yeah, God bless my mama!'

Forward scratch

Use the fader to cut out the back-stroke so you only hear the forward-stroke.

1 Hold the fader with one hand and the record with the other.
2 Do a single *zig-zag*, forward then back.
3 Open the fader for the forward-stroke and close it for the back-stroke. So you just hear the forward-stroke, ie the *zig*.

Exercises
- Make your scratches longer or shorter.
- Make the scratch sound as clean as possible. Move the fader quickly, just ahead of the record.
- Join a series of forward scratches together – *zig, zig, zig*. Make them sound rhythmic, like drum-beats.

Back scratch

Use the fader to cut out the forward-stroke so you only hear the back-stroke.

1 Do a single *zig-zag*, forward then back.
2 This time, keep the fader closed on the forward-stroke and push it open for the back-stroke. You should just hear the back-stroke, ie just the *zag*.

Exercises
- Make your scratches longer or shorter.
- Join a series of back scratches together – *zag, zag, zag*. Make them sound rhythmic, like drum-beats.

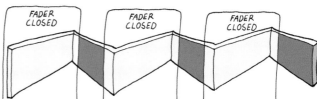

Scratch to the beat

Now you've got a few scratches up your sleeve, it's time to play along to something. Put a simple beat track on one deck and let it play. Put your scratching record on the other deck and play along using all the scratches you've learnt. The record gives you a beat and a bassline; you're playing lead. Get funky.

195

Transform

The aim is to create a nice long scratch with the record, using the fader to cut it up into a series of sharp, rhythmic noises. You start with the fader closed and open it to play bits of the scratch. Each time you open the fader you get a blast of noise. Think of it as a drum-beat or a stab on the horns.

1 Find a really long oooh or aaaw sound to practise on.

2 Do a smooth, slow zaaag-ziiig, back then forward. You could let the sound play normally some of the time.

3 Start with the fader closed, and rapidly push it open and closed to make whatever rhythms you want.

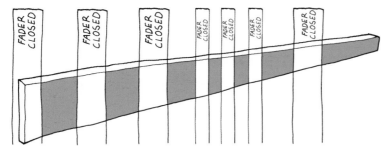

Exercises

● Experiment with different speeds and sounds and slurs and pulls.

● Try to be rhythmic; pretend you're a musician.

● Play around for as long as your housemates can bear it.

Using line/phono switches

Because it's all about on-off, you can also transform using the line/phono switches on your mixer to chop up your sound.

Using transform buttons

You can also use the transform buttons if your mixer has them. These are springy buttons, usually just next to the crossfader, which cut in the opposite channel when you tap them.

The transformation of scratching

Transforming is the foundation of much of today's turntablism techniques. Named after the 'Transformers' – cartoon robots who made scratch-like noises when they changed into trucks and cars – transforming is said to have been first practised by Philadelphia's DJ Spinbad. It was perfected through heated competition between DJs Cash Money and Jazzy Jeff. Cash Money showcased the transform to great effect in 1988, winning the DMC World DJ Championships in the process. Jazzy Jeff (DJ for the Fresh Prince, aka Will Smith) was the first to put it on record, in 'The Magnificent Jazzy Jeff'.

Flare

Flares are sometimes called reverse transforms. In a transform you start the scratch with the fader closed and use it like an on-switch. In a flare you start the scratch with the fader open and use it like an off-switch.

Clicks

Flares are measured in 'clicks', named after the noise the fader makes when it hits the off position at the end of its slot. Each click in a flare is a gap you've put in the sound – a chunk you've taken out of the scratch.

The classic flare has one less click on the back-stroke than on the forward-stroke, so

- A one-click flare has a click on the forward-stroke and none on the back-stroke . . .
- A two-click flare has two clicks on the forward-stroke and one on the back-stroke.

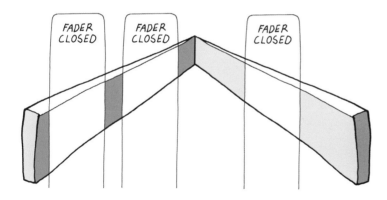

'The flare is just another scratch. Go back to the old school records with the old school scratches. Learn the basics, learn transforming. Transforming brings it all together.'

DJ Flare, DMC Turntablism video

197

Crab

A crab is a fast four-click flare which can sound a bit like a drum roll. You flick your four fingers one at a time against the fader in a kind of stroking action (a bit like drumming your fingers on a table), while your thumb works as a spring pushing it the other way. If you do this right over the cut-in point you'll turn your scratch off and on four times in rapid succession.

Practise by clicking all four fingers against your thumb – like snapping your fingers four at a time. Then do the same thing with the fader between them (with a kind of stroking action).

Twiddle

The predecessor to the crab. It's the same idea but with just two fingers and your thumb. Your middle finger and index finger push one way; your thumb pushes the other. It's a good idea to try this as a warm-up for learning crabs.

Orbit

An orbit is very much the same as a flare except it's symmetrical. So if you do two-clicks on the forward-stroke you'd also do two clicks on the back-stroke.

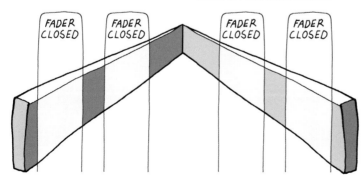

FADER CLOSED   FADER CLOSED   FADER CLOSED   FADER CLOSED

Scribble

Instead of smooth scratches, you're aiming to do superfast jud-ders. Tense up your arm and hand muscles to make your hand shake in fast little shiver movements. Careful you don't make the needle jump.

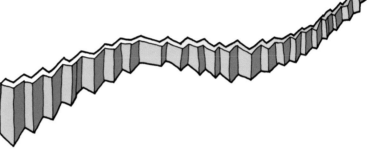

'When I started it was quite weird to be into scratching. It was like the goalkeeper job of music.'

Mark Rae

199

Some more scratches

Here are a few more scratches to play around with. Don't get hung up on names and definitions, and don't worry about how other people do things (even famous ones). Just get busy.

Drag/push
A baby scratch with the speeds changed. Slow the back-stroke down for a drag; speed up the forward-stroke for a push.

Chop/stab
Do a forward scratch but only fade in the first bit of it, so you get a short, stabby little scratch. These guys often travel in rapid-fire bursts.

Chirp
Do a forward scratch and fade it out towards the end, then make a back scratch and fade it back in. The result is a short, expressive chirp sound. It sounds simple but it's very hard to get right. Worth it, though.

Echoes/fades
Do a series of repeat forward scratches and use the upfader to lower the volume a little for each scratch. Often used with a vocal sample to make a single word repeat in a kind of dying echo fashion.

'When transforming came out it just flipped the whole scratching world around. They brought out all these weird styles and ways of scratching that had never been done before.'

Q-Bert

Tweak
With your motor off, push the record one way, then the other, transforming as you like. Without any power, the record goes wherever you push it, dying down in speed each time.

Bubble
Instead of using faders, you transform using the EQ controls to get a kind of wah-wah pedal effect. Depends how good the EQ cuts on your mixer are.

Hydroplane/rubs
Both your hands are on the record, working against each other. As one hand moves the record forwards, the other acts as a kind of half-brake, letting your fingers lightly judder against the record, without stopping it, to get a nice vibrato friction sound.

Tones

With a really long tone, such as a sound effects track, you can actually play notes. Let the record play then mess about with the speed control (33/45) and the pitch control.

Lyric-cutting

Similar to beat-chopping (See p202 *How to beat-juggle*). Here you're scratching audible lyrics, joining phrases from two different records to create a patchwork sentence, usually about how great you are.

Further information

Magazines
Hip-Hop Connection www.hiphop.co.uk
Knowledge www.knowledgemag.co.uk
The Source www.thesource.com
XXL www.xxlmag.com
Vibe www.vibe.com
Wax Poetics www.waxpoetics.com
Touch www.touchmagazine.co.uk
Hip hop record shops have no end of fanzines, too.

Videos
Lots of them are rubbish. The best tutorial we've seen is DMC's 'The Art of Turntablism'. Order this or any of their battle videos from www.dmcworld.com

Books
Turntable Technique
By Stephen Webber (Berklee Press). If you can read music, this book will help you learn to scratch. If you can't, it's a piece of poo.

Record stores
Fat Beats www.fatbeats.com
The famous New York store.

Honest Jon's
278 Portobello Road, London, W10 5TE
020 8969 9822.

Fat City www.fatcity.co.uk
20 Oldham St, Manchester, M1 1JN
0161 237 1181.

Low Life www.lowliferecords.co.uk
Online store with great website dedicated to UK hip hop.

Scenario www.scenariorecords.com
12 Ingestre Place, Soho, London, W1F 0JF
020 7439 0055

Sounds Of The Universe
www.soundsoftheuniverse.com
7 Broadwick Street, Soho, London, W1F 0DA
020 7494 2004

Websites
You'll find hundreds of websites devoted to turntablism.
www.dmcworld.com
www.turntablism.com
www.bombhiphop.com
www.sphereofhiphop.com
www.asisphonics.net
www.b-boys.com
www.battlesounds.com
www.skratchworx.com
Good website with scratching tutorials.
http://forum.djpages.com
DMC's very active turntablists forum.

34. **How to** beat-juggle

The zippiest turntablists can take a couple of beat tracks and whip up completely new rhythms of their own. They are so skilled that they can pick up a single drum-beat and put it exactly where they want. There's no way you can learn beat-juggling from a book. But these exercises should get you moving in the right direction.

How to beat-chop

Beat-chopping is using your decks as a drum machine – by scratching drum-beats. Beat-chopping uses a lot of the techniques you've already learnt in scratching and gives you some of the skills you'll need for beat-juggling.

Play a single kick drum

1. Use a record with a simple, clear kick-drum beat.
2. Find the kick-drum beat and move it back and forth.
3. Use the fader to hide the back-stroke.
4. Practise this until you can play the kick-drum beat at will.
5. Concentrate on making the beat sound clean.
6. Now play around with the kick-drum sound. Make little rhythms with it.

Play a kick and a snare

1. Use a record with a strong beat that has a kick drum and a snare close together with nothing in between – a simple *boom-bap* (or *bap-boom* if they're closer).
2. Find a kick-drum beat and play it as before (the *boom*).
3. Find the snare beat next to it (the *bap*) and play with it in the same way.
4. Go between the two, using the fader to hide the joins
5. Now play around with these two beats. Make little rhythms with them.

Play with the whole rhythm

1. Use a record with a clear, simple looped beat.
2. Play individual drum-beats as before – the kick, the snare.
3. Now, in between playing individual beats, let the record run free so a bar or two of the rhythm plays normally.
4. Mess around combining the record's rhythm, bits of the record's rhythm and individual beats.

How to beat-juggle

If you can chop beats up convincingly you'll start to see the possibilities of doing something similar on two turntables. The secret of beat-juggling is knowing the records in front of you so well that you can just *feel* where each individual beat is hiding and control them like a drummer. If this makes beat-juggling sound like some seriously esoteric Zen meditation, that's because it is.

Beyond beat-chopping
Get two copies of a simple looped beat track. Play one copy normally and use it as the background for a beat-chopping jam on the other turntable. Practise switching decks so your chopping record becomes the playing record and vice versa.

Looping
This is our old friend the back-cue, done at supernatural speed (see p184 *How to back-cue*). One fact helps you considerably: because you're back-cueing very short passages (maybe less than a bar) you'll only be rewinding the records a small amount.

Strobing
With two decks you play just a single beat from each record, one after the other – *boom*, *boom*, *bap*, *bap*... It's all about pausing or pulling back each record as soon as it's played the beat (or beats) you want from it. Concentrate on slowing the whole process down as much as you can.

Fills
Here you double-up beats by cutting fast from one record to another.

1 Get two copies of a track playing in synch, with record 1 playing out loud.

2 Pull record 2 back half a beat.

3 Cut from record 1 to record 2. Because record 2 is half a beat behind, you should now hear the same beat repeated.

If you're really fast you can quickly pull record 1 back a whole beat and cut back a third time to triple-up the beats.

(Fills use the same technique as a Detroit trick known as 'tripling', which Eddie Flashin' Fowlkes likes to pull off.)

203

The industry

>>

35. **How to** graduate from the bedroom

A DJ without an audience is nothing more than a chancer with some records. But everyone (and their mum) is a DJ now, and that means some serious competition. So how to showcase your golden genius? A DJ needs to play out – it's the only way to learn the vital secrets of driving a dancefloor. Otherwise you'll end up a socially retarded hermit who has amazing technical skills but can't make anyone dance (unless you're a turntablist, in which case lock the door and carry on). Go on, tell me, I'm begging you, how do you get out there?

Know your enemy

Older DJs

They've been around since the year dot, with vast experience and awesome record collections to keep them at the top of the pile. They learnt to spin before you were born, back when the only competition was the local mobile DJ with his traffic-light disco and his smoochy end-of-set 'erection section'. They started DJing for love, but now earn serious money. You'll never knock them off; all you can do is wait for them to go deaf or overdose on champagne and Prada.

Super-enthusiastic kids like yourself

A bit green, but what they lack in experience they make up for in sheer numbers. And in amongst these hordes there are inevitably a few who have something special. But don't kid yourself – there are an estimated 50,000 bedroom DJs out there. Maybe you're the lucky herbert who is so talented the world can't wait to discover you. But maybe you're not. Until you play out and see real people react to your music you won't know. Catch 22?

'People think my career started when I sent that tape to Renaissance. I'd actually been working hard for seven years before I got to that point. I was putting on parties and booking DJs around me to get my name on the flyer. I knew I had to do it for myself. I knew no-one was going to come knocking on my door. I knew it was up to me.'

John Digweed

How to
play dirty

Faced with this tricky problem, our advice is: play dirty. Forget the rules – they stopped working ages ago. These days only guerrilla warfare and disco terrorism will get you noticed. Don't expect anyone to discover you; instead, get out there and do it yourself. Throw your own parties, create your own gigs and make your own audience. That way you'll build the crowd you want rather than have to win someone else's over. Maybe start your own pirate station, or make your own tracks, or build a website to stream your mixes... Just get on with it and something will happen. If you're really ambitious, why not build your own superclub and install yourself as resident. Don't laugh, that's exactly what Justin Berkman did when he created the Ministry of Sound.

Get gigs, gigs, gigs
Wherever and whenever. Put nothing beneath you in your effort to play out. Playing your neighbour's 21st birthday party will teach you more about DJing in three hours than you've learnt in three years of lonely bedroom twiddling. House parties, youth clubs, even school or college events: if they need a DJ, make sure it's you.

Make yourself different
DJ agencies have big cardboard boxes full of tapes from people trying to be Sasha. They weigh them and laugh. It's great to have heroes, but unless you add your own twist you're just being a DJ impressionist. Concentrate on being *you*, not on copying anyone famous, and you'll have the right attitude to succeed. Whether it's spicing up your set with re-edits and your own tracks, or just developing a sound which is sparkling, unique and unforgettable, the most important advice we can give is: be different, be yourself.

Never pay to play
Ignore ads or postings on bulletin boards offering to find you gigs if you send money with your mixes. You will be ripped off.

How to get a local gig

Like all freelance jobs, a lot depends on meeting people and being nice to them. Infiltrate the local scene and try to make friends with key players.

- The resident DJ
- The promoter of the night
- The manager of the venue

Other people might help you, like the bar manager or even a friendly bouncer – it all depends on their relationship with the others in the club. Whatever you do, don't burst in there brandishing a tape. You've got to be far sneakier than that. There's a thin line between infectious enthusiasm and being a pest. Be interested, ask questions, buy the DJ a drink after his set and talk about what he does and what it's like. Talk about music, talk about football, talk about the human genome project, talk about anything except the fact that your life has no meaning until you play records in his club. Play it cool, turn up a few times and chat chummily without ever mentioning this. Then, finally, after you've moved in together and started going out with his sister, casually mention that you've made a tape and you'd value his opinion, and does he need a warm-up, and...

Giving out mixes

So you make your super-hot mix and send it to lots of clubs and they all call you up and beg you to play for them... Wake up!!! Sending unsolicited mixes out is more or less pointless. It's not cheap and, realistically, there are so many other kids doing it that it's unlikely to get you a booking. Your time would be far better used building up a name on your own, rather than waiting for Billy Bigboots at Pants superclub to discover you. Here's how to use your mixes.

Making your mix

These days it should be a CD if you want anyone to listen to it. At least 40 minutes long, with a strong opening – something unique and unusual to grab their attention. Plan it carefully so it feels like it's going somewhere. Try and avoid obvious hits and include a few surprises. Print a nice design on the CD if you can but don't bother about fancy packaging – a clear plastic sleeve will do. Remember to put your name, email and/or phone number on the disc. For details of how to record your mix to a computer so you can burn it to CD, see p99 *How to record to a computer*.

Use it as a business card
Always have copies of your latest mix to give to interested folk as deal clinchers and memory joggers. Maybe they liked what they heard you play, they'd like to book you for their club, but their partner needs to hear you first. Bingo, give them a mix. And give them to girls/boys you really fancy. Obviously.

Give them to your mates
Don't think the only reason to record a mix is to get a job. What about sharing your love of music? Mix tapes are great presents. Your nearest and dearest will definitely give them an airing, and you never know who might be listening.

Put it online
These days, a great way of getting yourself out there is to have mixes online. Either on one of the many DJ or community sites, or on your own site. For more on publicising yourself this way, see p240 *How to promote yourself online*.

Send them to competitions
Here someone's making a vague promise that they'll listen to at least some of your mix and judge it in some way. Pick me, Nigel.

Send them to Raw Talent
iDJ magazine's monthly Raw Talent competition is now an established part of the dance industry and it may even get you noticed. Winners are added to a pool of new DJs to play gigs at their Raw Talent nights across the country.
Send your mix on a CD, Minidisc or tape – any style. Include a full tracklisting (artists, titles, labels), name number email and passport-sized photo.

'I would blag my way into clubs for nothing by saying I was the DJ. I'd just turn up with my box of records and stand there waiting, in case the booked DJ didn't turn up. As soon as somebody didn't show up, I'd get on the decks.'

LTJ Bukem, *Muzik*

LTJ Bukem appears by kind courtesy of Good Looking Organisation Ltd. www.glo.uk.com Photograph by Gareth Jones

Raw Talent
iDJ,
7th floor,
Tower house
Fairfax Street
Bristol
BS1 3BN

209

How to join the DJ community

Sorry, that sounds a bit sociological. What we mean is that you need to get yourself on the inside track somehow, so you're no longer just a clueless chancer. Here's how to be a fully clued-up chancer.

Get to know DJs

Lots of them are knobs, and the big names are hard to meet without protective clothing (eg a furry G-string), but several DJs are lovely, friendly people who'd be only too happy to have someone to talk to over a pre-set port and lemon.

Get a job in a club

It sounds stupidly obvious, but if you can't get a job as a DJ, get a job in a club: work behind the bar, help set up the sound system, do the lights, do the cloakroom. Doesn't matter. You're still nearer the action than you would be mithering in your bedroom. You wouldn't be alone if you take this route. Larry Levan started out doing lights and got his big break when the DJ didn't turn up. John Digweed used to be a bar manager. Laurent Garnier worked in the kitchens at the Hacienda-owned Dry Bar to get his foot in the door. Plus you get pissed for free. Can't say fairer than that.

Hang out on forums

Forums are where DJs, clubbers and industry folk hang out when they've got nothing better to do (which, let's face it, is most of the time). They're great places for exchanging information, hooking up with like-minded souls, finding out about new parties and nights in your area and, most importantly, for selling your DJ talents.

DJ cyberspace

www.globalunderground.co.uk/forum.php
The Global Underground CD series bulletin board. Very active.

http://forum.djmag.com
DJ magazine's lively meeting place.

http://deephousepage.com/cgi-bin/ultimatebb.cgi
Chicago based forum, dealing in house history.

www.soulstrut.com/ubbthreads/ubbthreads.php
Excellent US-based crate-digging forum.

www.vinylvulture.co.uk/forum/index.php
The meeting place for vinyl-obsessives and their dependents.

www.ukhhf.co.uk/forum
Hip hop specialists.

http://brownswood.5.forumer.com
Gilles Peterson's forum.

www.undergroundhouse.net/forum
Busy UK house forum.

www.djhistory.com/forum
Our very own forum.

Get a job in a record store
The nearer to the centre of things you are, the better. Working in a chain store will give you experience of the retail music industry, but get in at the best independent shop and you'll be right in the hub of the local dance community, the place where DJs congregate, hang out and share information. Granted, the wages will probably be derisory, but it's a great way to meet the movers and shakers in your scene, some of whom might even give you a gig. Oh, and what better place to get access to new records, huh?

Get into dance journalism
An increasingly popular route into dance music is through the ever-mushrooming dance media. Ten years ago there were only a few outlets for dance music writing, now there are a dozen or more UK titles, as well as a bunch of online sites. Start a fanzine, send story ideas to editors (ask if they need a club correspondent from your part of the country), build an interesting website... Journalism is good for contacts (and free records). But don't kid yourself that spelling is the same as writing. It's a skill, love, innit.

Get a job in the music industry
Not the easiest thing, we know (especially as it's in recession right now), but if you swing it you've got all the connections plus a real job with money you can live on while you hatch your plans for DJ domination. Don't expect to walk straight into an A&R job, but with a few exams under your belt and some musical nous, a job in record promotion is completely plausible. Check out the jobs in *Music Week*, the industry bible, and abuse any contacts you might have, however tenuous. The advantages are that you get to work with dance records and talk to DJs, though by the time you've finished you will be stuffing mailers in your sleep (entry-level music biz jobs mean making tea and posting out records five days a week). As well as the labels (both major and independent) there are also independent promotion companies who specialise in dance music, such as Power Promotions and Hyperactive.

DJs who started in record stores
Ross Allen Inner Rhythm, Streatham
Ashley Beedle, X-Press 2 Black Market, London
Nicky Blackmarket Blackmarket of course
Joe Claussell Dance Tracks, New York
DJ Cosmo Dance Tracks, New York
Ray Keith Black Market, London
James Lavelle Honest Jon's, London
Simon Lee, Faze Action Reckless, London
Trevor Nelson Red Records, London
Mark Rae Fat City, Manchester
Justin Robertson Eastern Bloc, Manchester
Rocky, X-Press 2 Flying, London
Luke Slater Our Price, Croydon
DJ Sneak Gramophone, Chicago
Junior Vasquez Downstairs, New York

DJs wot have written stuff
Paul Oakenfold Blues & Soul
Pete Tong Blues & Soul
Ross Allen Straight No Chaser
Judge Jules Update
Dave Clarke Update
Dave Seaman Mixmag
Bill Brewster This book, dummy

36. **How to** get free records

Don't bother. You're a muppet if you think free promos are your short-cut to stardom. Sure, once you're a household name with a national radio show you won't need many skills beyond lifting future number ones out of the mailbag. But when you're starting out, you've got to prove you've got style, not just a few chart tunes ahead of the pack. Quality always beats quantity, and six quid well spent will do your box more good than a whole month of mailing list fodder.

Why you don't need free records

>> **Most of them are crap**
Good tracks are serviced early to important DJs, while the bad and the ugly are chucked at everybody in the hope that some one's dumb enough to play them. A decent DJ will ditch most of what arrives unrequested because it's weak or irrelevant.

>> **Being individual beats being upfront**
No-one got big by sitting back and waiting for the mailman. Put your energy into finding unique imports, great obscurities and forgotten classics. Don't waste time lying to promotion people.

>> **Everyone else will get the same tracks**
On the same day. How unique does that make you? You won't distinguish yourself by spinning the same tunes that landed on everyone's doormat.

>> **You still won't get the hotties**
The classier the tune, the fewer promos get mailed out. There's a pecking order and until you're spotted in *DJmag* you're at the bottom.

>> **Postman Pat will 'lose' them**
Or leave them on the doorstep for your neighbours.

'I get a lot of records sent to me, usually shit records that are good for making ashtrays.'

Darren Emerson, *DJ Times*

How promotion works

Why do DJs get free tunes? Because they promote them – they play them, talk about them and put them in their charts. A label's promotions people ('press officers', 'PRs' or 'publicists') give influential DJs free records ('promos') so lesser mortals will drop dollars for a full-price copy.

'We're here to make hit records and get good club chart positions,' says Matt Waterhouse of promo company Hyperactive. 'Our aim is to get our records played to as many people in a club as possible. We need to know they're reaching the right people.'

The golden goose is cooked

The era of getting enough free records to earn a separate income down at Record & Tape Exchange is over, sunshine. Outside of the majors, few labels are mailing out vinyl now. Many are only dealing in CD-Rs and several have already moved to download-only servicing. Nowadays, if you really want vinyl, the only way to get it is down the record store.

It's highly strategic

If a major label wants to make a new artist seem really underground they might send a tune to a small number of DJs on a certain scene. Or maybe they want it to chart right when the album comes out – in which case it might go to radio jocks at the same time as club DJs.

Tunes are targeted

Labels and promo companies have many different DJ mailing lists, all cross-referenced according to different genres, different regions, different audiences. There is never one list.

Numbers are limited

The average mail-out will be a few hundred copies, but a hot tune might only go to the country's top 50 tastemakers. Even the biggest mail-out will be 1,500 copies, maximum.

One in, one out

If they add a DJ to a mailing list they kick someone off. So to get on it you have to show you're more useful to them than someone they're currently servicing. A big promotions company has perhaps 50 new DJs a month scrabbling to get on their lists.

213

How to get on mailing lists

Are you worth it?
Ask yourself, 'Would I spend money giving me free music?' How many people hear you play? Who? How often? To get on the most basic list you'll need to be playing at least a couple of times a week to 200 people or more, preferably somewhere 'relevant'.

Calm your expectations
If it's a big mail-out (eg 1,000 copies) maybe you're in with a chance, but if it's only 50, are you one of the top 50 DJs in the country (or on that scene)? Possibly not.

You won't fool anyone
If you're just blagging they'll bust you. Promotions people know which DJs are useful to them, and until your sets are reaching the right ears it won't include you.

Prove it
Most often, a DJ is added to a list through personal recommendation (by another DJ or someone in the industry). Otherwise you have to state your case. Don't be pushy. Call or email, explain who you are and where and what you play. They might want proof, like flyers with your name on and promoters' or club managers' phone numbers.

Reviewing
Some reviewers get freebies, but there's no end of mags and web-sites out there and times are tight. Will you really help them sell their releases? Send an issue or email your site's address and mention your eight million readers.

Be discerning
Labels are happier sending you tracks you've specifically asked for and will definitely play out, rather than putting you on a list to receive everything. It shows you know their music and earns you more respect.

Be specific about your style
If you never play breaks, ask them to send only their more housey stuff. They don't want to waste postage on records you'll just sell for drugs.

How to stay on mailing lists

Return the reaction sheet
This will be a corny description of how great the track is and a witty questionnaire about whether you agree. This is market research so the label knows who's playing their tunes. Most insist you fax this back if you want to stay on their list.

Don't return the reaction sheet
If your credentials are shaky you'll have a better chance if you avoid attention. In this case never ever return reactions. They'll get you with the 'mailing list update' form, though.

Chart their records
Show enthusiasm. Fax or email them your playlist to show you're hammering their tunes. Even better – get it in a magazine.

Don't lie
Charting records you don't like or don't play just to stay on a list will damage your reputation (and is pretty pathetic). See p216 *How to use your chart*.

Be friendly
Behind every list is a human being. Treat them as a future business contact, not just a record dispenser.

Be friendlier
Drop by to pick up your records and say hi (and save them some postage). Spot them next time you're out and buy them a drink. Start sleeping with them.

'I don't want to be playing the same records as the guy playing in the Mecca club round the corner. That means playing more obscure records, not the records I get sent in the post, otherwise you just become a jukebox.'

Terry Farley, *Mixmag*

215

37. **How to** use your chart

The chart is a DJ's business card. It's invaluable self-promotion because it indicates your taste, style and current playlist to potential employers. Charts are the FT share index of the profession – examined obsessively by other DJs and industry folk looking for new tracks and trends.

How to compile your chart

You should post, fax or email your weekly top 20 (or top 10 if that's what they publish) to the places listed below. Include:

- artist, title and label for each track
- your DJ name, a contact number and where you play.

Don't send out different charts

You're working a commercial club but your taste is more under-ground – should you chart what you like or what you actually play? Chart editors will expect your true playlist, but it will do your career more good if you show off your personal tastes. Don't send two or more different charts to the same place – it will just confuse people.

Be honest

Don't chart records just to curry favour with a hot promotions company or record label. No-one will want to book a DJ whose taste changes with the wind. We've got jukeboxes already, thank you.

Where to send it

Labels whose records you play

If they see you charting their tunes they'll be more inclined to send you (or keep sending you) free promos. The same goes for promotion companies.

Magazines

Anywhere that publishes individual DJ's charts. The more distinctive it is, the more chance it will be printed. Even if it's not published, it will be used to help compile the magazine's club chart.

DJ forums

Make friends with DJs who have similar tastes to yours and share tips and vinyl discoveries. Who knows what potential employers might also be looking.

Anywhere you send your mix

A chart is a snapshot of your set, so include it with any mixes you send to clubs, promoters or agencies. It gives an idea of your style even if they don't have time to listen to your mix.

Club charts

Each dance magazine has a chart that reflects what's going on in the clubs, made by compiling playlist information from as many as 1,000 personal DJ charts each week (plus retail information from specialist stores). Any DJ can send in a chart – in fact it's crucial for their accuracy that DJs like you send in yours. However, if you play more obscure music, your chart won't make much of a dent. If that's the case it might be worth concentrating on more scene-specific charts which you'll find in magazines like *DJmag*.

Music Week's Club Chart
Alan Jones, Music Week, 7th Floor, Ludgate House, London, SE1 9UR.
Fax: 020 7579 4168.
charts@dotmusic.com

DJmag Club Chart
DJmag Club Chart, DJmag, Future Publishing, 2 Balcombe Street, London, NW1 6NW
charts@djmag.com

DMC Club Chart
Pete Roberts, DMC, PO Box 89, Slough, SL1 8NA
www.djpages.com
peter@dmcworld.com

Buzz charts

These sniff out the big records of the future. Their influence is less than it used to be because the dance scene is much less homogenous these days. They're created from the personal charts of leading DJs and industry types, and it's an invite-only affair, so wait until you're asked.

Buzz chart
Published weekly in Seven and used on Pete Tong's 'Essential Selection' on Radio 1. If you're asked to contribute to this chart, you'll be so upfront you'll be getting records before they're even made.

Hype chart
Published every fortnight in DJ, this takes a wider sweep than its two 'rivals', using more DJs and reflecting perhaps more underground tastes than the other two. Less concerned with 'crossover' potential of records in favour of club play.

Coolcuts
The original. Published weekly in *Music Week* (it started in the now defunct *Record Mirror*). It's also broadcast each week on Tall Paul's Kiss 100 and every Friday between 4.30–5pm on Ministry of Sound Radio.

Zzub
Launched by *Seven* magazine (now *DMC Update*) to support small scenes that more mainstream charts were ignoring, this includes everything from techno to downtempo electronica.

217

38. **How to** get paid

You reckon you're worth the price of admission? You probably are. But there are literally thousands of other DJs who are worth it, too. It's a dog-eat-dog industry and more than ever it's about connections and marketability rather than just pure talent.

Basic advice

Value your skills
At first you'll play for free for anyone. But if money's being made from your music, you should be on the payroll.

Be friendly
A dying art! It's good for business.

Be part of a scene
Most underground scenes are cliquey and impossible to break into. But if you're not on the inside you're nowhere.

Make tracks
The best way of getting noticed. These days it's almost compulsory.

How to avoid rip-offs

Hard cash only
Never accept a cheque – boinng! Even better, try and get paid before you go on. What do you mean the promoter's gone home?

Try to get a deposit
Agencies demand a 50% deposit upfront. This can be a friendlier way of protecting yourself than a contract.

Beware out-of-pocket expenses
Don't trust anyone to pay you back. If they're covering travel or accommodation as part of the deal, make sure they pay for it upfront.

Get a contract
A contract protects you legally but it can send out a message of mistrust. Given that many of your gigs will come from personal contacts, you should think carefully about whether or not you use one. Booking agents insist on a written contract and DJs like this because it insulates them from the heavy business stuff. You should always use a contract for gigs abroad and out of town. At the very least get a solid verbal agreement, and write down the details. Or simply write out today's date, the gig details and the agreed price, and get whoever's booked you to sign it. Even on a bar napkin, this is a legal contract. For a sample contract see p288.

How to build your reputation

Turn up
Obvious, really. A single no-show can ruin things for you. If it's unavoidable, let the promoter know as early as possible and be truly apologetic.

Don't be too available
'I'll just check my diary'. Make people think you're in constant demand, even if you haven't played out in weeks.

Know what you're worth
Figure out how many people you're bringing through the door. Know your market value and don't be pushed around.

Watch for your name on flyers
You weren't booked, but everyone thought you were. This can be as bad as a genuine non-appearance. Hard to prevent, but you can sue.

Be wonderful and unique
Of course you are.

Money and taxes

Be businesslike
Watch your earnings and compare them to how much you're spending on records. Ouch!

Save your receipts
Travel, records, magazines, stationery, audio and computer equipment, petrol, hotels, your mobile phone bill ... all legitimate business expenses for a working DJ (or even an aspiring one). This means they're tax deductible, so when the Inland Revenue works out your tax bill, they'll knock off a healthy proportion of what you've spent on these things.

Get an accountant
At least to do your tax returns. They save you more than they cost. Find one who has other DJs on their books, preferably by recommendation.

Fear the taxman
He knows DJing is now a lucrative cash business – start earning and he'll start watching. Several middle-ranking DJs were recently caught for not declaring all their income.

219

How to get a manager

A manager does all the things you would do yourself if only you had the time, the blag, the blinding ambition or a tiny bit of common sense. This includes whatever it takes to make you rich, famous and oh so stylish. A good manager will run all aspects of your career, from getting bookings to arranging production and remix work, boosting your profile, making unwise investments on the stock market and getting you in *Loaded* photo-shoots.

And of course they'll tell you how wonderful you are whenever you're having a bad hair day.

- Many DJs manage themselves, but lots pick up a manager along the way, often a mate or lover who believes in them more than they do themselves.
- Managers usually take 15–20% depending on your agreement. If you have a booker as well, the booker gets their cut first and the manager takes theirs out of what's left.
- If you start doing well a manager may farm out responsibilities to specialists, such as a booking agent, a publicist, a driver, an accountant and a Swedish head-masseur/patisserie-handler.

'Most DJs start off because they love music and because they think it's a cool thing. After I tried it one time, I just got hooked. Then it changed from this cool thing to do, where you're the centre of attention and you control the crowd, to where that became a very driving force. It became a need, as opposed to something I wanted to do. You don't have a choice. You have to do it. You fiend for it. It's a gravity well. It sucks you in.'

Roger Sanchez, DM

220

The league

Top of the Premiership
Big enough that your dad's heard of them (eg Oakenfold, Sasha, Digweed, Tiësto). They earn so much they rarely play more than once a week. Offers considered between £5,000–£20,000, which must include flash hotels, business/first-class air tickets and other perky inducements.

Rest of the Premiership
Big names but still gigging hard rather than resting on their laurels (eg Tall Paul, Judge Jules, Seb Fontaine, Jeremy Healy). These types burn up the miles headlining all over the country and beyond – they get £2,000–£5,000 for each one.

Championship
Make £500–£1,500 per gig. Some (eg Terry Francis, Mark Rae, EZ) are happy to avoid commerciality and think this is more than enough reward for doing the best job in the world. Others are gagging to make it into the Premiership and will rack up maybe six gigs a week to boost their profile.

League One
Breathe the same air as their nameable brethren, but rarely eat in the same restaurants. Their names appear in the middle of lots of flyers, they make £150–£600 a shot and play loooads of gigs. The kings and queens of local scenes, residents at carpet-and-chrome Cinderella's, or the big names on an underground tip.

League Two
A rag-tag bunch – from professional pub'n'club jocks who clear a regular £100 a night, to lesser players on the fringes of more credible scenes making £100–£200 a couple of times a month – because they work in a record store/label/DJ agency. Won't give up the day job.

Vauxhall Conference
Pub DJs. Your local club's warm-up fella. The keen amateur who makes £50 here and there as he starts his (long) journey to stardom. Will work for drugs, drinks, taxi fare and a go on a decent system.

Hackney Marshes
Occasionally released from the bedroom to play for family and friends. See them banging out their full-on Cream set at an empty house party, or trying some amazing scratch tricks for an audience of bemused cub scouts.

How to get a booking agent

An agent (or 'booker') gets you gigs, simple as that. They will send out your mixes, negotiate with promoters, draw up a contract with them (which will include taking a non-refundable deposit of 50% of your fee), and may organise travel, accommodation, visas and work permits where it is part of the deal. They sound wonderful, but they won't touch you unless you can make them some money.

- They take 10–15% of any bookings they get for you. (US agents usually take 20%.)
- They will know what you're worth better than you do, because they have a broader perspective of the scene.
- They'll bust a gut to get your price up.
- If they represent you exclusively, they'll look after your work diary.
- Some are motivated by money, but for most their job satisfaction comes from seeing their jocks rise up the ranks of a particular scene.
- Agents hate to be treated like managers, so don't ask them to help you find your lost car keys 20 minutes before a gig or help you choose a new bandanna to play out in.
- If you vomit on someone's decks, don't expect your agent to keep getting you work.

'The best advice I could ever give to anyone who wants to DJ is to get another job. If you have no responsibilities it is much easier to lose the plot. It's important to get some kind of grounding. It gives you responsibility and money, which means you never have to do other things for cash.'

Pete Tong, *Muzik*

222

Who are they after?

National agents are choosy about who gets on their books. You might be making good money DJing five nights a week, but unless they think you have some kind of star potential, at least within your genre, they won't be interested. You must:

- have a strongly defined style
- be making tracks
- be getting dubplates
- be drawing crowds on a particular scene.

If you're a less-established DJ an agent may occasionally take risks for you and make you a pet project, but only if:

- you are known within a specific genre's scene
- you've been personally recommended
- she's heard you live and been very impressed.

Some DJs choose to be represented by several agents/agencies at once (usually because they don't trust anyone). This works well if you're getting a lot of your own bookings, but it's rarely the way to get your price and stature rising.

Local agencies

What you've just read applies to the major players, but you'll find local DJ agencies in most cities and big towns now. For most of these it's less about pushing individual DJs and more about running a pool of talent and connecting it with the requirements of the area's pubs and clubs. As a rule, these guys don't care about your musical aspirations or your love of your genre, they just want to know that you're hard-working, reliable and unpleasantly flexible. This often means having a box full of chart cheese and some wacky microphone skills.

39. **How to** be a mobile DJ

'Who can do the Macarena?' Seen against the lifestyles of superstar DJs, the workaday craft of mobile DJing seems like a distinctly unglamorous career choice. Weigh it up against a dull office job or life on a production line and you realise it's actually quite an attractive proposition.

On with the show

Arrive at a venue, set up your gear, figure out the lie of the land and get on with playing tunes, while a party grows around you and someone enjoys a turning point in their life. Your songs will be obvious and commercial, you'll spin some of them at every event till they drive you nuts, but you'll be making good, regular money for playing music. Plus, you'll be learning invaluable lessons about reading and controlling a crowd, so if your true ambitions lie elsewhere, you'll have plenty of experience to turn to your advantage. Not to mention enough equipment to throw your own more underground parties whenever you like.

Part DJ, part comedian

The successful mobile DJ is an entertainer as much as a provider of music. You're there to spark up the party and break the ice, often for a group of people who are quite reluctant to let their hair down. This might mean starting party games, conga lines, getting people to pass a balloon between their knees... They'll be expecting you to get on the mic to entice people onto the floor, you'll certainly have to announce requests and dedications, and maybe even get out on the floor and dance.

Karaoke

Most mobile DJs have a karaoke set-up. It's a sizeable investment – you'll need a player unit, a TV monitor and a serious collection of karaoke CDs. But it's incredibly popular and you can usually hire out the gear without having to be present.

DJs who started as mobile jocks

John Digweed
Carl Cox
Gilles Peterson
Pete Tong
Lee Burridge
Dave Seaman
Timo Maas

How to build up your rig

Once you decide to go mobile you need a whole lot more equipment. To fill a decent-sized venue with sound and light will take gear costing several thousand pounds. You'll need some powerful amplifiers and some hefty speakers. Then there's lighting and other visuals, plus plenty of cables. And don't forget rugged flight cases to protect everything (including decks and mixer) now that it's going in and out of vans all the time. You may be able to hire stuff at first, but this will cut your profit margin right down. You should also consider whether you have enough technical know-how to avoid big repair bills when things need servicing.

Equaliser
Not a key part of your home hi-fi perhaps, but when you're setting up a big system in places with uncertain acoustics it becomes essential. Use it to cut frequencies that are causing feedback (very important when you're using a mic), and to get the best sound possible for each room. See p162 *How to improve your sound*.

Lights
You're expected to turn up with enough lights to transform a church hall into the Ministry of Sound. A clutch of programmable disco lights should do the trick, then you'll need stands and trusses to stick them on. A smoke machine is a nice touch, too.

A van
You won't get far without wheels big enough to stash your whole set-up in. And you'd better make sure you have a good lock-up.

MP3
American mobile DJs are quickly moving to an all-digital format – not just because it lets them bring hours and hours of music on a few CDs, but also because the player software is so sophisticated that it can mix and programme the night for you. This gives you more time and energy to devote to entertaining and silliness. See p96 *How to DJ digitally.*

225

How to make it a business

A proper business

Some mobile jocks build up their rig piece by piece, adding and upgrading until they have a fearsome set-up, perhaps taking out loans to cover big-ticket items. Others get a convincing business plan together and buy the lot with a start-up loan from the bank.

Small Business Service www.businesslink.org
Advice on all aspects of starting a UK business.

Licences

A PPL licence lets you play recorded music in public (the money collected goes to the music's performers). Many venues will have their own (displayed over the door along with their alcohol licence if they have one), and certain types of event, eg birthdays and weddings, don't need one. You should have your own PPL licence to play one-off events like fêtes, outdoor shows, sports club discos and office parties. You need 'Tariff 004 Mobile DJ' which costs a flat fee of £98.28 plus VAT per DJ per year.

Phonographic Performance Limited www.ppluk.com
1 Upper St James Street, London W1. 020 7534 1000.

Liability insurance

You need liability insurance in case a speaker stack falls on a gang of dancing ten-year-olds, or the bride's grandma electrocutes herself on your karaoke mic. All public places will have their own liability insurance, but it won't cover injuries caused by you or your equipment.

Equipment insurance

You should also get some serious insurance for your gear. If it's nicked or damaged you're out of a job. It's probably too valuable to be covered by your regular household insurance, so get some proper cover. It's not cheap but it's worth having.

Expenses

Save receipts for everything that could conceivably be a business expense, from records and petrol, to smoke fluid and laundry bills. Get an accountant to do your tax return and advise you about VAT.

A second rig

Sooner or later you'll find yourself with so much equipment sitting in your garage that you might consider sending two or more discos out on the road. You've no doubt got a trustworthy mate/assistant/son/daughter. Just train them up as a DJ and get your hands on a second van.

How to promote yourself

If you're the kind of personality that's cut out for mobile DJing in the first place, self-promotion should be no problem. Get friendly with local event organisers and venues (pubs, hotels, social clubs, etc). Maybe find a pub that needs a regular Friday-night boost. Make contacts with local businesses ready for Christmas party season, and with schools, colleges and youth groups. Also watch for local events (fêtes, festivals, etc) where you might be able to offer your services. If you're starting up it's sometimes worth knowing the other mobile DJs in your town in case they have jobs they can't do that they might pass over to you. Have a huge supply of business cards. Many DJs print their contact details (including rough prices) on the request cards they hand out at their events. Aim to get work from each event you play at.

Further information

DJ Times www.djtimes.com
Even though it is firmly aimed at the US market, this excellent magazine and website is essential reading for any mobile DJ. In between coverage of clubland's more underground DJ stars, you'll find tons of detailed information relating to mobile DJing.

DMC www.dmcworld.com
Tony Prince's company DMC (Disco Mix Club) has been at the forefront of DJing in the UK and around the world since 1983. It's most famous for its annual turntablist mixing championships, and for launching original UK club magazine *Mixmag*, but DMC also remains a solid support network for mobile DJs. Its DJ-only remixes and megamixes are just part of the many services worth checking out.

Disco City http://www.dfb-uk.com/DJ%20Guides/dj_guides_index.htm
This Nottingham-based equipment store sells new and secondhand gear and has an excellent guide and very busy forum full of mobile DJs and their fans (www.dfb-uk.com/phorum).

Disco Search www.discosearch.co.uk
There are several UK directories of mobile DJs. Most are very patchy, but this has over 100, listed by region.

American Disc Jockey Association www.adja.org
Almost a union for mobile DJs. There's no equivalent UK body.

227

40. **How to** be a radio DJ

Hi there, pop-pickers! Whereas a club DJ performs music, a radio DJ presents it, so a lot more depends on your entertainment abilities. Radio is an intimate medium. The listeners at home need to feel they have a one-to-one relationship with you, so get close – real, real close. Now over to . . .

Got what it takes?

'I am trying to expose a creative, social commentary dynamic related to a DJ. I'm not just time and temperature. I'm not just a voice on the air. I am just as creative – frankly more creative – than some of these people you hear on one of these records.'

Gary Byrd

Personality is vital in most types of radio DJing. Are you funny, interesting, do you draw people in like a magnet? Can you gab on for ages without prompting? Do you have the skill to ad-lib when something goes wrong, or would you be risking the ominous silence of 'dead air'? Your voice is important, too. Thanks to a little EQing and compression you no longer need an especially deep one. But you do need to learn to speak clearly and grammatically without swearing or, erm, saying 'umm' too much. What kind of disc jockey do you want to be?

Club DJ on radio
In the mix, playing just as you would in a club. Maybe exchanging a few grunts and introducing the traffic report.

Musicologist
A keen collector and discoverer. Eclectic like John Peel, Gilles Peterson or Ross Allen, or a genre specialist like Tim Westwood (hip hop) or Fabio & Grooverider (drum & bass).

Commercial
Playing rapid-fire music, commercial dance or top 40 with short bursts of chat.

Personality
An entertainer. On a morning or drive-time show, where there's a lot more talking than music: 'human zoo' where you have a gang of foolish mates, or 'Shock jock' where you try and offend the world. Chris Evans, Sara Cox and Chris Moyles fit this category.

Talk radio
A journalist. Either interviewing guests or taking calls from listeners. Call-in hosts are usually right-wing misanthropes because this annoys more people into picking up the phone.

The technical skills you need

The basic skills involved in presenting a show are: using a microphone, 'driving the desk' (fading different sound sources up and down), cueing up records, playing jingles, taking calls, linking to news, weather or outside broadcasts and dealing with competitions. Your producer or engineer may take care of some of these. The more production skills you have, the more employable you are.

Programming
A show has a prepared running order. Learn how to follow one. Smaller stations still use written 'timesheets'; bigger ones use automation software like AudioEnhance www.audioenhancedps.co.uk, Simian www.bsiusa.com/software/simian/simian.php or Raduga www.raduga.net.

Editing
Pre-recording jokey skits or serious reports is the key to adding interest to your presenting. In some stations this still means splicing quarter-inch tape. Elsewhere it's done using software like Pro-tools www.digidesign.com.

Signal processing
At the very least, understand how to get your levels right. Radio transmitters are less forgiving than clubbers' ears.

How to make tapes

Tapes (or ideally a CD) are how radio jocks get work and move stations. Yours should be presentable and eye-catching, with clear contact details and a CV. A Programme Director will be looking for experience to back up your obvious talent.

Edit the music right down
All but the 'tops and tails'. It's your skill *between* the songs people want to hear.

Start off with your killer link
Not loads of jingles. You've only got 30 seconds to win them over.

Send tapes to the right places
To stations you want to work for; to stations that might employ you. Think of their format and their size.

229

How to break into radio

Be yourself, sound natural

They're after a relaxed pro; so you can't sound forced or nervous. Raw enthusiasm is the way in. Radio is filled with stars who started as gabby teaboys or enthusiastic receptionists. Radio stations rarely have a huge staff, so even in the most dogsbody work-experience job it's not impossible to get noticed. Competition is fierce though, so you better also have some experience – in student or hospital radio, on an RSL station, or even a pirate. Get some proper training under your belt, and go the extra mile in everything you're asked to do.

Student radio

Whether part of a proper course or not, most colleges and universities support some form of broadcasting.
Student Radio Association www.studentradio.org.uk
Forum, links and list of college radio stations.

Hospital radio

Be a Florence Nightingale of the airwaves.
Hospital Broadcasting Association www.hospitalbroadcasting.co.uk
UK charity supporting hospital radio, with links and local station-finder.

RSL (Restricted Service Licence) radio

These are licences issued by the Government to local community stations (among others), allowing them to broadcast for up to 28 days at a time.
Community Media Association www.commedia.org.uk
Your gateway to community media organisations in the UK.

Pirate radio

The equipment may not be the latest, but it's seat-of-the-pants broadcasting at its most 'educational'. See p236 *How to start a pirate station*.

Internet radio

The easiest way to get on the radio is to do it online.
www.radiofeeds.co.uk
www.radiotower.com
www.last.fm
www.npr.org
www.shoutcast.com

Further information

Radio Now www.radio-now.co.uk
Massive directory of UK stations, including webcasts and satellite.

FM Jock www.fmjock.com
A UK-based commercial site offering all sorts of strange services to the professional radio disc jockey. A great insight into the profession.

Ofcom
www.ofcom.org.uk/radio
UK Government body that licenses radio stations.

Broadcast
Weekly industry magazine, good for job ads. Monday's *Guardian* is good too.

Courses

Look for one that covers production and presentation. This will teach the technical skills you'll need to impress employers, as well as on-air motormouth experience. Most have arrangements with community broadcasters. Some are free if you're unemployed. If you've got a job there are many part-time ones. The courses at Bournemouth University www.media.bournemouth.ac.uk/courses/marp.html are reckoned to be some of the best in the country. You'll find a useful directory of UK courses at www.radioandtelly.co.uk/courses.html

The BBC

The good old Beeb remains a fine paternalistic educator. Get your foot in the door and free training runs like water. They definitely look after their own, so a job on a local BBC station is perfect for getting you noticed on a bigger one.

www.bbc.co.uk/jobs/gettingintobbc
www.bbc.co.uk/newtalent

Who's who in a radio station

Programme Director

Approves playlists, invents new programmes and formats, worries about audience figures and usually hires and fires DJs. Often a former DJ.

Head of Music

Works under Programme Director. Chooses music, draws up playlist (with DJs and producers). Deals with labels and promo people.

Producer

Works under Head of Music to create and run individual pro-grammes. Mollycoddles the talent (DJs, etc), prepares records and running order.

Engineer

The techie who makes the studio work. Worries about signal and sound quality.

231

41. **How to** throw a great party

Jeez! Stop moaning that no-one will give you a gig; get off your arse and make one. By far the best way to establish yourself is to create your own little scene – with you cleverly showcased playing great music.

How to fill a party

- It's a party, not a club.
- Don't try to make a profit.
- Start small and grow.

A great party takes planning and hard work and it starts with the right people – a roomful of sexy boys and girls who'll dance all night. Begin well in advance, pick a date without too much competition and work hard inviting people. If you can sell tickets upfront you'll have a smaller drop-out rate.

Friends
Get personal. Don't just leave flyers in the record shop (next to 3,000 others) and hope for the best. Put in the hours calling, faxing, emailing everyone you know. Invite all your friends and make them invite all their friends. You'll soon be into three figures.

Party monsters
The popular people, social captains with big phone books, friends having birthdays. Suck them into your party-planning circle and the masses will follow.

Girls, girls, girls
Where the girls are, the boys are, too. Girls bring more friends, work hard on looking great, and they're first on the dancefloor.

Your gay mates
They party harder and dress better than mere mortals and always know where the drugs are.

The general public
Try to manage without them. The best parties are where everyone is connected. If you can make it invite-only/word-of-mouth you're doing great.

The key is to find a place you can put your stamp on – a small club midweek, a pub or social club's function room, a restaurant basement, a village hall, an empty warehouse, a millennium dome... Look for places down on their luck and start talking.

Money
The usual deal is that you fill an otherwise quiet night with drinkers and the manager lets you charge on the door. Some may want paying as well, while some may want a deposit which you get back if you bring enough people or if they make enough money at the bar (or if they feel like it). Negotiate. Be clear on what's been agreed. Try to ensure against double-bookings and resident DJs who turn up expecting to play.

Security
Nothing spoils your night more than unexpected trouble when there's no-one to squash it. In a licensed venue the management are responsible for providing bouncers. But they may charge you for them. Elsewhere, you'll have to find someone experienced and scary with a heart of gold (see Gangsters).

Licences
What time's the last record? When do they turn off the booze? Will they serve soft drinks after that? Can you charge on the door? These usually depend on the venue's licence. Pubs, bars and social clubs may need to get an extension to go late.

Sound system
There's not much point to all this if you end up on some shitty karaoke set-up. Check what's provided and if it's not enough, a small-to-average system can be hired for £150 to £400. Mates in a band might have a PA you could borrow (test it first). Check with the venue that you can bring your own sound; use this to argue their price down.

How to choose a venue

'I think there's a whole element that's lost out there of how grand a party can be. What drama, and what can really happen when somebody plays music that's not just a succession of beats or a collection of this week's new releases, but is actually an inspired reading; it's a message; it's a telling.'

François Kevorkian

233

How to turn it out

Music

Vitally important. We're trusting you to be amazing. If you're not up for playing all night, make sure the other DJs fit your style and give a lot of thought to the running order. Argue it out *before* the night.

Booze

If you're doing your own bar expect lots of carrying, guarding and thieving, and then there's barstaff to find and pay. Get the drinks sale-or-return in case you don't sell out. If it's bring-a-bottle make sure everyone knows.

Drugs

We never do anything stronger than Sherbet Dib-Dabs, but we've noticed that drugs make a huge difference to the atmosphere. Obviously you should never invite a friendly dealer, and you should never suggest what they might bring. Scientists have proven that cocaine makes individuals high (and mighty), but ecstasy brings up the whole party. Let ketamine in and you won't hear the music for snoring.

Lights

Darkness encourages dancing, but you also need movement (ie flashing lights). If there's nothing provided, get a mirrorball (£40), a pin-spot (£20) and a small strobe (£20) as your party-starter starter pack.

Decorations

Hard work but worth it. Balloons, streamers, murals, fabric, hangings... Party wholesalers and pound stores are good sources. Keep it fireproof. Themes and other silliness make people have more fun.

Doorpeople

A friendly welcome and someone responsible to collect the money. We're lucky to know two goddesses who always look fabulous and are happy to stay in one place. Start looking.

What party is this?

Marxist-Leninist principles aside, we know the power of branding. If you throw a great party, give it a name for everyone to remember. Ours is Low Life, what's yours?

How to avoid failure

Gangsters
Because it involves drink, drugs, cash, expensive equipment and hired muscle, the world of partying is not entirely controlled by angels. Be careful. If you're using an unlicensed venue in a dodgy neighbourhood, be very careful.

Location
Make sure people can find it and get there easily. Have some cards from a local cab company on hand for home-time.

Flyers/invites
Include the when and the where (plus hints for how to get there) and your best attempts at humour.

Easy, tiger
Aim to start with memorable one-offs. Then, if the numbers grow and you have a regular venue, try a monthly, then maybe a weekly. A successful party builds its own momentum.

Invite us
We are great fun and very good-looking: billandfrank@djhistory.com

For more party advice: **www.urban75.com/Rave/party.html**

Basement Jaxx at the Junction

A great illustration of the power of a party comes from Basement Jaxx, who for four years promoted sweaty nights in dark Brixton pubs. Creating their own scene meant they could play exactly how they wanted. 'They were always in small venues and it's always been just like a party,' said Simon Ratcliffe in DJ Times. 'We felt very at home. We started playing there together, inviting different guests to play around us, or just playing all night – music we love, cool music. We were trying to recreate what we thought the ideal underground Chicago or New York house club would be like. So it was dark, it was very underground, not shiny, not flash at all, just music, people sweating, jacking.' After a couple of years the parties were infamous, undoubtedly helping the Jaxx boys on their rise to international album stars. And their advice for a fine shindig? 'It's the people that make it. There's no point standing there with your bottle of beer expecting things to happen. You have to start dancing; it's you that makes it.'

42. **How to** start a pirate station

Pirate radio is totally, completely illegal and we advise you not to even consider starting your very own radio station. Don't look at any of the websites listed below (the work of deviant anarchists), don't talk to anyone involved in pirate stations, and whatever you do, don't imagine using it as a surprisingly accessible broadcast medium through which to promote your DJing skills and the underground music scene you're part of. Got that?

Hopefully this should deter you

- Almost everyone on Radio 1, including Pete Tong, Danny Rampling, the Dreem Teem, Gilles Peterson and John Peel, started as pirate broadcasters.
- Since the sixties, pirate radio has been home to the hottest, most underground music.
- There are an estimated 200 pirate stations successfully operating in the UK; more than 80 in London alone.

Don't touch that dial

Pirate radio takes its name from the outlaw stations of the sixties which broadcast from ships out in the North Sea and English Channel. Most famous were Radio Caroline and Radio London (from which Radio 1 took almost all its disc jockeys when it launched in 1967), as well as land-based Radio Luxembourg which blasted its way across the Channel. The seventies brought stations like Invicta and DBC (Dread Broadcasting Corporation), which changed the tastes of a generation as they boomed out soul and reggae to London's growing black communities. Acid house saw a huge explosion in pirate broadcasting, as the rave movement used outlaw stations like Kiss FM (now legal, of course) to advertise its events. These days, despite three decades of government efforts to silence them, the pirates are healthier than ever, and continue to offer an exciting alternative to legal radio. This means a constant diet of upfront garage, ragga and drum & bass – plus, of course, whatever's next.

Don't ever do any of these things

We'd hate for you to be stupid enough to put music and free speech ahead of respect for the rules of a democratic capitalist society. As long as you don't do any of these things you will be perfectly within the law.

- Find a group of people who share a passion for illegal broadcasting and underground music.
- Including people who are more technically minded than you.
- Including people who are more streetwise than you.
- Find a handy tower block, preferably where the streetwise people know who's who and what's what.
- Find a gap in the radio band in that area (at least 0.2 MHz clear of any other station) and make sure no other pirates are using it or planning to use it.
- Beg, borrow, buy or build a transmitter. (In the past, evil criminals have bought them abroad for as little as £200, built them from plans on the internet, or made them from kits legally available in the UK.)
- Build an antenna and attach it to the tower block. (Radio baddies resort to the internet for their law-breaking antenna designs, and they've developed despicable diversionary tactics for erecting and protecting their equipment.)

'I would convince my dad to drive us up to Epsom Downs where it was quite a bit higher and we'd connect the transmitter to the car battery, put an aerial on the highest tree and we'd pick up phone calls from the local telephone box while my dad sat in the pub. We'd get one call and it'd be incredible!'

Gilles Peterson

237

Don't go to any of these websites

Pirate Radio Kit Site http://members.tripod.com/~transmitters
A monstrous site, showing how far these thugs will go. Dedicated to giving criminals all the technical advice they'd need to run rampant on the airwaves.

How To Be A Radio Pirate www.irational.org/sic/radio/
Filled with dangerous anarchist-led advice and criminally minded technical details, this evil UK-based site has no doubt spurred many towards a life of depravity and imprisonment.

Free Radio Network www.frn.net/
Let's just hope the FBI are keeping tabs on this American affront to decency. No end of technical information, masquerading as innocent circuit diagrams. Plus links to other suspect groups throughout the world.

Pirate Radio Central www.blackcatsystems.com/radio/pirate.html
Disguised within a commercial software operation (including downloadable software for designing antennas) is a devious and highly organised nerve centre for US pirates, listing many law-breaking examples.

'Everything was going fine until we heard we were about to get raided. I called Goldie up on my mobile to tell him to get rid of the transmitter quick. When we got to the flats all we could see was a big crowd of people looking up towards Goldie's window where he'd chucked the thing out. The only problem was he'd forgotten to unplug it.'

Tall Paul, *Mixmag*

Some final warnings to make sure you never ever get involved with illegal broadcasting.

Other pirates

Pirate radio can be big business, so new broadcasters would have to tread carefully around any existing stations. And evil gangs, drug dealers, filthy DJs and professional criminals are never far behind. You'd be nuts if you tried it.

DTI

Thankfully the DTI (Department of Trade and Industry) is extremely vigilant in policing the airwaves. Their Radiocommunications Agency makes sure no-one messes with frequencies used by the emergency services (although 88 to 108 MHz is earmarked for FM broadcast radio so anything within this wouldn't run the risk of upsetting ambulances, etc). And they track these rotters down in a snap. In London they can pinpoint a transmitter to within 20 metres, less than 10 minutes after it's switched on. They usually monitor new pirates for a few months to figure out what they're up to, and will record as evidence anything broadcast which isn't straight music.

The penalties

If caught, these cowardly airwave bandits get the book thrown at them. Offenders have been fined as much as £1,000 and had all their equipment seized (including turntables and records). The latest figures (for 2000) show that out of 1,494 raids the DTI secured 40 convictions, with an average fine of £377. That's a whopping 2.6% conviction rate.

Outside London

The DTI concentrates almost all its resources on policing the London area. Other places might not be as well covered, but let's hope they manage to plug those gaps before lunatic pirates go crazy in small towns across the country.

Given this kind of opposition you'd have to be completely crazy to try and get away with it. You'd certainly need a lot of luck and best wishes.

And in case you were still considering it

'I was on LWR and Invicta. When I started doing pirates it didn't seem to be an illegal thing to do. It was like a hobby, and the fact that you were so bothered about doing it, and you would bother to go to such great lengths to do it, it seemed like, "What do you mean, it's illegal?"'

Pete Tong

239

43. **How to** promote yourself online

Until you're appointed the new resident of Centro-Fly in New York or Zouk in Singapore, the best way to let your music earn some air miles is by putting it online. All you need is a computer and an internet connection, and it can be pretty easy and cheap to do.

The basics

The web is full of great places to publicise yourself, but you're going to have to put in some work to make anything happen. Don't think you can simply upload your mix somewhere and the world will suddenly discover you. There are lots of sites which will host music (some free, some for a charge), but unless you tell anyone to go there, your mix will simply sit gathering dust among thousands of others.

How to get a mix online

See also p208 *Making your mix.*
See also p99 *How to record to a computer.*

The easiest way to get a mix online is to upload it free to a website like yousendit.com. These are really easy to use, and you can have your mix on the net in minutes. Once it's uploaded you get an exclusive web address where anyone who knows about your mix can download it. You get free space for a limited time (usually around seven days), or for limited downloads (yousendit.com gives you 100). If this isn't enough you can pay to upgrade to their premium services, although once you do this, you might want to consider buying your own webspace somewhere.

www.yousendit.com
www.megaupload.com
www.rapidshare.de

How to publicise your mix
The best way to get people listening to your mix is to post the link for it on a relevant DJ forum. This way you reach likeminded people who are into the same music as you. You can also email the link to your mates or to contacts like club and bar owners, or simply post it in your blog. If it's any good, your mix will soon start doing the rounds. Think of yourself as a one person viral marketing campaign.

www.service.real.com/learnnav
www.recess.co.uk/genfaq.html
www.irational.org/radio/radio_guide
www.streamingmedia.com/tutorials

Streaming mixes
A streaming mix is one which people can listen to but not download. The advantage is they can start listening to it without waiting.

The downside is that if they like it they can't copy it or send it on to anyone, and that's why we advise against streaming – you want your little babies zinging about the net like ants at a picnic. Think viral. Think shameless promotion. The other reason we don't recommend streaming is that it's much more complicated.

How to upload a podcast

Podcasting is a simple method of getting your music out there, and can turn your bedroom into a one-man radio station. The beauty of a podcast is that you can regularly update it, so you could post a new mix every month and anyone who's enjoyed a mix of yours in the past will automatically receive your latest offering.

How does podcasting work?
A podcast is an online audio broadcast that people can subscribe to. This means they don't have to log on to a particular website and manually download it each time. Instead their music program (eg iTunes, Juice or Doppler) will automatically download the latest podcast you've uploaded. The subscription is handled by some nifty software called RSS (Really Simple Syndication).

How to make a podcast
If you simply want to post regular mixes for people to download, then all you need is an MP3 file of your mix, a place to host it (eg your blog) and a podcast program like Podcastmaker or Pod Producer to do the rest (setting up an RSS feed to it). If you've got ambitions of becoming the next Pete Tong or Westwood and you want to mix speech and music, it's a little more complicated (but only a little).

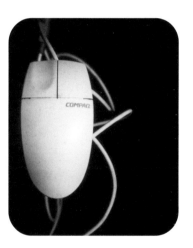

> **Detailed guides to creating podcasts**
> www.how-to-podcast-tutorial.com
> www.jellycast.com
>
> **For making programmes with speech**
> Garageband (Mac only) www.apple.com/ilife
>
> **For turning mixes and programmes into podcasts**
> Podcastmaker (Mac only) www.potionfactory.com/podcastmaker
> Pod Producer (PC only) www.podproducer.net

Where to get noticed online

Now we've got DJ forums and social sites like MySpace we don't need pubs or partners any more, just a computer, a good connection and a serious lack of real friends. Nowadays you can boost your DJing career or promote a successful party without printing up flyers or posters or even leaving your bedroom, thanks to the joys of the net. And forums, those buzzy bees full of enthusiasm and vituperation, are great places for learning about music, as well as making friends and contacts.

Forums we like

www.djhistory.com/forum
It's ours (blush).

www.faithfanzine.com/phpBB2
Come and get ravaged by acid house warhorses.

www.vinylvulture.co.uk/forum
Possibly the most knowledgeable board on the net. Great for breaks, beats, soul, jazz and folk.

http://brownswood.5.forumer.com
Gilles Peterson's site.

www.zrecords.ltd.uk/mb
Disco, disco, disco. And house.

www.soulstrut.com/ubbthreads/ubbthreads.php
Occasionally incomprehensible, always entertaining hip hop culture site.

www.littledetroit.net/forums
Excellent techno forum.

http://deephousepage.com/cgi-bin/ultimatebb.cgi
For Chicago house and disco heritage (and arguing).

www.tranceaddict.com/forums
Incredibly vibrant trance forum.

Online tips and etiquette

- It's up to you. Get out there and interact with people. Don't expect the world to beat a path to your door just because your music is online. Despite what you heard, no one really became famous purely from having a blog on MySpace – its success stories always have a PR machine or an existing fanbase behind them.

- Don't barge straight into a forum with shameless self-promotion. If you hang out on message boards purely to big yourself up, you will get short shrift.

- In the digital world as in biblical times, give and ye shall receive. If you're generous with your own knowledge, information and contacts, you will find other board members regard you in a similarly benign way.

- If you find a forum you particularly like, it pays to do a spot of lurking before diving in there like a hillbilly on crystal meth. That way, you get to know the board characters and you're less likely to end up in a cyber scrap over catalogue numbers or mixing techniques.

242

How to make your own website

We're not going to get all HTML on you. But if you're keen to strike out on your own and build a personal site to promote yourself, here are some ideas to get you all the attention you deserve.

What to include

- **A bio** Tell the world who you are, how you got here and where you'd like to be. Make it short and funny. Maybe list where you've played and what residences you've had.
- **Photos** Some shots of you in action so they can see how gorgeous you are.
- **Dates** A calendar of your upcoming gigs.
- **Mixes and tracks** Your greatest moments for them to stream or download.
- **Your chart** What tunes are you caning right now?
- **A blog** Your witty thoughts on life as you DJ your way to fame and fortune.
- **Other useful stuff** If you know something helpful or interesting, share it – more people will visit. In the past DJs have built sites about scratch techniques, or sample-spotting, or taking Technics decks apart...

Keep it simple. Make it easy to get around. Clear sections, a simple menu and quick-loading pages mean happy visitors. Lots of complicated Flash designs and clever animated menus mean it won't work on all browsers or it'll take hours to load.

Internet radio

If you have some technical wizardry and a decent budget for hosting and software, you could get into the world of live streaming. These companies offer expertise and, more importantly, server space.

www.planetwideradio.com
www.streamguys.com
www.mediacast1.com

243

44. **How to** make a re-edit

For spice, get splicing! There are few better ways of making your set unique than producing your own re-edits. A clever DJ uses re-editing to make songs longer, shorter, or just better. Most importantly, make a great re-edit and you have a version that no-one else can play.

What's a re-edit?

Not to be confused with a remix. A re-edit is a cut-up or rearrangement of an already completed and mixed song, whereas a remix goes back and plays with individual elements from the multitrack recording (for more on remixing, see p258 *How to make a remix*). Re-editing is a natural extension of DJing. In essence, you are reproducing in a studio what a very clever DJ might do live. Until the arrival of digital technology, editing was done manually using razor blades and tape, but these days anyone with a computer can re-edit a track.

Why make re-edits?

Re-editing is a chance to show the world *exactly* what you love about a song. Find its essence and share it. Extend and rearrange the best parts, remove the bits you don't like or that don't work on the dancefloor. It's the musical equivalent of shuffling a deck of cards.

- **Exclusivity** Make a song yours. Make your set more individual.
- **Better music** Your version is a huge improvement – that's why you did it.
- **Experience** Easier than making a track, but a great introduction to producing.

Cutting up history

Hip hop was founded on live re-editing – DJs like Kool Herc and Grandmaster Flash extended the break using two copies of the same record. Chicago house, too, was all about re-edits – Frankie Knuckles and Ron Hardy spliced new versions of old songs and beefed up their percussion with drum machines and rhythm tracks.

Before this, though, it was disco that made re-editing a key tool in the DJ's armoury. 'In the seventies, before direct drive turntables, samplers and computers, DJs like Walter Gibbons would splice together a reel-to-reel tape of a special party version of a track,' explains veteran DJ and master re-editor Danny Krivit. 'These tracks were exclusively theirs and you had to hear that DJ play to hear them.'

'It was difficult for a DJ to do all these fancy moves all the time, all night,' adds François Kevorkian, a DJ whose career was based on a series of incendiary re-edits, 'so I started making all these little dubplates. My dubplates were a kind of concentrated energy at the time, really a kind of greatest hits formula.'

Take a good song and make it better, or take a crap song and make something worth playing.

Change the length
The song's great, just too short for the dancefloor, so extend those groovy parts and percussive passages. Maybe loop a section of a break to make some DJ-friendly intros and outros. Or perhaps a track's too long. Cut it down; condense the excitement.

Take out the trash
Get rid of extraneous bridges, bad choruses, tacky chord sequences. Replace the crap bits with some good bits – find a groove section and use it as a bridge to link the verses.

Create your own dubs
Take out the vocal. Use instrumental passages to replace the singing parts.

Change the breakdown
If you're a breakdown-happy breakdown-lover you could extend it for added drama. Or maybe it sucks the energy from the floor. Take it out.

Extend the intro of a familiar tune
People know it, but not like this. Your edit teases them and adds drama by holding back the familiar pay-off.

Emphasise a sampled classic
If there's a current hit using a sample from a classic record, make a re-edit of the classic tune that emphasises the sample so the dancefloor can't miss it.

Boost the percussion
Layer a new drum loop under an otherwise untouched song. Update old tracks with a little extra bass or some FX on the intros and breaks.

Save your effort
Blending an acappella over a dub; editing together elements from two versions of the same song. Why sweat over really impossible mixes in the club when you can do them at home as a re-edit.

Some re-editing ideas

'The thing about doing your own re-edits is that you can play them for ages, because no-one else has got them.'

Dave Lee

245

Editing software

Editing used to require Scotch tape, razor blades and a reel-to-reel machine, plus the skills of a brain surgeon and the patience of a ninja. Now you just need a computer, a decent sound card and the right software. All these packages give you a visual representation of the track you've recorded, letting you cut, paste and tweak different sections. You'll quickly see how the scratchy graph on the screen relates to the song.

Audacity
http://audacity.sourceforge.net/
(Mac/PC freeware) For a start-up editing package you can't beat Audacity, not least because it's free. Simple, flexible, with unlimited tracks.

Adobe Audition
www.adobe.com/spe
cial/products/audition/syntrillium.html
(PC-only; £250) Sadly, the cheaper Cool Edit 2000, is now no longer available, although current users can upgrade. Still has a full range of features and effects.

Logic Express
www.apple.com/logicexpress
(Mac-only; £200) The replacement for MicroLogic, sitting between Garageband and its big brother, Logic Pro. Has 255 tracks, 37 plug-ins, 24 bit/96khz recording. For taking music seriously, while still being user-friendly.

Pro Tools
www.avid.com/products/xpressStudio/pr
oToolsLE (Mac/PC) More or less an industry standard, certainly the most popular re-editing tool on the market, used by all

the pros. Full version comes complete with a soundcard. There's a free demo version available.

Tracktion 2
www.mackie.com/products/tracktion2
(Mac/PC; £110) Easy to use and a great start-up package for beginners. Its single-screen interface keeps the screen clutter-free since it's been designed to keep the technical stuff in the background.

Sound Forge
www.sonymediasoftware.com
(PC-only; £200) Now owned by Sony and up to version 8 it's still an enormously popular editing suite with a full range of sound effects and an intuitive interface.

WaveLab 6
www.steinberg.net
(PC-only; £250) Rival to Sound Forge and Pro Tools (and equally pricey), but still enormously popular. Now includes features such as pitch-shifting and timestretching, along with the usual array of FX and plug-ins.

How to re-edit

Before you start
- Don't just re-edit any old track. Before you start improving things, make sure there is something good to begin with.
- Are there enough good bars to work with? Re-edits have been made from as little as one or two bars of a track, but this is hard. If the good stuff is only tiny you could use it as a sample on another track instead.

Arrangement

When re-editing you need to give your new version a solid shape for the dancefloor. For more about song structures see p74 *How to place a mix*. If you're not sure, copy the structure of songs you know.

- Get two copies of the song you want to re-edit and DJ with them. A live re-edit like this is a great way of getting unexpected ideas.

Edits and overhangs

You need clean edits, but don't be too hygienic: smudges and accidents are often where great ideas come from. Your biggest problem comes when an unwanted sound runs into a bar you're trying to loop. These 'overhangs' mean that the end of your loop won't match up with the beginning.

- Watch for overhanging reverb and sustained chords at the start of your sample. One solution is to take a single bar from another part of the break and drop it in.
- Reversing the last part of a bar masks any loose edits (it mimics the effect of a crash cymbal at the start of the next bar).
- When editing old records, beware of live drummers who waver in tempo. If you're extending their breaks, make sure the edits are in time.
- If you add EQ and FX into old tunes, be careful of distortion.

After you finish

- Leave it for a few days before listening to it. Does your new arrangement still make sense? Do the edits work?

'You're saying, "That's not the way this music should be. I can make it work." Then you get those moments when they recognise what the piece of music is but it doesn't sound like it should do. Joe Public will go, "This is great, I can dance to it" and the spotters will wonder what the hell is going on.'

Luke Solomon

247

45. **How to** make a track

What's the best way to get yourself known as a DJ? Make tracks instead! Most DJs these days are also producers, but while the two jobs are intimately linked, they're not the same. There are DJs who rarely produce (Danny Rampling, Tony Humphries), there are dance producers who don't DJ (BT, Arthur Baker), and there are plenty of DJs who'd do us all a favour if they stayed well away from the studio.

How to make a hit

'Everybody thinks they can write and everybody thinks they can take a photograph,' said writer Nick Hornby. And every DJ thinks they can make a hit record.

Get good ideas
Essential. A DJ knows what will make people dance, so work on ideas from your set. Maybe there's a tune with an amazing break and the rest is arse. Maybe there's a tiny noise in an intro that's just dying to be a whole record. Maybe there are two songs you mix that you'd like to combine more intimately.

Don't reinvent the wheel
Do like everyone else and steal creatively. Recognise the bassline on The Temptations' 'Papa Was A Rolling Stone'? Thought so; we've heard it a hundred times, too. Or look at Raven Maize's chart hit, 'The Real Life'. The main sample was Simple Minds' 'Theme From Great Cities'. Add Queen's 'Bohemian Rhapsody', stir in some beats and a bassline – Top 10 hit!

Combine things creatively
'Go take your ten favourite records of all time, and make your own record out of them,' advises Danny Tenaglia. 'And when you listen back to it, it won't sound nothing like those ten records.' Dance music genius lies in seeing how different elements from disparate styles of music can fit together to create something new and unique.

Keep it simple
Don't overload your track with 25 ideas – it'll sound like a scout troop being thrown down the stairs. Hitmaker Dave Lee (Joey Negro, Jakatta) says simplicity is the key: 'Your average big track rarely has much to it, maybe only two or three elements, but if those elements are memorable it'll drum its way into people's brains.'

248

Choose a minor key

The majority of dance hits are in minor keys. Rob Davis, who co-wrote Spiller's 'Groovejet', argues, 'You can make a sweeter vocal line on minor keys and you can make it more plaintive.' Despite having a major-key hit with 'Big Love', Pete Heller agrees: 'They're easier to work with and to introduce a sense of depth. To work in major chords is quite hard to do without it sounding cheesy and commercial.'

Include memorable hooks

'With writing hooks, keep it really original,' says Rob Davis. 'Don't just stop at your first idea unless it feels really fantastic.' But what's a hook? 'An instantly memorable, simple, melodic, rhythmic or harmonic component of a piece of music,' explains Tom Middleton of Global Communication. Pete Heller has a simpler definition: 'When people go into record shops and say, "Have you got that record that goes der-der-der-der-der?" That's the hook.'

Create drama and tension

'It's drama,' says Middleton. 'The anticipation of something that's going to happen.' 'Breakdowns and build-ups are the key,' adds Heller. 'Build the track up and then strip it down. Use different methods. You can bring everything down to just a kick drum and a bassline for a clap-along moment, or you can stop everything and have a big snare roll and it makes everyone realise it's about to go off again. Careful, though,' he warns, 'or it becomes a cliché.'

How do you know if it's a hit?

Sometimes even the most experienced producers have no idea of the monster they've created. Rocky of X-Press 2 remembers being distinctly underwhelmed after recording seminal tune 'Muzik X-Press'. 'We were just sitting there going, "Well, it sounds alright, but I don't know if I'd play it." ' Says Pete Heller of his huge hit 'Big Love': 'Well, I thought it was a nice demo for something I'd finish one day.'

See you at the mixing desk!

'Make what you're able to hear.'

Arthur Baker

The basics

MIDI

You better get your head around MIDI right away – it's a key part of any modern recording studio. MIDI (Musical Instrument Digital Interface) is a computer language invented in 1983 that gets electronic instruments talking to each other. Everything in a studio has a MIDI-in and MIDI-out connector to daisy-chain them together. Most importantly, your sequencer program records and plays in MIDI. This means that instead of recording musical notes it records a sequence of instructions (digital control codes) for synthesisers and other instruments. For more about MIDI:

www.midi.org/about-midi

Samples

The starting point for most dance producers. Dig deep and raid your record collection. Dig deeper and trawl your friends' collections. There are commercial CDs full of copyright-free samples and, of course, the internet.

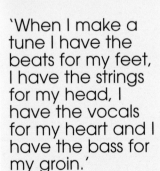

www.audiogalaxy.com Great for acappellas (and much more).	**www.drummachine.com** Samples of every drum machine ever.
www.beatsandsamples.com	**www.ontology.com**
	www.samplearena.com
www.dailywav.com Speech samples from movies.	**www.samplenet.com**

'When I make a tune I have the beats for my feet, I have the strings for my head, I have the vocals for my heart and I have the bass for my groin.'

DJ Rap, *DJ Times*

Tracks and channels

A simple cassette recorder tapes everything onto a single track (or two, if it's stereo). But a song made in a recording studio can have maybe 48 separate tracks (in a 48-track studio), each recorded from a separate channel of sound on the mixing desk. You put the kick drum on one, the tom toms on another, the hi-hat on another, the vocals on another, the guitar on another, and so on. You generate stereo effects by doubling an instrument onto two channels (or by panning individual elements to different positions). You can add as many elements as you like, up to the capacity of the mixing desk, and you can play around with each channel without affecting any of the others. The more channels on the desk and tracks on the tape, the more fun you can have.

Mixing

The mixing desk is essentially a huge version of your DJ mixer. It lets you hear channels separately or together, and when you're happy with everything it combines them all ('mixes them down') to two channels for a stereo record or CD. You decide which channels appear at what volume on each part of the finished track. After the mix you take the results to be mastered, which is the first step in turning it into a record. See p260 *How to release a record*.

How are you going to make your track?

● **p252 USING A VIRTUAL STUDIO**
All the kit you need is just software in your computer.

● **p256 HIRING A REAL STUDIO**
Get a clever engineer to do all the dirty work.

● **p254 USING A HOME STUDIO**
Drum machines and synths – real gear and real wires.

Using a virtual studio

Now that we live in the future, you can have all the different clever boxes of an expensive studio sitting on the desktop of your computer. A virtual studio is just that: it exists in your computer purely as software. Samplers, a sequencer, synthesisers, drum machines, a mixing desk and a digital recorder are all either included in these packages or available as plug-ins. Provided you have enough memory and processing power, you can get started right away.

This is by far the cheapest and most accessible method of making tracks. Make music any time the inspiration hits you – there's no plugging wires into the back of hot boxes, and you avoid playing pool with heavy metal bass players.

For a great introduction to making music this way, go to Music Maker at www.musicmaker.demon.co.uk which is unbeatable for demystifying things.

What you'll need

Computer
Mac or PC? Most bedroom producers tend to work on PCs, yet most professional producers use Macs. There are also the Luddites who insist on using knackered old Ataris, a throwback to the days when sequencer packages like Notator were Atari-only compatible. Provided your chosen software is compatible, stick to what you're comfortable with.

Soundcard
To boost your computer's musical abilities. The more you spend, the better you're going to get. But you can still produce release-quality material on a cheap soundcard – Four Tet's album, Pause, was recorded using a SoundBlaster Live 1024, which is as little as £50. For serious use, buy a soundcard that is ASIO-compatible (Audio Stream Input Output).

Speakers
There's nothing wrong with using add-on computer speakers (especially the kind with a nice sub-woofer), or even doing everything on headphones, but for better results you should output your sound from your computer into an amplifier or stereo system. For the best sound, invest in a pair of studio monitor speakers.

'I think DJs who don't want to make their own records are soft, because no one knows better than a DJ what creates a buzz on the floor.'

Sasha, *Mixmag*

252

The packages

Live www.ableton.com
(PC/Mac; £235) Famous as the latest high-tech DJing tool, Live is actually brilliant studio software, with a revolutionary approach and a super-intuitive interface. Lets you combine sampled, synthesised and even live instrumentation.

Acid www.sonymediasoftware.com
(PC-only; various prices) Popular loop-based (non-MIDI) production suite with different versions from freeware right up to the £200 professional package.

Reason www.propellerheads.se/products/reason
(PC/Mac; £240) Hugely popular among users with no previous experience because of the brilliantly obvious interface. Visually arranged like a studio set-up, it's intuitive, easy to master, supports MIDI and is capable of producing release-quality productions.

Logic www.apple.com/logicpro
(Mac-only; £639) Logic 7 is the program that had a generation of producers ditching their PCs for Macs. You can run it on a series of networked Macs for ultimate processing speed. For about £180 there's Logic Express.

ReCycle www.propellerheads.se/products/recycle
(PC/Mac; £105) A production package aimed at people making loop-based tracks purely from samples (non-MIDI). Eagerly pounced on by drum & bass folk.

Soft synths and other plug-ins

Add endless extras to your main package. Look hard enough and you'll find the software equivalent of just about any electronic instrument and studio kit that ever existed. These bits of software are known as 'plug-ins', because they 'plug in'. See?

K-v-R www.kvr-vst.com
A variety of plug-ins to download. Also news, a bulletin board and user reviews.

Plugin Spot www.pluginspot.com
Synths and effects boxes for fruity-loops.

QuadraSID www.refx.net
Soft synths and effects.

Reaktor www.native-instruments.de
If you really have no life, custom-make your own soft synths.

Steinberg www.steinberg.net
Huge site from the people who make Cubase. Samples, synths, effects and a soft version of the Prophet 5, a classic analogue synth that went out of tune faster than a pissed-up folk singer.

Theremin www.bbc.co.uk/science/playground/theremin1.shtml
Download a Theremin for your desktop. Go on, you know you want to.

253

Using a home studio

Despite the wonders of virtual studios, plenty of producers still lust after sexy synths and classic drum machines. Yes, you can get them as software these days, but it's not like being able to fiddle with those oscillator knobs. This is where the home studio comes in. You still programme the music through a sequencer on your computer, but now you've got some proper gear to get your mitts on.

Sequencer

At the heart of every studio is a sequencer program like Cakewalk or Cubase. This records music, not as a series of sounds, but as a series of instructions – all written in MIDI. You see the song you're making as a timeline on a computer screen, and you can add or change whatever elements you like. When you play the song back, the sequencer becomes a robot conductor, sending out all the necessary orders to the music machines you have plugged into it. If you could speak MIDI you'd hear it say things like 'Play a C on the synth for 2.5 seconds. Then play a G on the squawk sample for 0.8 seconds...' It's like a digital version of an old-fashioned player-piano. These days most sequencers have the ability to play and process audio alongside MIDI.

Cubase www.steinberg.net
(PC/Mac) Probably the most popular sequencer among UK producers. Prices range from around £60 for Cubasis up to £650 for the full package.

Logic Audio www.emagic.de
(PC/Mac) The equal of Cubase but perhaps harder to use. Packages range from £100-£550.

Cakewalk www.cakewalk.com
(PC-only) Hugely popular with home producers, with a wide variety of different packages (£35-£300).

Controller keyboard

You drive your sequencer with a controller keyboard (the piano type rather than the typewriter sort). As you play this the sequencer records the tone and duration of the notes (but not any actual notes). This creates a series of MIDI instructions which the sequencer can use to drive the keyboard itself or any other MIDI device, including triggering a sample. Classic controller keyboards are synths like the Korg M1 (now discontinued, but still easy to find), the Nord Lead (both Leftfield and Chemical Brothers use this) and Roland A-33. Fatar and BCK make keyboards starting around £100, while a basic Roland is about £300.

254

You don't have to use a keyboard, MIDI controllers include drum pads from Akai or Roland; you could even use a MIDI guitar.

Samplers

The cornerstone of modern dance music, a sampler is simply a machine that records sound digitally without tape. Most people use an AKAI, a firm which has been making samplers for years; they're now up to the S5000 and S6000 models. Fatboy Slim claims he recorded the whole of his last album using two AKAI S950s, a sampler so old it comes fitted with a teasmade.

Drum machines

For more than you'll ever need to know about drum machines, plus downloadable samples, visit the Drum Machine Museum at:
www.drummachine.com

Studio monitors

Speakers to you (very precise ones). If you want to upgrade from your normal hi-fi ones you'll need to spend at least £300. Yamaha NS10s are very popular in home and professional studios (almost an industry-standard piece of kit).

Online equipment outlets

www.synthesisers.co.uk
Hardware and software and a great links page.
www.digitalvillage.co.uk
Hardware and software.
www.soundslive.co.uk
Hardware, software and traditional instruments.

Secondhand gear

Sound On Sound www.soundonsound.com/adverts
An excellent readers' ads section.
Vintage Synths www.vintagesynth.org
For those of you who get strange trouser movements at the mere mention of TBR-303s and AKAI S950s.
eBay www.ebay.co.uk
Did we mention we're addicted to eBay?

'To get started I bought about nine grand's worth of equipment. That night my friends all came over and laughed at me. "Stupid mother-fucker bought all this shit and don't even know how to play nothin'." Because of all their abuse I made my first track after only two days.'

Marshall Jefferson

255

Hiring a real studio

'I get started with a bunch of pretty melodies, put it to a hard beat and bassline, and take out all the melody after the song is done. Those pretty pianos? You'll never hear them on the record. I use them to make the track but then I take them out and I put in some harder elements. It's a trick actually.'

Todd Terry

This option requires the least effort on your part, although you'll need some wodge instead – you'll be lucky to hire a studio for less than £100 per day (top-of-the-range places are more like £250 per *hour*). If you just want to fiddle about with some samples, it would be much cheaper to do it at home. On the other hand, a real studio has some major advantages.

- Better access to good equipment.
- An engineer who instantly knows how to do things. Behind every successful DJ/producer there is invariably a talented (and unrecognised) engineer.
- Essential for live instruments or vocalists (like your concept album with the London Philharmonic strings and full Baptist choir).
- Fuller, bigger, better sound.

Finding a studio

Look under RECORDING SERVICES – SOUND in your local Yellow Pages. What you pay depends largely on what equipment it has. The more channels it can record (eg '24-track', '48-track'), the more expensive it'll be. Unless you're recording live instrumentation or vocals, it's possible to make and mix a track in a day.

What you're looking for

- Get the rates from each studio and make sure they include an engineer.
- Ask if they have cheaper 'downtime' rates (usually through the night).
- Make sure the studio is equipped to make dance music (you don't want to turn up and find Iron Maiden packing up their gear).
- If possible, find an engineer sympathetic to your style of music; a good engineer will vastly improve the sound (and probably content) of your track.

How to prepare

- Go in ready to start recording – don't waste expensive studio time trying to come up with ideas.
- Bring all of the samples you want to use (if they're on vinyl, check the studio has a turntable).
- If there are other tracks you've nicked ideas from (for arrangements, breakdowns, rhythm patterns...), bring them to play to the engineer, even if you don't need to actually sample them.
- Sketch a plan of how the track appears in your head. Draw a horizontal line with groups of bars across it representing the structure of your song. Most sequencing programs (eg Cubase) have a similar graphic look.

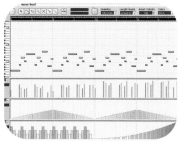

'Before, if you couldn't play notes or you couldn't sing then you couldn't make music. Now all you've got to be able to do is type. If you can type, then you can make records, produce them, remix them.'

Norman Jay

What do I say to the engineer?

Don't be afraid of his superhuman grasp of technology – he has a mother just like you do. If you're a complete studio virgin, admit it right away – you're paying him to be cleverer than you so why fake anything? When you arrive, have a chat and tell him what you're looking for. Play him your samples and any other tunes you're ripping off and say, 'Something like this.' Let him take control of the process, but make sure you're in charge of what things sound like.

Who's the musician?

Provided you have strong ideas of how your music should sound, you don't need to be able to play an instrument. However, you will need someone to tap in a few notes on the keyboard (most likely the engineer). You can always correct it on the sequencer later so they hardly have to be Gershwin. When Marshall Jefferson played the piano for 'Move Your Body' he was so useless he recorded it at half-tempo and speeded it up afterwards.

257

How to make a remix

For most dance producers remixing is the same as making a track, except they start with some ready-made bits from an existing song.

Remix vs re-edit

A re-edit is a finished song cut up and rearranged like a patchwork, with some passages repeated and others removed. See p244 *How to make a re-edit*. A remix is made from the separate components (vocals, percussion, bassline, etc) lifted from the original multi-track recording.

How close to the original

This is a matter of choice (and record company 'suggestions'). Some remixers keep much of the original song intact, just adding a few new elements and removing others (and maybe changing the tempo). Some might use only the vocal track and float it over some beats they made themselves. At the most extreme, a remixer might make a completely new track but throw in a tiny snippet – a guitar lick, half a word, a horn blast – from the original.

How do I get to do a remix?

- Be cheeky. If there's a song you really like, call up the A&R department of the record company and ask if you can do a mix 'on spec'. This means they're not committed to paying you anything – unless they like it and decide to release it. They may at least send you some parts to work from.
- Approach DJ organisations like DMC that produce remix packages for DJs every month. They're always on the look-out for hot young talent. DMC 01628 667124.

'I try to live with a song before I go into the studio. I start to hear it in my sleep and a lot of the string and rhythm arrangements come to me. So when I get into the studio I know if I'm going to embellish the song or if I want to strip away everything except the vocals and reconstruct it.'

Frankie Knuckles

258

Sound engineering courses

These will teach you the basics of sound engineering and help you start making tracks, but you'd need a lot more than a weekend course to qualify you for a job in a studio.

Music Education Directory
www.bpi-med.co.uk
The British Phonograph Industry's database of popular music courses.

The Recording Workshop
www.recordwk.dircon.co.uk
Based in West London. Various specialist modules (around £300 each).

The Academy of Music & Sound
www.theacademy.uk.com
Studios in Birmingham, Torquay and Hartlepool, running various accredited courses, including BTEC (around £800).

Manchester MIDI School
www.midischool.com
Everything from weekend courses (£315 for two weekends) to full-time (£2,475 for nine-month course). They can help you find funding.

Touch IMW
www.imw.co.uk
London-based, with courses from £200 (just £100 if you're unwaged).

Books and magazines

The Manual (How To Have A Number One The Easy Way)
In 1988 Jimmy Cauty and Bill Drummond (the KLF) delivered their manifesto for the future of music. Despite its age, this tiny book remains an essential text for sample-based hit-making. Cynical, enthusiastic, hilarious.

Computer Music
www.computermusic.co.uk
An excellent techie's magazine. Great for information on new packages, upgrades, downloads, expert advice and free cover mounts.

Future Music www.futuremusic.co.uk
Groovier competitor to SOS. Similar to Computer Music.

Sound On Sound
www.soundonsound.com
The drier elder statesman of music technology magazines. Their brilliant website stocks editor Paul White's books which we also recommend: strong guidance without confusing jargon.

Websites

www.tweakheadz.com
Great source of information for anything remotely connected to studio production, including excellent step-by-step beginner guides.

www.sharewaremusicmachine.com
Musicians' site with heaps of software and hardware advice. Parts are members-only (around $60 a year), but there's a lively and useful noticeboard: **www.hitsquad.com/smm/wwwboard** for techie queries and conundrums.

www.futureproducers.com
www.musicianstechcentral.com
Diverse American-based site that covers all styles of music, but has a DJ section. Lots of links to free downloads.

www.recording.org
Excellent central resource, created by musicians for musicians, with a very active bulletin board offering advice on all aspects of music, from studio software to which strings Jimi Hendrix used on his Stratocaster.

www.dancetech.com
Vast and phenomenal site with reviews, forums, downloads, samples, links and interactive tutorials... and more!

www.musicplayer.com
From a group of US magazines, Music Player Network is a vast site aimed at producers and musicians of all levels. Endless advice and information.

46. **How to** release a record

You've finished your track, mixed it down, dubbed it on to a DAT or CD and want to unleash it on the world. It's a hit – you're convinced of that. But what do you do next?

How to press up white labels

The quickest way to get a record on to the streets. Avoid all the trappings of bureaucracy (and legality). Bang it out and see who salutes.

Brokers

A one-stop shop: they'll take your track and artwork, sort out mastering, deal with the pressing plant and present you with finished vinyl. These days pressing plants are mostly on the Continent, so turnaround can take as long as four weeks.

Magic Wand 01784 253534
Uses UK-based plants. Costs start at around 58p per unit, plus £70 processing per side (plus VAT). Minimum order is 1,000.

COPS 020 8778 8556
Based in Bromley. Acts as agent for two pressing plants in France. They can produce 500 white labels for around £600 (plus VAT).

Impress Music 020 8795 0101
Prices change all the time; call for current rates. Presses for Ninja Tune, Azuli and, er, Oasis.

Mastering

Mastering is where a sound engineer with valuable ears gets your track ready for the pressing plant. A broker can sort this out but many producers organise it themselves and 'attend the cut'. It's about getting the EQ and volume levels of your track as perfect as possible to bring out the different elements and eliminate any distortion. Good mastering will make your track sound vastly better, even if you thought it sounded pretty good already. The 'cut' creates a 'lacquer' which is used to make the metal stampers (the vinyl equivalent of a jelly mould).

The Exchange 020 7485 0530
Masterpiece 020 7731 5758
Town House 020 8932 3200
Whitfield Street Studios 020 7636 3434

Test pressings

TPs usually come as part of the package (check that they do). Your last chance to rectify any mistakes before the plant presses your order. Listen for drops in volume and pops and clicks. Always insist on 'virgin' vinyl for your records.

How to distribute your record

Get those boxes of vinyl out of your kitchen and into the shops.

Do it yourself
Lug your records around independent dance stores. London is your best bet, where all stores regularly take stock from walk-in customers on SOR (sale or return). They'll listen to the tune, give you a receipt for any they take, and you come back to collect the proceeds. There's no guarantee they'll sell any, but a mysterious white label builds a fine buzz.

Independent distributors
These guys operate from white-van mini-warehouses and provide the bulk of the records you see in your local store. Send them a copy of your tune. Wait a week, then call to find out if they're keen. The average distributor only takes on about 10% of the material they are sent, but any hype and promotion you can do in advance will increase your chances.

Amato 020 8838 8330
Distributes Junior, Bedrock, Newkleuz, Tidy Trax, Anodyne...

Essential Direct 020 7375 2332
Distributes Strictly Underground, Relentless, So Solid, Public Demand, Bingo, Platipus...

Unique 01204-393710
Distributes Dorigen, Envision, Poodle, Rotunda...

How to promote your record

Let the world know it exists. A great white label in the right stores will create its own word-of-mouth. After that, promotion is about trying to get radio and club play plus DJ charts and editorial coverage (magazines reviews and features). A professional promotions company will have names, addresses and phone numbers of everyone you want to reach, plus personal relationships with the right DJs and journalists.

Rocketscience 020 7033 4000
Underground house, techno and electronica. To mail out 120 records (25 to press, 15 to radio and 80 to DJs), costs around £375 (plus VAT). Used by 2020 Vision, F Com, Tortured, Tummy Touch, Novamute...

Zzonked 020 8503 1880
Hip hop, drum & bass, breakbeats, electronica and downtempo. Promotion to DJs costs around £2.65 per record (plus VAT). Used by Compost, Talking Loud, Source, Dada, Ninja Tunes, Warp...

White Noise 020 7729 3320
Everything from underground house, downtempo, electronica to crossover dance. £2.60p per record (+ VAT) or for 50 records (the minimum) it's £150 (+ VAT). Clients include Skint, Catskills, City Rockers, Ultimate Dilemma.

How to sell a track to a label

This relies on you convincing someone that your *meisterwerk* is worth releasing. Either send them a CD of your track(s) with your contact details and some attention-grabbing packaging, or you can stick your amazing white label in the shops and sit tight.

Licensing

You never actually *sell* anyone your track. You 'license' it to them (a legal term for lending) for an agreed period of time. After that, the full rights to that piece of music will revert back to you.

A typical deal

If a label wants your track, they will send you a 'Heads of Agreement' or 'Deal Memo', which is an outline version of the contract. Once you sign this you have agreed to the deal. You don't get a full contract – many pages of legal jargon – until later. A Heads of Agreement will include:

- **Time period** Usually ranges from three years to perpetuity (never ever license anything in perpetuity – it means forever).
- **Advance** How much they'll pay you upfront for your track(s). This is 'recoupable', meaning that your initial royalties go towards paying it back. Only when your royalties have covered the label's outlay (the advance plus any ancillary costs (eg remix fees)) will you actually get any paid to you.
- **Royalty rate** The percentage you get of either the dealer price (what a store pays) or the retail price (what a customer pays). Known as 'points', short for 'percentage points'.
- **Territories** You only license a label to release your track in certain countries. If it's a hot record, only include the territory in which the label's based (eg UK & Eire). This way you're free to license the same track to other labels overseas.
- **Options** When the label signs your surefire hit, they may ask for first dibs on your next single, or even an album. This is an 'option'.
- **Third-party rights** This gives the label the right to sub-license your track to another label (if it gets so big they can't handle it, or for compilations).

Top tips

- Remember what your dad always told you and don't sign anything without a grown-up present. Get a proper music business lawyer to look over the contract. It's worth the expense. And we don't mean the solicitor who helped your aunt buy her retirement bungalow.
- If possible, don't sign under your own name. Use a production alias (eg Fatboy Slim, Aphex Twin, Tiny Trendies). This leaves you free to record for other labels under another name.
- Check out the label you're going to sign to. Make sure they have a good reputation. It's a sad fact that many labels do not pay the royalties they are legally supposed to. If artists have stuck with a label – and it doesn't just have an endless succession of new producers – it's a sign they're keeping people happy.
- Make sure you have a clause giving you remix approval. All those pricey Puff Daddy and David Morales remixes? They're coming out of your royalties, baby!

If only I'd got some advice

The music industry is littered with talented saps who've been ripped off because they simply didn't understand what they were doing when they started out. The way the industry works can be frighteningly complex and anyone who doesn't pay attention to what they are signing could well lose thousands of pounds from bad deals. Don't be one of them. Question everything, assume nothing, make sure you understand what you're agreeing to. The music biz is famously corrupt and a healthy level of paranoia is definitely good for you.

All You Need To Know About The Music Business
by Donald S. Passman
www.donpassman.com
This great book will help you understand things better. Although it's written for an American audience (UK entertainment law can be slightly different), it's witty, concise and easy to read.

Copyright, samples and bootlegs

Copyright

Usually, when someone creates something original – a book, a movie, a piece of music – they own the 'copyright' to it. This means that, by law, no-one else can come along and copy it. There are two kinds of copyright in a record.

- The song (that was written by the songwriter).
- The performance (that was recorded onto the record).

Bootlegs

A bootleg is any recording that breaks copyright law – from illegally copied albums made for pure profit to your wonderful dance tune with its tiny uncleared Boyzone sample. In the dance world 'boot-leg' is mostly used to refer to records that use blatant samples of big artists or famous songs.

Sampling

Whenever you use bits of existing recordings to make a new piece of music, it's 'sampling'. Old buffers and dad-rock fans argue that this new-fangled idea is killing music. Bollocks. Nicking someone else's music to make a new tune is as old as music itself; it's just that before the Akai 3000 came along you had to do it on a guitar and it was harder to prove.

How to sample without going to jail

When you sample someone else's record, unless they give permission, you are infringing their copyright and breaking the law. Getting their permission is called 'clearing' the sample and usually means paying them money. Luckily for you, no one's too concerned if you make a little record using uncleared samples. Everyone does it. However, people will start to get very interested once you make any real money from it. If a song looks like it might cross over into the pop charts you should definitely worry about sample clearance.

>> **Clear samples before your record's a hit**
Wait until after your tune's blown up in the clubs and you'll get stung. When Fatboy Slim failed to clear the string sample in 'Right Here, Right Now' he had to concede all of the publishing rights to The James Gang, the band that wrote the track he sampled.

264

>> ## Watch it Stateside

Few UK dance labels bother to clear samples (few could afford to), and the industry here is relatively laid back about it. But the USA does not take such a sanguine approach – sample James Brown at your peril, son!

>> ## Offset a sample with an original composition

If you release a big tune with an expensive sample on it, write a (sample-free) track yourself to go on the same record. However bad it is, this self-penned track will make you song writing royalties to offset the royalties you've lost through the blatant Abba sample on the main track.

How to clear a sample

You have to negotiate with whoever owns the copyright and pay them either money or a share of the new record's royalties in order to get permission to use the sample. Certain artists may refuse permission altogether (some old coots will regard you as a musical burglar).

The basic rule is very simple: the more you sample, the less you'll earn. You'll end up giving away some or all of your publishing royalties and you'll have to share a songwriting credit with the old rockers whose guitar riff you nicked. If they are very famous old rockers and you've sampled a very famous guitar riff, expect to pay a whole lot more than if it's a two-bar loop from an obscure funk record. In some extreme cases (eg if you've sampled two different tracks) you may even end up paying more than 100% of the publishing royalties to someone else. Think carefully before you raid your dad's Stones collection.

Replay it

If they can't clear a sample, producers sometimes get a band to recreate it. This might sound identical, but legally it's a cover version, not a sample.

Sample clearance

These guys will sort it out for you. It's not always quick.

Sample Clearance 01273 326999 www.sampleclearance.com Clients include Skint, Wall Of Sound, Azuli and most major labels, plus artists including Gorillaz, Jamiroquai, David Holmes, DJ Shadow and Fatboy Slim.

Music Admin www.musicadmin.com Northern-based company whose clients include Belgian label R&S, plus lots of artists whose names they keep confidential.

265

Publishing and royalties

The real cash in music is in songwriting. The wealthiest musicians are filthy rich because they write songs as well as perform them. Publishing is the industry that collects money (royalties) on behalf of songwriters for the use of their songs. A hundred years ago, publishers made their money from the sheet music your gran bought to play on the old joanna. Nowadays they make it from anyone (record labels, advertisers, movies, manufactured cover bands) who want to use other people's songs. Once a publisher is interested, get a lawyer to sort it out.

Publishing royalties

- **Performance** Money you get each time someone plays your song in public, eg on the radio or in a club.
- **Mechanicals** Money you get each time someone (eg a record company) makes a physical copy of your song.
- **Sheet music** Money you get each time someone prints a paper copy of your song.
- **Synchs** Money you get each time someone uses your music for things like advertising or soundtracks.

If you have no publishing deal
Print 'Copyright Control' on your records. This is a warning to copyright thieves and also an ad to potential publishers, because it says, 'I haven't got a publishing deal, but I'm open to offers.'

Join an established publisher
Eg Warner-Chappell or Universal. Could make you some money and bring greater exposure.

Set up your own publishing company
You keep control of your copyrights, but it's an extra amount of admin and your songs won't get the push a big publisher can give them.

Get an administration deal
You keep control but someone manages your songs on commission.

Let your label organise it
Quite common, but actually a conflict of interest. Your label will be collecting your publishing royalties from itself.

266

UK publishing royalties are collected by ...
- MCPS (Mechanical Copyright Protection Society)
- PRS (Performing Rights Society)

These operate in tandem as the MCPS-PRS Alliance (020 7580 5544). They license public places in which music is played and collect money for the songwriters. You have to be a member to benefit.

> For more advice about publishing
> **Music Publishers Association**
> 020 7839 7779 www.mpaonline.org.uk
> email: info@mpaonline.org.uk

American copyright organisations
- ASCAP www.ascap.com
- BMI www.bmi.com

How to start your own label

Since the punk DIY revolution, independent labels have been the creative life-force of the British music industry. Ear to the ground, nose to the grindstone – running a label puts you at the centre of the action.

As a P&D deal
This stands for 'pressing and distribution', and that's what you get. The idea is that you run your label within the security of an existing one. You scout the talent, choose the tracks and artwork and organise the promotion. And in return for a slice of your profits, your parent label lets you use its established manufacturing and distribution network (two areas where a tiny independent could otherwise easily get shafted). It's like instead of an artist, they've signed a label. You won't have to sleep on unsold records and there's no huge capital outlay on your part. However, P&D deals usually go to people sitting pretty at the heart of a particular genre or scene – established producers, successful A&R people or powerful DJs.

As a stand-alone independent
This is the big one. Here you'll need to have a proper business head with a proper business plan and some proper start-up money. You won't leave the office for the first three years, and the risk of failure is high. However, you keep full control of your music and your release schedules, you take a larger cut of the profits and maybe one day you can buy an island off Richard Branson.

Small Business Service www.businesslink.org
Advice on all aspects of starting a UK business.

47. **How to** be a girl

It shouldn't be an issue whether you arrive in possession of a willie or a fanny as long as you show up with your records. Sadly, as any female DJ knows, it is. Clubland is far more likely to champion women's cleavage than women's equality. You're going to change all that. Say it loud: 'I'm not *with* the DJ; I *am* the DJ.'

The situation

DJing has always been a little boys' club. The modern profession emerged in seventies New York, when women in straight clubs were seen as decorative accessories, and women in gay clubs (where most of the action was) were rarely seen at all. And like most crafts in which there's a long apprenticeship, DJ skills have been passed down the male line in near-masonic secrecy. Wider cultural biases didn't help either. While boys were encouraged to play with gadgets and technology, the notion of girls tampering with anything that wasn't a typewriter, cooker or cash till is, sadly, relatively new.

The good news

DJing's maleness is largely a historical thing, and the proportion of DJs who are women, while still small, is growing rapidly. Although the UK DJ Premiership is still a boys-only arena, Lottie is knocking at the door and the First Division now includes DJs like Lisa Lashes and Anne Savage. Acid house veterans like Smokin' Jo, Lisa Loud, Sister Bliss and Rachel Auburn are still wowing the crowds, and even in the far more sexist US, women like Sandra Collins, Jeannie Hopper and DJ Heather are breaking through, following trailblazers like Teri Bristol, DJ Moneypenny, Anita Sarko and Susan Moribito. Newer forms of music have less ingrained prejudices. 'Techno and drum 'n' bass – those scenes are more open to female DJs,' says New York's DJ Cosmo. 'These girls grew up with computers and electronics, so it was no big deal to them.' Sure enough, drum & bass gave us DJ Rap and Kemistry & Storm, while the UK garage scene is producing talented female DJs like Donna Dee and DJ Touch. 'Things are changing,' says Cosmo. 'It's not that big a deal to be a female DJ any more and I think that's great. The less people ask me about it the better.'

How you can help yourself

Abuse your 'rarity value'

You have a huge advantage over your male brethren: novelty! Promoters care more about marketability than music, and a woman DJ on the bill gives them something different. Forget the politics of why you got a gig and rejoice in the fact that you got it. Take advantage – any DJ starting out needs every bit of help they can get. Now blow away any charges of tokenism by showing them you have the skills to match.

Play girls-only nights

Take the pressure off by playing (or creating) events/nights/a room where female DJs are the norm. Power up together with some sisters and show that while your dancefloor is red hot, your sex is no big deal. Promoters see all-girl nights as a marketable idea, and as long as they're promoted tastefully, you're not compromising yourself in any way.

Be part of a scene

Any DJ has an advantage if they're inside a close-knit scene. Whether based around a particular place or a specific genre, it gives them the support network they need to develop. Underground scenes can be very supportive of women, though you'll have to prove yourself worthy.

Do it yourself

Throughout this book, our advice is to get off your arse. Don't wait for favours and don't expect anyone to 'discover' you. If you find it difficult to break into an existing scene, build your own. Throw your own parties, promote your own nights; don't depend on anyone but yourself and your mates.

Be a show-off

Fight any feminine tendencies to be humble and retiring. If you want to DJ, do it. 'Women tend not to put themselves in the spotlight or make fools of themselves,' says New York DJ Lucy Walker. 'Music was always a private passion for me. It was only recently that I went more public with it. I think this happens with a lot of women.'

'I used to dress quite scruffily. I wanted to be sure I was getting booked because I was a good DJ, not because I looked nice.'

Lottie

269

What you should expect

It's tough for everyone
You're going to have to struggle to break into DJing whatever your sex. Maybe the goalposts are further if you're a girl, but they're pretty distant for boys, too.

Expect to be judged harder
Thanks to the relative novelty of a girl behind the decks, you will get more attention than a male DJ of a similar standard, and you'll have your share of dumb beer-boys watching keenly for you to mess up. How to deal with the extra pressure? All you can do is be excellent. It cuts both ways, though – if all eyes are on you, your mind-blowing set will make even more of an impression.

Expect to be patronised
A guy in a record store asks if you're sure about a record; a warm-up DJ takes a little too long explaining the booth set-up; a promoter expects you to be grateful for the gig. A DJ is a very controlling role, and sometimes this is hard for the men in the room to deal with. Women DJs often notice a sound engineer or another DJ giving them far more 'assistance' than their male counterparts – tweaking the sound levels, checking equipment. You have to expect this kind of nonsense. Rise above it. Laugh. Prove how unnecessary it was.

How to approach DJing

Be confident, informed, obsessed
The industry no longer finds good women DJs a huge surprise; what does impress is a woman who can hold her own in obsessive trainspotting and shop-talk. When the subject turns to studio gear or editing software or records, records, records, you're going to floor them with your knowledge.

Embrace technology
When your brother got a Scalextric you got a My Little Pony. When you asked for a chemistry set you got another fucking Barbie. Now you're free from all that pink-for-girls shit. DJing and technology go hand in hand and whether it's streaming media, signal-to-noise ratios or MIDI, you've got to love the machine.

Be competitive
Never before was DJing so hard to break into. You've got to be ruthless whatever sex you are. Grrrls don't take no for an answer.

270

Dare to be dolly?

Most women shudder at the idea of using their looks to get ahead. 'I think it's really unfortunate that some female DJs exploit their sex to get work,' says London's DJ Touch. 'It's important to be good at what you do and not rely on getting recognition because you're a woman.' She's absolutely right – if you want respect for your music, no-one's going to give it to you because you're wearing a push-up bra and hotpants.

However, if you just want to get out there, maybe the issue is not so cut and dried. In the spirit of disco terrorism, any method that gets you gigs is worth considering. If you're a great DJ who's desperate to crash through that glass ceiling, what's wrong with using sex appeal to get where you want? Provided you have talent to win respect once you get on the decks, maybe it's a 'by any means necessary' situation.

DJ Dazy, who runs an email forum for women DJs, agrees, though she insists that if you adopt this tactic to get ahead, you'd better have the skills to justify yourself. 'Do whatever you want to do, as long as you can cut it up on the decks. Just don't wear a bikini top while you're train-wrecking records. If you don't have the skills, don't embarrass the rest of us women DJs who have worked really hard to get where we are.'

'I have always kept my gender separate from my DJing. The name DJ Touch does not give away any detail about me being a woman – I cringe when people call me Lady Touch – it just freaks me out!'

DJ Touch

More information

www.shejay.net
Vibrant international site with wide variety of content.

www.sistersf.com
A San Francisco female DJ collective. Sound advice on all aspects of DJing from a female perspective.

www.wigmag.com
Website from NYC's Women In General magazine. Includes interviews with several female New York DJs.

www.pinknoises.com
NY-based writer/musician with lots of DJ-related interviews/articles.

48. **How to** play bigger gigs

'On tour' used to mean four spotty lads with guitars piled in a Transit with a mattress in the back. Now it means a permanent tan, a taste for Virgin choc-ices, mates all over the world and an aching shoulder on your record bag side.

How to break out of Norwich

'I was always the guy from the countryside. You have to work at least twice as hard when you're living away from the big cities and you don't have contacts.'

Timo Maas, *Muzik*

Or Ullapool, or Bedford, or Market Rasen... If you thought it was hard to get out of your bedroom, wait till you try to get an out-of-town gig. Sadly, the only reason anyone in the outside world will book a small-town DJ is if you have something amazing that they can't get at home.

- Be mindblowingly different.
- Move to the big city.

Most opportunities to play guest spots, like everything in the DJ world, come from personal contacts. So network, kiddo! Be friendly, meet people and infiltrate a big-city scene. Make sure you have business cards and/or a mix to give people (even when you're playing home-town gigs – you never know who might drop in). And try our little guerrilla tactic...

Peer-to-peer guest spots
You're the top DJ in a little town in Wales. You play the big Saturday night there but nowhere else will give you the time of day. Meanwhile, in a small town in Finland, Elli has exactly the same problem. Her 'Moomin' parties are the hottest thing around, but like you she's a big fish stuck in a tiny pond. Suddenly, with a sprinkling of internet magic, you become the best of online friends. After meeting on a DJ bulletin board, you exchange tapes, you love each other's music and agree to give each other a guest spot. So instead of hitting Magaluf you jet off to Helsinki, take a train deep into the Finnish forests and become an international DJ overnight. (Six months later you settle down together in Lapland to raise reindeer.) Get on those bulletin boards and plan your world tour. (Be careful, though – make sure Elli isn't secretly a middle-aged DJ-molester.)

How to play an out-of-town gig

Pack your box carefully

The most important thing is to be ready for an unfamiliar crowd. Don't just cross your fingers – put some effort into finding out what the night is like and what music they'll be expecting. They may want it harder, deeper or more commercial than you're used to playing. Be aware that other cities and countries often use genre terms slightly differently; make allowances for promoters who can't describe music very accurately; and double-check by asking other people (ideally other DJs who've played there). Take a much wider selection than usual, with more records than you need, and if you can play them, a big stack of CDs, too.

Get a contract

It shows you mean business. It's best to use your own contracts. Send two copies out with your signature on and ask the promoter to sign them both and mail one back to you. You're not fully booked until you get it back, with a deposit (50% of your fee). Leave the contract at home but take a photocopy to wave at the promoter. For a sample contract, see p288.

Travelling expenses

Unless you're flying, promoters hardly ever pay for travel within the UK. However, if you're playing for less than normal or for free, your expenses should be taken care of. Don't buy a train ticket until everything's confirmed.

Accommodation

It might be a hotel, a B&B, or a sleeping bag next to the promoter's dog basket. They may have hooked you up or they may be expecting you to fend for yourself. Ask. Don't assume anything.

Get there early

Make sure you know exactly where you're going and have at least two phone numbers to call when you get there. Allow lots of extra time for the inevitable flat tyres, late trains, rubbish maps, wrong addresses, floods, tornadoes, wars, etc.

Driving

Don't be stupid. If you know you'll drink, snort or take bonkers conkers, plan to stay over rather than drive back. And don't make plans which depend on staying sober and awake when you know you never will.

273

How to play abroad

All the out-of town advice applies (times ten). Have a passport, of course, a visa and/or working permit, if required, and a return ticket to prove you're coming back. Is someone meeting you at the airport?

Work permits

UK nationals can visit and work in any EU country, no problem. Anywhere else, check the rules with their embassy. In some countries even DJing for free counts as working. It's always the responsibility of the promoter to organise work permits. Don't take off without one in your hand. Being busted for not having the right paperwork means you'll be barred from that country for a number of years. The xenophobic USA is the hardest to arrange. For more on working abroad:

www.direct.gov.uk/BritonsLivingAbroad
Government advice, innit.
www.support4learning.org.uk/jobsearch/working_abroad_ _overseas_ _from_the_uk_ _
_international_work_opportunities.cfm
Limited advice but extensive links.

Contract

You might risk having no contract for gigs in your own country, but for overseas work they are essential. If things go wrong abroad it can cost you plenty, and a contract means at least you'll get paid. Don't fly without one and stash a copy at home.

Records

All airlines will insist your record box is insured and as safe as houses. But you've got a lot to lose if it gets 'misdirected' by a vinyl junkie baggage handler. If you're checking it, use a sturdy, lockable box that looks as boring as possible, with your name and address all over it, inside and out. A good antitheft idea is to disguise your box by taping it up inside a cardboard box. Maybe take your most prized records (ie the hardest to replace) in a shoulder bag so you can play a set whatever happens. The airline's Customer Service (or an extra nice flight crew) may let you take your box as hand luggage. It depends how busy the flight is. And get some wheels for it.

A second ticket

You have to be big before your mate or lover comes free. Women have a better chance because they are less likely to want to travel alone. Unless you're First Division, dahling, you'll be in cattle class with the rest of us.

274

How to play stadiums and festivals

If you've reached this stage it's a good bet that you're a household name. This makes things very easy because the crowd will go crazy for you however rubbish you are. Get their attention by building a set with lots of changes, fresh starts and reliable big-room tunes. The larger the crowd, the harder it is to see how they're reacting or how the atmosphere is building, although once you've got them going there'll be a lot of momentum. If it's a festival, make sure your rider includes a Winnebago with a jacuzzi and satellite positioning so you can find it when you're stumbling back naked from the tent with the Pontefract acid dealer.

How to open for a rock band

Play tunes you know their fans will like (cover versions or records by similar groups), but avoid playing any of the band's actual songs. This is because the records were made when they were 20 years younger and will sound miles better than their actual performance. The only exceptions are songs from their early career that they are completely embarrassed about. How could you warm up for David Bowie without playing 'The Laughing Gnome'?

How to play celebrity parties

Apart from a few renowned party monsters, celebs are dull as dishwater on the dancefloor and have the musical taste of bus drivers. Fashion parties are the worst. Treat celeb bashes like weddings: make sure you have obvious chart tunes and any records connected with the event or with people who might be there.

How to get into a helicopter without looking foolish

Duck a little but not too much. Try to act nonchalant, like it's a Fiesta.

'I DJed at the Spice Girls' album launch and played Spiller's "Groovejet", forgetting that it had just beaten Posh's debut single. It was a big track at the time so everyone was going nuts – except the Spice Girls. They came over and stared at me and told me they were never using me again.'

Sam Totalee, DJ to the stars, *Mixmag*

275

49. **How to** be famous

Plenty of great DJs get by without being famous. They concentrate on their music and don't worry about celebrity status unless their talent brings it knocking. But you're young, you're foolish, you want the world at your feet and a mink-lined swimming pool.

How to generate fame

Make a track. Make a track. Make a track. The fastest way to get yourself known is to make a fantastic track that charts (or a crap track that charts). You may be a lousy DJ but people will flock to hear you because of your record. This illustrates the basic rule: being a famous DJ often has nothing to do with being a good DJ; it is much more about getting exposure and being marketable.

Name recognition is your goal. Get on as many flyers as possible and fool people into thinking you deserve their attention. Be pushy and get higher billing than you deserve. Hire a publicist. A good one will think of endless stunts to get you in the pages of the dance mags. Being messy or a 'character' and causing 'incidents' is tried and trusted, as is celebrity shagging/thumping. DJ PLAYS AMAZING SET is hardly news, but DJ SPINS NUDE or DJ SLAUGHTERS GOAT DURING IAN VAN DAHL BREAKDOWN might be worth a few column inches in *iDJ*.

And marketability. Sad to say but an averagely talented one-armed DJ who does lesbian porn movies in her spare time will immediately get more bookings than an averagely talented DJ who has his own plumbing business. Don't go chopping limbs off, but think up a USP (Unique Selling Point) for yourself. Top ruse is claiming your music is a new genre. The mags are so scared of missing the boat (like they did with jungle) that they will immediately hail you as the saviour of dance music. Speed something up a bit or play bad records for people who can't tell the difference, then simply coin a new name: 'handbag hip hop', 'polka trance', 'weekend breaks' are all up for grabs. You'll soon be getting on famously.

How to sustain fame

Much easier – once you're on the gravy train it's hard to fall off. Celebrity DJs enjoy a lot of clout so you'll be sent all the best records well ahead of the pack. You'll get peak slots where you're expected to play big tunes, so you won't even need to work too hard on your set. And unless you're stupid, you'll have set up endless remixes, a label deal, a radio show, a few advertising endorsements, a management/publishing company and all the other intertwined business interests of the average superjock. If you were good to begin with, remember that believing your own hype will quickly erode your talent. Don't forget to change your style completely whenever your genre looks like it's going to fall from favour.

276

Fame or greatness?

We've been a little scathing about the pursuit of fame, but the choice is yours. Is it a frantic scrabble into the *DJmag* top 100, or do you prefer to bide your time and perfect your craft? To start on the long path toward true greatness, follow the tips on the left. To be successful at any cost, follow the tips on the right.

Great DJ	Ruthless DJ
Do it to share great music with people.	Do it to be famous, rich and more sexually attractive.
Be yourself.	Get an image.
Concentrate on finding great music.	Concentrate on getting in the dance press.
Learn the history of the music you love and buy classic records.	Try to jump on the next big thing before anyone else.
Find floorfillers that no one else will ever get hold of.	Find floorfillers that everyone else will play, but get to them first.
Have fiercely individual taste and carve out a unique style that no one can easily describe.	Make sure your style can be pigeon-holed so dumb promoters don't have to think too hard.
Don't restrict yourself to a narrow style of music.	Figure out upcoming trends and play lots of records from that genre.
Take risks with strange and unfamiliar records.	Play only what you're sure the crowd will approve of.
Have fun; imagine yourself on the dancefloor.	Take it seriously; imagine yourself in *Mixmag*.

50. **How to** be great

Putting a roomful of people in the moment; amazing them, surprising them, challenging, even confusing them; teasing, loving, electrifying them; carrying them with you towards a higher place; shaking the dull daylight out of their bones and waking them into their other life. You don't need telling how much power and mastery a DJ can exercise. That's why you're reading this book.

Express yourself

Greatness? It's about showing your personality. It's about being unique. It's about taking music made by somebody else and making it undeniably, demonstrably *yours*. Own your own style. Know who you are musically. Have a sound that could come from no other DJ. On a purely commercial level a distinctive style makes you marketable. In a more personal sense it's an essential part of being creative. 'A good DJ should show where they're coming from,' insists Mr Scruff. 'They should reveal their influences and stamp their personality on a performance. A bad DJ will put technique before the choice of music, and box themselves in with preconceptions about how and what they play.' Only play what you love. Play tracks that excite you and move you. Don't play records – however amazing or effective – if you don't feel some kind of connection to them.

Make records yours

When you start DJing, the records you buy will define your style. But once you find your feet your style will define the records you buy. The ultimate is to have such a signature style that when people hear a record they connect it to you or your club rather than to the producer that made it – 'That's a real Digweed record' or 'That's a classic Sound Factory tune'. As Tony Humphries points out: 'Anybody can play last week's hits and have people screaming. But people won't remember you; they'll remember the records. You have to make them think, "That's the record I heard Tony play at Zanzibar." If you don't do that, who are you?'

'There's a lot of fun when you're DJing. Seeing people dance. Seeing what records make them get frenzied and let the God spirit travel out of their body. It's the thrill of just controlling the music and seeing the people on the dancefloor partying, or just playing some records that makes them think, or some that makes them just shake their booty.'

Afrika Bambaataa

Develop your tastes

Music, not mixing, is your prime concern. The most common mistake young DJs make is to perfect the technical side without ever developing their musical taste buds. Established DJs do it, too: ploughing their way through an impeccably stitched landscape of upfront but uninspiring (or overfamiliar) tunes. 'Sadly, a DJ's technical ability has become more important to a lot of people than taste in music,' says Terry Farley. 'Don't think that being technically perfect and having every record Pete Tong played last week in your box makes you a good DJ.'

Show your feelings

'The thrill of DJing is being able to express myself,' says DJ Pierre. 'So the best thing is to have a crowd that lets me express everything I'm feeling.' We're all emotional beings and music is an emotionally charged artform, so let your records speak for you. Play a track that reflects a certain emotion and there'll be someone in the crowd who feels the same way and understands why you're playing that tune. 'Big record after big record – that's going to work anyway,' says Mick Wilson of Parks & Wilson. 'If you want to make it a bit more special and memorable you have to put in a little bit of yourself and how you're feeling.'

Share your excitement

Please yourself? Sure, as long as you please others along the way. DJing is about sharing music. Do it for purely selfish reasons and you'll get so far but no further. 'Do it because you love it,' insists Funkmaster Flex. 'When I hear a DJ who says, "I'm going to blow up and get paid," I think, that's not going to happen. But do it because you love it and you always get better.' Approach it right and DJing is its own reward. Norman Cook sums it up wonderfully: 'On a good night, you're in the middle of a crowd of people, a lot of whom are your mates, and you're having fun. And you're the centre of the party. And you're making them dance. And getting paid to play your favourite records. What a way to make a living!'

'DJing is a two-way effort. It's not just about me and what's in my mind. It's always about engaging contact with the crowd and feeding off them and vice versa. So you're really building a rapport. The best nights are ones where it's a team effort. You're playing with the crowd and you're bouncing off each other.'

Danny Howells

279

Enjoy your freedom

Now that the world is clogged full of DJs we need a few more wild ones. We need people to remind us that playing records is fun; that up in the booth you have a joyful freedom which you can really take advantage of. Kick off all that pressure on yourself to be clean and neat and precise. Safety = boredom. Play weird records, be a little daft, go for the unexpected and see what happens. Have a laugh, for fuck's sake. DJs who make no mistakes are just not taking enough risks. There's no safe road to paradise. You are free to do anything you like with any piece of recorded sound you can lay your hands on. Today's technology makes this so easy it's almost your duty. 'You're the key to the lock,' says DJ Dimitri. 'Behind you is the treasure room with all the records that were ever made, and before you is the dancefloor. It's up to you what you give them.' Be a kid in a candy store, not a mechanic on an assembly line.

Fight against perfection

You mixed from that weird slowing down bit in the jazzy Detroit track into an amazing funk song with a live drummer. Those two records next to each other made people literally *screammmm*. So what if the mix was pretty rough? The musical moment it created was unbelievable. Only by doing things that could go horribly wrong can you pull off amazing things that go horribly right. Experiment, take risks, try new ideas, test out weird possibilities. 'At our parties we like completely throwing the audience, giving them something they don't expect, trying to mash the sounds around as much as possible to make it alive and to put some energy into it,' says Felix Buxton of Basement Jaxx. 'If the record jumps everyone cheers because it's kind of anti the whole thing of being a smooth DJ. It's about having a good time.' So lighten up. It's music: it's for dancing. It's not major surgery. No one will die or lose an eye if you make a mistake.

'My friend taught me to look on it as a lot of fun. Not to look at it in a mechanical way, like you got to be better or you've got to innovate. Look on it more in an emotional way, like you're touching people and helping people enjoy music, and everything else will come. Your style will develop, you'll get better.'

Rob Swift

'You got to play everything; you got to move the crowd. I don't think it should all be a house set or all a drum 'n' bass set. It should just be little snippets of every-thing, a variety. A lot of DJs stopped being diverse, stopped trying new things. They started to get more safe. They probably just didn't know better.'

Todd Terry, *DJ Times*

Create your own freedom

If your audience is unadventurous it's your duty to re-educate them, not to join their ranks. Now that dance music is everywhere a real conservatism has crept in. People seem to think there's a right and a wrong way to play records. DJs worry that if they don't serve up exactly what's expected, they'll lose their place in the queue. This is bullshit. You have all the freedom in the world and if you don't you only have yourself to blame. OK, a generation of bad DJs has trained audiences to expect a snare roll every two minutes and a tempo that would wear out a bluebottle, but it's your respon-sibility to fight this, not to meekly accept it and then moan to anyone who'll listen.

Explore other genres

A great DJ should only play one kind of music – good music. Genre categories are artificial boundaries and the best DJs stride over them. Pick up great tunes whatever their style, otherwise you'll get stuck in a cupboard. Genres help us talk about music, help us describe a song or a scene, but the only reason to keep different kinds of music apart is for marketing: it makes it easier to sell tick-ets. Admittedly, as Pete Tong points out, for a DJ trying to get out there's a lot of commercial pressure to stick to a narrow style: 'It's quite sad if a DJ's starting today, and wants to make his reputation. He has to be very niche and has to have a sound. Whilst I under-stand that, I think that's quite limiting.' Damn right it's limiting. So don't stand for it. It's good for establishing yourself, but at home, at your mates' parties, once you're established, play what the hell you like. To be a great DJ you have to keep your ears open.

What great DJs can do

Get inside people's heads

For some reason a series of musical notes has the power to conjure genuine emotions. More than this, records can have powerful associations for people. Play an old record and there'll be someone in the room who's broken up to it, someone else who's fallen in love to it, someone who's cleaned up a flooded kitchen to it. Play that record and those people will feel you know them in some way. This is an illusion, of course, but it's a powerful one. The best DJs seem to do this more often, not because they have psychic powers, but because they play better records – memorable records, emotionally powerful records, records that people notice.

Play like musicians

Music has rules – about regularity and repetition, anticipation and resolution. Most of these are traditional – set down by ancient composers, ancient bluesmen and ancient African drummers. Even if you can't describe them, once you've listened to a few records and danced on a few dancefloors, you'll have felt them in action. A good DJ plays by the same rules as his records, so rhythms and melodies fit together beautifully, and mixes and changes sound as though they were part of the song. At its basic level this is about avoiding key clashes and incompatible rhythms; done with style, each record speaks to the next in an elegant musical conversation.

Respond to the audience

The greatest DJs have a sixth sense for feeling where the dancefloor wants to go. Or, more accurately, they have an acute sense of how closely the dancers are following them on their musical journey. 'A good DJ can relate to the audience,' says Gilles Peterson. 'I think that's really key. A good DJ gets inside and connects with the energy and ambience.' A lot comes from imagining yourself down on the floor – how would you be feeling if you were dancing rather than DJing? You watch their reactions to your music like it's an experiment. 'It's a very powerful position,' says Tom Middleton. 'You're taking people on an emotional rollercoaster ride. You're so lucky to have these people to play with! You have these people there to do what you want to do with them. You're a scientist.'

Create a narrative

Take me to the promised land! The best DJs use music to tell a story. They make sure one record has something to say to the next, so their rhythmic, melodic and stylistic similarities give some sense to the sequence of records and the changing energy on the dance-

282

'It's pretty damn hard to get a thousand people together and make them all happy.'

Derrick Carter

floor. Think of journeys, or of how music works in films. Even without lyrics, some tracks are about anticipation, some about action and others about resolution. For New York DJ Johnny Dynell this is the satisfaction of DJing: 'When you're creating that magic on the floor. When they've thrown their hands up in the air, and they're totally lost and abandoned into this other world. And you've taken them to that other world. That's what DJing is. Otherwise you're just playing records, which is not DJing at all.'

Recontextualise records

'A really great DJ is totally capable of making a bad record sound okay, a good record sound great, and a great record sound fantastic – by the context they put them in, and what they put around them. How they steer them.' So says former *Mixmag* Editor Dom Phillips. It's all about similarities and contrasts. A slightly discoey record will sound really discoey after a completely non-melodic track. A slow house track will sound quite zippy after an R&B number. And an ancient classic will sound pretty startling if there's a crap cover version of it currently running up the charts. The best DJs can make you listen to a song with fresh ears.

Stay excited

If DJing loses its spark you're becoming lazy and not putting in enough effort. The best DJs never lose that hunger: the drive to seek out amazing new tunes, the drive to create an unbelievable atmosphere. 'For me as a DJ, I still have the same attitude,' says Anthony Pappa. 'I still work as hard now as I did when I was trying to get my first gig. I love it as much. I treat it with the same amount of respect.'

Obey the first rule of show business

Always leave them wanting more!

283

The extras

Further information

Books
History and culture

Sean Bidder	Pump Up The Volume (Channel 4, 2001)
Bill Brewster & Frank Broughton	Last Night A DJ Saved My Life (Headline, 1999)
Mel Cheren	Keep On Dancin'
	My Life & The Paradise Garage
	(24 Hours for Life Inc., 2000)
Matthew Collin	Altered State (Serpent's Tail, 1997)
Mark Cunningham	Good Vibrations – A History Of Record Production
	(Sanctuary, 1998)
Jim Fricke & Charlie Ahearn	Yes Yes Y'All – Oral History of Hip Hop's First Decade
	(Perssue Press, 2002)
Sheryl Garratt	Adventures In Wonderland (Headline, 1998)
Dave Haslam	Adventures On The Wheels Of Steel
	(Fourth Estate, 2001)
Simon Reynolds	Energy Flash (Picador, 1998)
Peter Shapiro	Turn The Beat Around – The Secret History of Disco
	(Faber & Faber, 2005)
Dan Sicko	Techno Rebels (Billboard Books, 1999)
David Toop	Rap Attack 3 (Serpent's Tail, 2000)

Industry

Sarah Davis and Dave Laing	The Guerrilla Guide to the Music Business
	(Continuum, 2001)
Donald S. Passman	All You Need To Know About The Music Business
	(Simon & Schuster, 1995)
Music Industry Manual	www.mim.dj

Websites

www.recess.co.uk
www.djmandrick.co.uk
www.dj.deft.ukgateway.net
www.djprince.no
http://dju.prodj.com/v2/index.php
http://music.hyperreal.org/
www.berkleepress.com/links/djing_turntablism.htm
www.sistersf.com/
www.adja.org/
www.dmcworld.com/
www.djhistory.com
www.deephousepage.com

Magazines

Computer Music www.computermusic.co.uk
DJmag www.djmag.com
DJ Times www.djtimes.com
DMC Update www.dmcupdate.com
Fact www.factmagazine.co.uk
Future Music www.futuremusic.co.uk
IDJ www.i-dj.co.uk
Keep On www.keeponmagazine.co.uk
Mixmag www.mixmag.net
Sound On Sound www.soundonsound.com
The Source www.thesource.com
XXL www.xxlmag.com
Vibe www.vibe.com
Wax Poetics www.waxpoetics.com

Videos

DMC battle series www.dmcworld.com
So You Wanna Be A DJ www.dmcworld.com

Sample DJ contract

Engagement Contract

AN AGREEMENT
made on the _____ day of_____
BETWEEN _____
hereinafter known as the Management of the one part
AND_____hereinafter known as the
Artiste of the other part
WITNESSETH that the Management hereby engages the
Artiste who hereby accepts the engagement
TO PRESENT_____

SCHEDULE

The Artiste agrees to appear at 1 performance(s) for a
fee of _____ plus VAT where applicable.
Advance payment of _____ (inc. VAT) payable to
_____ to be
paid no later than _____.
Balance of _____ in cash
UK sterling on engagement day prior to performance.
Artiste will bring VAT invoice on engagement day if VAT
is required on the balance.

VENUE(s)_____

DATE(s)_____

Management agrees to provide the following at their own expense and at no expense to the Artiste:
    Hotel accommodation (if applicable)
    Ground transport and flights (if applicable)

CONDITIONS

1. The Artiste will perform for a total of 1 x ___ minutes.
2. Arrival time: _____ On stage time: _____
3. Cancellation of this engagement Contract will only be acceptable under the terms of Force Majeure.
4. Artiste may terminate this Contract forthwith by written notice to Management if: a) Management commits any breach of any obligations under this Contract; b) any sums payable under this Contract by Management are not paid on or before its due date for payment in accordance with the above Schedule. In the event of termination all outstanding sums shall be paid by Management within 5 days of receipt of the notice to terminate. Upon occurrence of a breach of Contract by Management, Artiste shall be entitled to: a) discontinue performance of its obligations under the Contract; and/ or b) seek to recover damages from Management.

I / We the undersigned acknowledge that I/we have read the above terms and conditions and agree that they will be adhered to in full.

_____DATE_____
SIGNED *for Management*

_____DATE_____
SIGNED *for Artiste*

289

Glossary

A

acappella from the Latin 'with the voice'. An unaccompanied vocal. Great for sampling and clever mixes.

acetate (also 'dubplate' 'slate') a one-off pressing made from soft vinyl. Expensive to make and with a lifetime of only 10-20 plays. Thanks to CD burners they're becoming a thing of the past.

acoustics the science of sound. Mostly used to refer to the way sound behaves in a certain room.

amplifier the piece of sound equipment which makes the music loud enough to power the speakers.

analogue non-digital. Sound processed in the old-fashioned way (and the equipment which processes it this way) is analogue. This means that changes in the sound are a direct result of similar changes in something else (eg an electronic signal, a magnetic charge or a groove cut in vinyl).

anti-skating a spinning record pulls the needle into the centre. An anti-skating system pulls it the other way to correct things.

B

baby scratch the simplest kind of scratch.

back-cue to loop a section of a record manually by cutting between two copies of it very fast. The basis of hip hop and all other breakbeat music.

backspin see **spinback**.

bar a division in musical notation; a section of a song. In almost all dance music it is four beats long. 'Measure' in American.

beat a particular kind of rhythm – a constant pulse, a regular tick, tock, tick, tock, a heartbeat. The regular 1, 2, 3, 4... that you can count out.

beat-juggle to play individual drum-beats from a pair of records so you create an entirely new rhythm. Possibly the hardest technique in this book.

beatmatch to adjust the speeds of two different records so they match and their beats are synchronised. The basis for most kinds of mixing.

beatmix to mix using beatmatching. Usually means some sort of blend.

blend a smooth and gradual transition from one record to another with the beats synchronised.

booking agent someone who gets a DJ gigs.

bootleg a record which is illegal because it's used copyright material without permission.

May be an illegal copy of a rare record, or these days most likely to be a track using samples of big artists without paying them.

bpm (beats per minute) the measurement of a record's tempo, ie how fast it is. House is around 125bpm, hip hop around 90bpm.

break the part in a record where the track is reduced to just the rhythm. The song takes a breather, drops down to some exciting percussion and then comes storming back in again.

breakbeat music made by looping up a section of a break. Sometimes used to refer to original songs which have great breaks in them.

breakdown call the RAC! A breakdown is when the rhythmic part of the track takes a rest ('breaks down') leaving just the musical and vocal elements and then builds up teasingly to a storming climax. It's the bit where you get to put your hands in the air.

C

cartridge the part of a turntable which converts the vibrations of the stylus (needle) into electrical signals.

channel an individual sound signal or pathway. A stereo system has two channels (left and right); a mixer has several channels, depending on how many things it can mix together.

chord a bunch of notes played simultaneously, eg on a guitar or piano.

counterweight the weight on the end of the tone-arm which balances the needle and stops it digging in to your records.

copyright if you make something original, you have the right to stop others copying it without your permission.

crab a clever finger movement that lets you do rapid-fire scratch techniques.

crossfader the control in the centre of a mixer that fades from one channel (or turntable) to another.

crossover the circuitry in a big system which divides the sound signal up and sends it to different speaker circuits (tweeters, mids, woofers, sub-woofers).

cueing (1) listening to the next record in your headphones while the dancefloor hears something else; (2) getting the needle in the right place and starting the record.

cut a sharp switch from one record to another, done without losing the beat. Sometimes called 'drop mixes'.

D

dat digital audio tape.

decibels (dB) the units in which sound pressure (volume) is measured.

delay a sound effect where the original signal is held back for a moment, creating a single repeat.

digital if sound is recorded digitally it is saved as

computer code, in millions of ones and zeros. CDs, Minidiscs and MP3s are digital, but records and cassettes are analogue.

distortion when a sound signal goes through a piece of equipment at too high a volume it will distort, losing its highs and lows, and start to sound like a Harley Davidson in a ditch. You can do this on purpose with sound effects.

distributor the person or company a record label (or unsigned producer) pays to get their records into the shops.

domestic a domestic release is a record made in this country.

download to take a file (eg an MP3) from a website and suck it into your computer.

dub the original Jamaican term for a radical remix (from 'double', as in make a copy). Nowadays a dub is usually a

simpler, stripped-down mix of a track, without vocals.

dubplate see **acetate**.

E

echo a sound effect where the sound is repeated several times.

eq (equalisation) adjusting separate frequencies in the sound (eg bass, midrange, treble). This might be to make the system sound clearer or it might just be to mess with the dancers' heads.

F

fade to gradually adjust the volume. You can fade a record in (from silence to music), fade a record out (from music to silence) or fade from one record to another.

feedback the nasty noises electrical equipment can make when it picks up its own signal.

filter a piece of electronics which lets certain frequencies through and blocks others. Put disco through a filter and you get a Daft Punk record.

flanging a sound effect which adds a whooshing sensation to the music. Similar to phasing.

flare a type of scratch where the fader is used like an off-switch to control the sound.

291

four-four music which has four beats in a bar. Dance music is almost all in 4/4 time. This is a time signature.

four-on-the-floor music, like house or disco, which has four kick-drum beats in every bar. A regular heart-beat rhythm. Also called 'four-to-the-floor'.

FTP (file transfer protocol) a way of sending files (including soundfiles like MP3s) from one computer to another over the internet.

FX (effects) electronic boxes (or circuits built in to something else) which mess with your sound in a certain way, creating echo, delay, distortion, phasing or a combination of these.

G

gain the knob on a mixer which turns up a particular channel as it enters the mixer. You use it to add volume to quiet records.

groove (1) the spiral scratch in a record which contains the song; (2) the repetitive pattern of drums and bassline which sits underneath the rest of the song and drives it forward, nailing dancers to the floor in the process.

H

harmony if two notes (or chords or voices or tunes) sound nice together, they are 'harmonious'

or 'in harmony'. In a song the harmony is an extra bit which adds to the melody without overshadowing it.

hook the memorable part of a song. The bit the postman whistles.

I

impedance how hard it is to push electricity through something.

import a record made in another country. DJs love imports because they're rarer than domestic releases. A song may one day get released domestically, but if you buy it on import, you're going to be first.

K

key a family of notes which sound harmonious together.

key clash the out-of-tune sound when you try and mix two records which are in incompatible keys.

kick drum (or 'kick') the big bass drum which sits on the floor. The driving pulse of dance music.

kill switch a switch on a mixer which turns off a particular range of frequencies in the sound. The idea is that you can 'kill' the bass or treble (and then bring it back in) and make the crowd wet their knickers.

L

level how big a sound signal is. Shown by the level meters.

license after you release a track in one country you can license it to be released in another (a different 'territory'). So a tune on a French label might be licensed by a British one and released in the UK.

loop a sample which repeats and repeats to form a constant rhythm or melody as part of a track.

M

mailing list a list of DJs who get sent promotional records.

manager someone who looks after all aspects of a DJ's business affairs.

mastering tweaking the EQ and volume of a recording so the finished result sounds as clear and impressive as possible.

melody the tuneful part of a song. The bit played on piano, guitar, sax, etc that sits on top of the drums and bassline. The bit you can hum.

midi (musical instrument digital interface) – a computer language that lets music machines talk to each other.

midrange the frequencies between the bass and the treble.

mixer a machine which lets you combine sound signals from more than one source.

mixing (1) joining different pieces of music together to create a DJ performance; (2) the studio process where different channels of sound are chosen and combined to make a track.

monitors the speakers near or inside the DJ booth which let the DJ hear the music as clearly as possible, sharpening up the booming and echoey sound from the dancefloor.

mp3 the most popular kind of computer soundfile.

P

p&d (pressing and distribution) a record deal where a smaller label is signed to a bigger one and gets its records manufactured and distributed in return for a share of the profits.

pa (public address) (1) a sound system – a big amplifier and speakers. (2) a 'personal appearance' – when a live act turns up during a club night for a lip-synching performance.

panning a stereo sound effect where the music seems to zip from one side of the room to the other.

percussion drums and other (largely non-melodic) instruments which are played by being hit.

phasing combine two identical soundwaves, with one that's delayed a little bit, and you get a watery whooshing effect. This is phasing (phase shifting). You can do it with a sound effects unit or two copies of the same record.

phono short for 'phonograph', another name for turntable. Often used to name the mixer inputs designed for turntables, and the kind of plugs which join stereo equipment together.

phrase a section of four bars. The building block of a song's structure.

pirate radio radio stations which don't have a government license. Named after sixties stations which broadcast from ships. Usually have the most upfront music and the shoutiest MCs.

pitch how high a note is, or how fast a record is. The two are connected.

pitch control sets the speed or tempo of a record.

pitch bend momentarily speeds or slows a record so it can catch-up with another.

programming the way in which a DJ puts together a set. The way you thread your records together and the order in which you place them.

promo records made to publicise or 'promote' a song before it is released. These are sent to DJs with notes begging them to play them. Now that everyone's a DJ, you can also buy promos in dance shops.

promoter someone who puts on club nights, booking the venue and the DJs and then working to fill the place with clubbers.

promotion record promotion is the industry which works to make people buy records and CDs. Sometimes it's a department within a record company, and sometimes it's an independent company. DJs like promotion people because they   send out free records – but only to DJs who can help turn them into hits.

publicist someone who can be hired to persuade newspapers and magazines to write about something (eg a record) or someone (a DJ).

publishing the business of selling permission to use songs written by other songwriters.

R

re-edit a new version of a song made by cutting up and splicing together chunks of the original song but rearranging them in a different order.

remix a new version of a song made by recombining parts of the original multitrack recording.

residency a regular gig at a certain club. Used to mean you were the main (or only) DJ that played there. DJs love residencies because they're a chance to build a real understanding of a certain crowd. And regular cash, too.

reverb a sound effect which adds lots of little echoes to the music. This makes it more 3D, as if you were hearing it in an echoey room.

rhythm a pattern of sound. Usually refers to the patterns and arrangements of a record's percussion.

royalties money you get for each copy of a record sold or each time someone performs or records a song you wrote.

S

sample a snatch of an existing record used as part of a new one.

sampler a machine which records sound digitally without tape.

scratching making rhythmic sounds by moving a record back and forth and cutting them up using the faders on your mixer.

sequencer a computer program which records music not as sound but as a series of instructions which other electronic instruments can follow.

signal-to-noise ratio how much interference or unwanted noise a piece of equipment adds to the music it's process ing (compared to the amount of music). The lower the signal-to-noise ratio, the better the equipment.

slipmat the felt mat that sits between the platter and a record so you can hold the record still without having to stop the turntable.

snare drum (or 'snare') the drum with a chippy-chip biscuit-tin sound.

spinback using your hand to spin a record into reverse for the crazy 'rewind' sound it creates.

split-cue a feature on some mixers which lets you hear one track in each ear of your headphones.

stab a short staccato sound (usually sampled from either strings or brass sections on old records) that accentuates the start of a bar. They're also called 'hits'.

streaming a streaming soundfile is one which you can play without having to download it all first. You hear one part whileyour computer is busy downloading the next bit. Makes the internet work like a radio.

strobe (1) a flashing club light; (2) a light which flashes 50 times a second on the dots on a turntable platter to show whether its speed controls are calibrated properly.

stylus the needle, diamond or sapphire, which sits in the groove of a record and vibrates to create the sound signal.

syncopation a way of making a rhythm bouncier or more funky. Syncopation means playing beats a bit early or late to make a rhythm more interesting.

T

tear a scratch technique where a gap is put in the sound by halting the record for a tiny moment.

tempo the speed of a song, measured in beats per minute (bpm).

test-pressing before a record is produced in any numbers, the factory will make test-pressings to make sure it sounds OK. Labels often give these to their favourite DJs so they can be the first to play the track. These days, labels sometimes call promos test-pressings to make DJs more excited about them.

time signature the numbers at the beginning of a piece of written music which tell the musician how many beats are in each bar and how long (relatively) each beat is. Almost all dance music has a time signature of 4/4.

timestretching changing the tempo of a tune (its speed) without affecting its pitch.

tone-arm the long part of a turntable which holds the cartridge.

trainspotter an obsessive DJ/collector with an unhealthy interest in obscure musical information. Named after the lads in anoraks who made a hobby out of writing down locomotive numbers.

transform a scratch technique where you use the crossfader like an on-switch and chop up a scratch into little rhythmic noises.

tripling a Detroit trick where the same beat is played three times using two copies of a record. The same trick is known in beat-juggling as a fill.

tremelo a sound effect which is the equivalent of turning the volume up and down very fast. Gave Buddy Holly that shimmery guitar sound.

turntables decks, record players.

turntablism using turntables and records as musical instruments. Once called scratching but now it's a whole universe of techniques.

tweeter a treble speaker. Small and piercing. In big clubs often hung from the ceiling.

W

white label a record which isn't from a record company, so it just has a plain label. These are usually made in small batches and sold directly to a shop by the person who made them. Record companies often make their promos look like white labels to make them seem rarer.

woofer a bass speaker.

>> Notes

>> Notes

Acknowledgements

2 x CD
mixed and compiled
by Bill Brewster
available to order from
www.hooj.com

A big shout-out to . . .

Design Julia Lloyd
Photography John Bland
Illustrations Trudi Cross

The wild world of publishing
Julian Alexander and Lucinda Cook at LAW; Doug Young, Cora Kipling, Lynne Eve, Emma Musgrave, Marina Vokos, Henrietta Lewis, Claire Evans, Alison Martin and Rachel Connolly at Transworld.

The bedroom consultants
Terry Weerasinghe (Pioneer), Matt Young, Rachel Badzire, Will Fulford-Jones, Kevin Ebbutt, Andy Frentzel-Beyme and Michael Cook.

The dancefloor consultants
Danny Tenaglia, John Digweed, Mr Scruff, Ross Allen, Jon Marsh, Danny Howells, Anthony Pappa, Gilles Peterson, Boy George, Dave Hucker, Derrick Carter.

The masterclass consultants
Rocky (X-Press 2), Dave, Sanjay and Fly (Fabric), Grandmaster Flash, Grandmixer DXT, Grand Wizard Theodore, Roc Raida, Mark Rae, Anthony Pappa, Mark Davis (Camelot Sound), Vikram Rai (DJ Prince), Tom Stephan, Paul Noble, DJ Dubious and Sean Johnston.

The industry consultants
John Digweed, Dave Lee, Pete Heller, Tom Middleton, Rob Davis, Matt Waterhouse (Hyperactive), Karen Dunn (Unlimited DJs), Rebecca Prochnik (Profile), Alexia Beard, Paul Coleman (Rocketscience), Quinton Scott and Toni Rossano (Strut), Leo Elstob, Stuart Patterson, Dave Jarvis, Chris Stella, Luke Solomon, Richard Brown (Swag), DJ Dazy, Asad Rizvi, Simon Marks (Azuli), Mario (Amato), Frank Tope, Ralph Pool and Simon Lindsay (MCPS), Elliott Lawrence (bigredfunbus.com), Jim Broughton, Jon Williams, Stephen Cooper, Arlette Dunn, Adam Goldstone, Pete Roberts (DMC), Tim Jeffries, Austin Wilde, Dom Phillips, all the staff at Sapphires, Dan Solo and Simon Burgess @ Space FM.

And all the DJs we've ever interviewed, especially
Afrika Bambaataa, Ashley Beedle, Boy George, Gary Byrd, Coldcut, Kenny Carpenter, Norman Cook, Cosmo, DJ Pierre, Dave Dorrell, Johnny Dynell, Terry Farley, Jazzy Jay, Norman Jay, Marshall Jefferson, François Kevorkian, Frankie Knuckles, Kool Herc, Danny Krivit, David Mancuso, David Morales, Paul Oakenfold, Dave Pearce, Danny Rampling, Q-Bert, Nicky Siano, Luke Solomon, Steinski, Rob Swift, Todd Terry, Pete Tong, Junior Vasquez.

Special thanks to
Liz McMahon, Imogen Crosby and Lola Brewster.